COMMUNICATE!

A Workbook for Interpersonal Communication

Sixth Edition

Communication Research Associates

Long Beach City College

KENDALL/HUNT PUBLISHING COMPANY
4050 Westmark Drive   Dubuque, Iowa 52002

Note: Unless otherwise noted, all exercises were written by the author team.

Cover photos courtesy of Digital Vision, Photo Disc, and University of Dubuque.

AUTHOR TEAM

Editor-in Chief

Linda A. Joesting

Authors-Editors

Richard Carroll

Gregg Florence

Linda A. Joesting

Betty Martin

Jim Ostach

Dianne G. Van Hook

Roger E. Van Hook

M. James Warnemuende

Special Acknowledgments

We wish to acknowledge the following educators for their years of professional dedication to making *Communicate!* the workbook that it is: Wes Bryan, Herb Caesar, Dianne Faieta, Frank Faieta, Lowell Johnson and Molly MacLeod.

iii

FROM US
TO YOU AND YOUR SELF

We,
with our thoughts of today,
wish you the words of tomorrow.

We

want you

to be you,

to smile and to cry,
to touch the sensations of each day,
of each new way
you grow in your self.

We
need you
to reach beyond our limitations,
to willingly open
your eyes to laughter,
your ears to the song,
your hands to feel your world
and your voice to speak
the greatness of the small.

We
want and need you now
to communicate today
the sounds of Your valuable Self
and the value of Others,
that you might be the words
of solidarity,
blending the breaks of Humankind.

LAJ

CONTENTS

A "✷" denotes an activity.

CHAPTER 11: JOB SEARCH SKILLS

Communication Foundations

DEFINITIONS

Following are some important definitions of communication, the three major types of communication and a definition of the term "process" as it specifically relates to the study of communication.

✳ **Communication**

General Definitions:

- Communication is the process of shared meaning through symbolic interaction. —D. Fabun
- Communication is the process by which we understand others and in turn are understood by them. (It is dynamic, constantly changing in response to the total situation.) —M. Anderson
- Communication involves the conveyance of something to someone else—our ideas, our aims, our wants, our values, our very personalities. —Robinson and Lee

✳ **Dyad**

A dyad is a group of two individuals.

✳ **Intrapersonal Communication**

Definition: Intrapersonal communication is the process of communicating with oneself, our self-talk; when we daydream, reflect on what we have done, what is presently going on, or what we will do in the future, we are engaging in intrapersonal communication.

Example: As we consider buying a car, we weigh the pros and cons of one model versus another model in our head before making an overt decision.

✳ **Interpersonal Communication**

Definition: Interpersonal communication is the process of communicating and interacting with other people.

Example: As we are buying a car, we interact with the salesperson, discussing equipment, pricing, financing. We try to work out a deal that is acceptable to both parties.

1

✹ Extrapersonal Communication

Definition: Extrapersonal communication is the process of interacting with beings or articles which are nonhuman.

Example: We can talk to a dog, a plant, or even yell at our car when it will not start.

✹ Process

Definition: When we speak of communication as a process, we are referring to the ongoing, continuous, dynamic sense of relationships existing in all communication. Communication has no beginning and no end.

Example: As I communicate with someone, I send a message to that person. The other person then receives my message and speaks back. As he/she speaks back to me, that person becomes the source and I now become the receiver of his/her message. Throughout the entire communication process, we are constantly changing—changing our roles, changing our language, changing our presentation, changing our attitudes and perceptions.

✹ Triad

A triad is a group of three individuals.

THE IMPORTANCE OF COMMUNICATION

Human beings are constantly communicating. In both sending and receiving messages, adults spend almost half of their total verbal communication time as listeners. We spend over one-third of our communication time as speakers.

COMMUNICATION IS A SKILL

Because we spend so much time in oral communication, effective communication skills are vital to all of us. Indeed, you may be enrolled in this communication course to improve your communication skills and to become a more knowledgeable communicator. Employers look for employees who are effective communicators. Generally, the most successful people in our society are those who have strong communication skills. In his autobiography, Lee Iacocca, the head of Chrysler Corporation, stresses how important both speaking and listening skills are to success in motivating people. *A*

course in speech communication can help you gain these skills.

COMMUNICATION LINKS PEOPLE

During any given day, you may talk to your friends, listen to members of your family, receive correspondence, observe and react to others' gestures and facial expressions, and even carry on conversations with yourself. You, like all humans, are a communicating being. "Communication is the way relationships are created, maintained and destroyed," observed one communication specialist. Every day, we depend on our abilities to speak, listen, write, read, think and interpret nonverbal messages. *Without these abilities, we would lose much of what makes us human,* and trying to be human in this very complex world requires all the help we can get. This chapter will show you just how vital communication is to our survival.

COMMUNICATION BEGINS RELATIONSHIPS

People often react very differently to the act of getting acquainted, of getting to know someone else. Some people seem to be able to hit it off very easily with people they have never met. Other people seem to get sweaty palms, heart palpitations, nervous stomachs at the very thought of having to meet another person for the first time. Why?

We are all human, aren't we? Of course we are, but the answer goes way beyond that.

It is true that in many respects we are all alike; however, as the following boxed selection indicates, we are all unique individuals with different personalities and needs, as well as different levels of socialization skills. The purpose of this text is to help you develop and expand these skills.

The Person Next to You

Who is the person sitting next to you?

What is the person's name? How tall is the person? I clearly see the color of my neighbor's hair and eyes, but I wonder what kind of clothes this individual likes? Where do you think the person lives? Does this person believe in evolution or creation? I wonder if my new neighbor will trust me? I wonder if we will enjoy talking about the same types of things? Is the person married . . . single . . . committed to another person . . . ?

Do these questions define who the person next to you is?

Not really; you see, the person next to you has a life story of extraordinary fullness. This living soul is a unique world of experience—a cluster of past memories, current actions, and expectations for the future. That person is a whole colony of people and events that have passed in and out of the person's life—parents, guardians, teachers, friends, enemies, jobs, schools, vacations, parties, problems, dreams, hobbies.

Much of the person next to you cannot be known immediately. How does the person make choices, accept responsibility, solve problems, perceive the world, work to capacity? How may I bring out the person's character as quickly as the photographer's chemicals bring out the forms latent in the negative?

How much does this person like himself or herself? How well does this person know and accept both his or her strengths as well as weaknesses? Is this person aware of how he/she fits into the scheme of things?

The person next to you is happy and sad, fearful and sure, content and wondering, shy and outgoing, asking questions and knowing answers—looking for respect, looking for love, looking for acceptance, looking for you . . . to reach out and care. . . .

How much is this person like you? You probably will never know until you reach out, reach out to meet that unique person sitting next to you.

Who knows—you might even discover that even though the two of you are very different, you are in many ways very much the same. It is this seeming contradiction of "uniqueness" and "sameness" which can turn the person next to you into a close acquaintance, into your next best friend. . . .

BARRIERS TO UNDERSTANDING COMMUNICATION

COMMUNICATION AS A NATURAL PROCESS

The major barrier to studying intrapersonal, interpersonal and extrapersonal communication is that most people have a tendency to see communication as a **natural process**, requiring little effort or training. After all, we can all talk to a person sitting next to us in this room—can't we? And we seem to make it through life (childhood, adolescence, marriage, relationships, adulthood) interacting with others at each stage—don't we?

The answer to both of these questions is "yes." But wait. True, we may have made it this far in our communicating with others and could make it the rest of the way through life continuing as we are. The point here is not whether we are "communicating" or not. The real point is whether we are **communicating with maximum effectiveness** or not. This effective communication is the major concern of this book.

As you study the principles and strategies presented in the following pages, you will begin to see that effective communication is not as simple as most believe. Each chapter presents different barriers that can interfere with or prevent effective communication from taking place. You may find, for example, that we do not always really listen to others. Or perhaps we may not describe what we perceive all that accurately. Also, we might not be as aware of ourselves—our values and attitudes or the way we think others see us—as we think. Finally, we might not be handling conflict or our personal relationships as effectively as we could.

Overall, communication requires a great deal of effort to overcome the many barriers that confront us. Our hope is that as you study this essential life skill, the barriers become easier to handle and your relationships with others become more meaningful.

COMMUNICATION AS A RISK

Many people have barriers toward classes such as speech and interpersonal communication. These barriers may have to do with our self-image and with our perceptions of other people.

SELF-IMAGE

Self-image barriers include poor self-esteem, shy behavior, lack of social skills and anxiety over how others may view us. For example, if we have not had a lot of experience in interacting with others in classes, clubs, families, etc., we may be afraid to try. We may be afraid of saying the wrong thing or if we do speak up, people may not like what we say and thus reject us. Therefore, classes such as this one must start with the requirement that we all respect each other, support one another and refrain from rejecting or judging others.

PREJUDGING OTHERS

Our perception of others can create barriers such as misjudging people, not giving others a chance, and/or stereotyping. For example, if we see someone sitting next to us who has a different hair style or who is from a different racial or ethnic background, we may not want to get to know him or her because of preconceived ideas or beliefs—i.e., long hairs take drugs; blacks don't take school seriously; football players are dumb; Asians are unfriendly, etc. These stereotypes have no basis in fact—the only thing they do is keep us from getting to know one another. When we get past these barriers and accept people individually, we find that each individual is unique and does not fit these preconceived notions.

TAKE A RISK

So, we challenge you to risk in this class. Risk getting to know others. Stay open to others and their ideas. Do not prejudge others. Remember to separate people from their ideas or behaviors. For example, others may wear their hair differently from you or have different ideas and values from your own but that does not mean that they are not worth knowing. Again, take risks, keep an open mind, get to know one another and make new friends in this course.

Communication Quiz

PURPOSE:

To consider some basic concepts about speech communication and to begin thinking about the communication process.

PROCEDURE:

Indicate your response to each of the following statements by circling either **T (True)** or **F (False)**.

True or False

_____   1. How you communicate has very little impact on what you communicate.
_____   2. Communication is a natural, human process requiring little or no effort.
_____   3. When communication is good, both people will understand each other totally.
_____   4. Dictionaries give us the meanings for most of our words.
_____   5. We learn who we are from others.
_____   6. People who talk to themselves are in need of psychiatric help.
_____   7. Your past experiences and future expectations do not greatly influence your present communication.
_____   8. Communication basically involves getting our ideas across to others.
_____   9. Listening and hearing are the same thing.
_____   10. We can't not communicate.
_____   11. Most of us perceive the world accurately.
_____   12. Once we communicate a message, we have no control over what will be done with it.

DISCUSSION:

As a class, discuss each question and its implications.

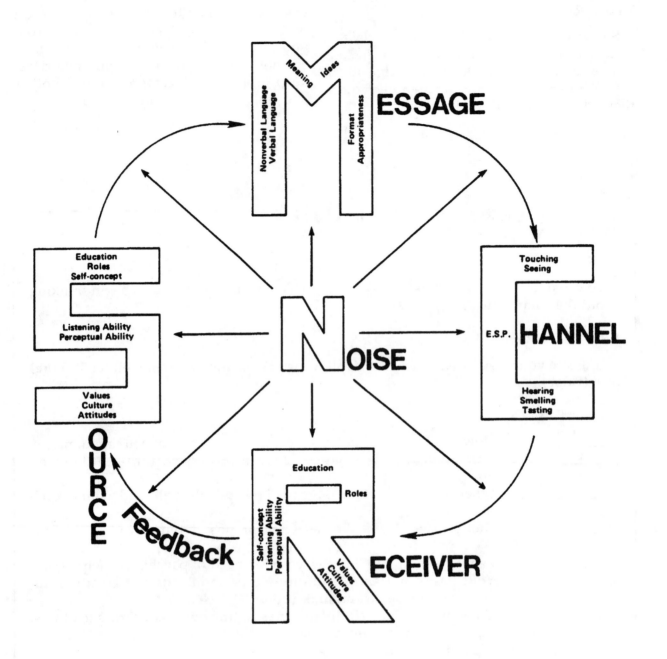

Circle

For all is a circle
Like the watch on my chain
The hands go to six
And back to twelve again.

Walking and sleeping
Living and dying
Summer and winter
Laughing and crying.

Nowhere on a circle
Does it begin or end
One message coming
One message to send.

Leslie Pasch
Utica, New York

Reprinted with permission from *Scholastic Voice,*
© 1975 by Scholastic Magazines, Inc.

BASIC TERMS

Following are some important terms related to understanding the process of communication.

Terms & Definitions	Examples
SOURCE: One who begins the communication through verbal or nonverbal means. Other names for source include encoder and speaker.	Pianist Instructor
RECEIVER: One to whom the source's verbal/nonverbal communication is directed. Other names for receiver include decoder, listener, audience.	Audience Students
MESSAGE: That information or product of the source's purpose which is coded into symbols/language and expressed through verbal/nonverbal means.	Music by Elton John Lecture-discussion, with visual aids, on why/how we communicate.

Terms & Definitions	Examples
CHANNEL: That sense-related medium by which a message is transmitted. Light-waves, sound, and airwaves are considered as channels.	Sound/airwaves—sense of hearing, lightwaves—sense of sight. Sound waves—sense of hearing, lightwaves—sense of light
FEEDBACK: The receiver's response to the source's message. Feedback indicates how well the source is doing in communicating his message.	Screams, applause, restlessness at performances; letters afterwards. Wandering eyes, nervousness, questions, attentive faces during lecture-discussion; good answers on exam afterward.
ENCODING: A process involving (1) selecting a means of expression and (2) transforming ideas into those means through appropriate selection of symbols/language.	Notes on paper are transformed into music as Elton John plays the piano. The instuctor selects appropriate language to effectively communicate his ideas.
DECODING: The receiver's interpretation of the message based on background, education and future expectations.	Audience interprets the music according to their capacity. Students interpret information according to their interest and educational background.
NONVERBAL: The use of hand gestures, posture, eye contact, vocal tone, personal distance, to emphasize or complement oral communication.	At the end of each song, the singer raises his arms, stands, faces audience and bows. On having two students talking in the back row, the instructor stops talking, puts hands on hips and glares in their direction.
FIDELITY: High fidelity is the ultimate goal of communication.	The audience understands the singer's song and begins to identify with its message. The students understand the instructor's assignment and complete it to everyone's satisfaction.
MECHANICAL (External) NOISE: Any external interference in the environment that prevents the message from being accurately encoded or decoded.	A defective microphone screeches through the auditorium. A loud group walks down the hall. A police siren blares outside.
SEMANTIC (Internal) NOISE: Any internal interference in one's mind that prevents the message from being accurately encoded or decoded.	The audience has never heard rock music and has difficulty understanding what it means. The instuctor refers to concepts the student does not understand.

Defining Communication

PURPOSE:

To start you thinking about communication and to determine how much you and the rest of the class already know.

PROCEDURE:

The class will be divided into groups and will be asked to discuss the following questions for approximately 30 minutes. Each group should try to reach general agreement on each of the questions. Everyone in the group should be afforded equal opportunities to contribute ideas.

1.   What are the major elements of any communication event? (See note below.)
2.   Why do you think communication is called a process?
3.   What is communication? Describe what you think communication is. Try to arrive at a definition that the group will accept. (Be sure to include the concept of *effective* communication.)
4.   What communication barriers did you perceive as your group discussed the above three questions?

DISCUSSION:

Record the responses of your group and be prepared to discuss the conclusion in class.

NOTE:

Which of these terms are *absolutely necessary* for communication to occur? These are the elements of communication.

Decoding	Intent	Stimulus
Noise	Understanding	Sender
Listening	Message	Response
Emotions	Process	Encoding
Context	Receiver	Channel
Feedback	Hearing	Transmission

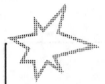

Veterans/Rookies

PURPOSE:

To analyze and evaluate a variety of definitions of communication.

PROCEDURE:

1. Rank the following definitions from 1 to 10, with 1 being your opinion of the "best" definition and 10 the worst.
2. In small groups compare your decisions with the other members. Explain why you ranked the definitions the way you did. Listen to the other members and see if you understand why they chose their rankings.
3. Your instructor will then show you how a group of 100 speech "experts" (professionals in the communication field) ranked the 10 definitions at a recent convention.

Rating Scale
1 Best
10 Worst

DEFINITIONS OF COMMUNICATION

_____ A. "In its broadest perspective, communication occurs whenever an individual assigns significance or meaning to an internal or external stimulus."

_____ B. "A communicates B through channel C to D with effect E. Each of these letters is to some extent an unknown and the process can be solved for any one of them or any combination."

_____ C. "Communication means that information is passed from one place to another."

_____ D. "All communication proceeds by means of signs, with which one organism affects the behavior of another (or more generally the state of another)."

_____ E. "The word communication will be used here in a very broad sense to include all of the procedures by which one mind may affect another. This, of course, involves not only written and oral speech but also music, the pictorial arts, the theater, the ballet, and in fact, all behavior."

_____ F. ". . . the intuitive interpretation of the relatively unconscious assimilation of the ideas and behaviors of one's culture."

_____ G. ". . . The process by which an individual (the communicator) transmits stimuli (usually verbal symbols) to modify the behavior of other individuals (communicatees)."

_____ H. "Communication does not refer to verbal, explicit, and intentional transmission of messages alone. . . . The concept of communication would include all those processes by which people influence one another. . . . This definition is based upon the premise that all actions and events have communicative aspects, as soon as they are perceived by a human being; it implies, furthermore, that such perception changes the information which an individual possesses and, therefore, influences him."

_____ I. "This definition (communication is the discriminatory response of an organism to a stimulus) says that communication occurs when some environmental disturbance (the stimulus) impinges on an organism and does something about it (makes a discriminatory response). If the stimulus is ignored by the organism, there has been no communication."

_____ J. "Communication is the assignation of meaningfulness or significance to one's perception of an arbitrary sign."

DISCUSSION:

1. Were you surprised by any of the "expert" rankings? Why?
2. Did your group agree that some (or one) definitions were better than others?
3. What did the definitions that were ranked near the top have in common?
4. What critical aspects of communication did the bottom-ranked definitions lack?
5. Would it be possible to write a definition of communication that would please everyone who studies it? Why or why not?
6. As you listened to the other group members, could you understand why they ranked the definitions as they did? Why or why not?

Julie and Mr. Conroy

PURPOSE:

To examine a communication breakdown and analyze how it could have been prevented.

PROCEDURE:

1. Read the following situation.
2. In groups of five to six, answer the questions that follow.
3. Try to achieve consensus as you discuss each item.

"I only figured that any kid who was messing around like that deserved some kind of punishment."

John and Patricia Conroy were apparently no more, no less perplexed by the generation gap than any other parents of a teen-age girl. Julie, their 16-year-old daughter, was a good student, reliable, known for her quick smile and friendly manner. She never caused her parents any great problems, though they had long since given up trying to make sense out of the exuberant and slang-filled speech she constantly used.

Julie was an only child and her parents were often quite restrictive as to where she went and with whom she went. Julie naturally complained occasionally, but there were never any major problems until one warm June evening.

School had just been dismissed for the summer and Julie was given the family car for the evening to go to a girlfriend's party. She was given careful instructions that she was to be home by 12 o'clock.

The all-girl party was a success, and the happy teenagers were so engrossed in talk that hours slipped by quickly. Someone finally pointed out that it was almost 1 a.m. Julie gasped with surprise and quickly told her hostess that she had to leave. Several of her friends quickly asked for rides home. Julie knew she was already late so why would a few extra minutes matter?

As she drove down the street toward the first girl's house, one of the other girls in the car spotted two boys she knew walking down the street and asked Julie to stop to give them a ride. Julie knew neither of them but stopped anyway to pick them up. At the next intersection Julie's car was hit broadside by a man who failed to stop at the traffic light. No one was hurt, but the car was inoperable. Police, after questioning all of them, took Julie home in a squad car. Both worried parents came running out of the house to see what happened. In the turmoil of Julie's excited efforts to explain, all her father heard was, "We were riding around with a couple of guys and some old man hit us." Visions of his daughter roaming the streets late at night in a car with boys she didn't even know combined with his built-up tensions and Mr. Conroy vented his anger by slapping Julie so hard she fell to the pavement. The patrolman attempted to intervene and Mr. Conroy hit him, breaking his nose.

Julie spent 10 days in the hospital with a concussion, the officer needed emergency treatment, and Mr. Conroy was fined $500 and given a suspended sentence for striking an officer of the law. It was months before father and daughter could even begin to talk to each other without anger and years later, there is still bitterness between them.

DISCUSSION:

1. Who was the sender and the receiver of the fateful communication?
2. What effect did the time, place and circumstances have on Mr. Conroy's action?
3. Did Julie's choice of words have any effect on Mr. Conroy's actions?
4. What effects did the emotions of both Julie and her father have?
5. Were both Julie and her father attempting to communicate? Were they listening to each other?
6. What roles do values play in this incident? What are the possible differences in orientation for Mr. Conroy and Julie?
7. Was the "punishment" by Mr. Conroy related more to what Julie did or what she said?
8. Did Mr. Conroy show any sensitivity to Julie's needs?
9. How could this incident have been prevented?
10. What sort of interference was there in this communication event?

Speech is a civilization itself.
The word, even the most contradictory word,
preserves contact.—It is silence which isolates.
—*T. Mann*

Things to Work On. . . .

Following is a list of 15 problems many individuals have as they try to communicate effectively. Read the list and rank your top five individual concerns from 1 to 5, with 1 being your top choice.

_____ A. I often speak before I really think.

_____ B. I usually speak rather than really listen to others.

_____ C. I feel that I am shy.

_____ D. I let others do most of the talking.

_____ E. I would rather communicate in writing rather than speaking face-to-face.

_____ F. People tell me that I speak too fast.

_____ G. I often misunderstand what people say to me.

_____ H. People often misinterpret what I say.

_____ I. When talking, I gesture more than others.

_____ J. I often interrupt others while they are talking.

_____ K. I feel uncomfortable looking into someone's eyes when talking.

_____ L. When meeting others, I tend to get very nervous.

_____ M. I have trouble when speaking to people in authority positions.

_____ N. I feel that others lose interest in what I am saying.

_____ O. I often find myself playing games with others instead of expressing how I really feel.

Course Goals . . .

Following is a list of 15 possible goals and reasons for taking this course. First, read the list and add other goals that might apply to your individual circumstances. Then, select those five goals you feel are most important and rank them from 1 to 5, with 1 being most important.

_____ A. To organize my thoughts more effectively.

_____ B. To overcome the shyness I experience in talking with people.

_____ C. To communicate more effectively with others.

_____ D. To increase my social skills.

_____ E. To gain confidence in myself.

_____ F. To make myself more marketable for a job.

_____ G. To increase my effectiveness in working in small groups.

_____ H. To increase my vocabulary.

_____ I. To become a better listener.

_____ J. To be more successful in interviews.

_____ K. To speak more clearly.

_____ L. To learn about the various theories of communication.

_____ M. To become more aware of how I perceive others and how others perceive me.

_____ N. To use my body language/nonverbal communication more effectively.

_____ O. To fulfill my Speech requirement.

_____ P.

_____ Q.

_____ R.

R E A C T I O N S

1. What is your personal definition of effective communication?

2. Give three reasons why communication is vital to your survival.

   a.

   b.

   c.

3. Many people feel that communication is an effortless, natural process, requiring little or no work. Do you agree or disagree? Why or why not?

4. Some authorities believe that all communication breakdowns are the fault of the sender. Do you agree or disagree? Why or why not?

5. What does it take for you to open up and disclose yourself to others when you first meet?

Listening

DEFINITIONS

Are you a good listener? Listening is a very important communication skill, yet we seldom receive special training for it in school. People often confuse listening with hearing. Some people play the game of listening by putting on a rubber reaction face along with occasional head nods and verbal sounds.

Listening requires time and effort. It involves much more than hearing. The purpose of this chapter is to provide information about listening and activities which will help you learn about this most frequently used element of communication. You must have a desire to apply what you learn if you wish to improve as a receiver.

First, let us understand four very important terms:

✱ Hearing

Definition: Hearing is necessary for listening, but is a separate process involving the reception of sound waves by the ear and brain.

Example: You may hear sounds but not necessarily pay any attention to them. Have you ever been guilty of staring at the speaker when she says, "You're not listening to me"?

✱ Listening

Definition: A mental process of interpreting sound waves in the brain. We focus our hearing upon the stimuli we wish to attend to. Listening isn't passive. You must interpret this stimuli into meaning and action.

Example: Mother, in the kitchen, may be slightly aware of children's laughter and noise coming from the next room, yet can still concentrate on a meaningful task without distraction. But let some unusual sounds occur; they are then interpreted as being significant danger signals.

✱ Feedback

Definition: Those verbal and nonverbal responses that affect the speaker in either a positive or negative way. Feedback may either strengthen or weaken communication. Feedback should express clearly what we want the speaker to know of our understanding about the message.

Example: A student speaker in a public speaking class would be more encouraged upon seeing affirmative head nods regarding a proposal than if he read anger, negative body language and glances at the clock.

✴ Empathic Listening

Definition: Listening to discover the sender's point of view. The speaker is encouraged to selfdisclose. Establishing trust, the listener enters into that person's world and attempts to imagine the thoughts and feelings of the speaker. Empathic listening responses should be a willingness to understand, but not give advice.

Example: Let us imagine that a fellow student is sharing with a classmate that Professor Jones hates him, is out to get him and will certainly fail him no matter how hard the student tries. An empathic response might be: "You don't feel Professor Jones is being fair with you?" To suggest that this person is irrational and should "talk-it-out" with Professor Jones is being judgmental and giving advice.

THE IMPORTANCE OF LISTENING

Most of us have, at one time or another, had the experience of talking with someone and getting the feeling that we weren't being listened to. At such times we may have felt frustrated or perhaps even angry. At other times we may have been in the role of the listener and experienced the embarrassment of being caught not listening. At these times, whether we have been the speaker or the listener, we may have become acutely aware that listening skills, whether someone else's or our own, were not as good as they could or should be. How many times have you made, or heard someone else make, the accusation, "You're not listening to me"? In trying to understand why we are not the listeners we could be, let's consider five questions essential to that understanding. How important is listening? How good are we as listeners? What are the various types of listening? What are the major barriers to listening effectively? How can we become better listeners?

LISTENING AS A BASIC ACTIVITY

How important is listening? Beyond our own awareness that it is important to have others listening to us when we are talking, research has indicated that listening is the most used basic communicating activity in our day-to-day lives. On the average, we spend about 70–80 percent of our time awake in some kind of communicating. Of that time, we spend approximately 9 percent writing, 16 percent reading, 30 percent speaking and 45 percent listening. Furthermore, of all the information we come to know during our lifetime, we learn over 90 percent of it through our eyes and ears. In fact, some people have even suggested that the causes of some of the major disasters in history were due to poor listening.

In addition to being the most frequent communicating task that we perform, the importance of listening is further amplified when we consider that listening to someone is a form of recognizing and validating that person's worth. This is probably why we get angry, frustrated or simply feel rejected when we are not being listened to. How often have you heard, or said, during an argument, "You're not listening to me"? Good, effective listening is a way of reducing hostility while poor, or withheld listening, is a way of creating hostility. In fact, intentionally withheld listening has been used as a form of punishment during Victorian times and by primitive tribes. Withholding listening is also a major element in brainwashing techniques. Obviously then, being listened to is a very real need we all have!

LISTENING AS A SKILL

Finally, when looking at how important listening is, consider your attitude about people you know who are good listeners. You probably like them more than others who you feel are poor listeners. Research has revealed that being a good listener is considered the most important management skill. So it seems that listening is very important—it's the most used communicating skill. We depend on it heavily for most of the information we come to know. It's important for our success in school, on the job, and in relationships, as well as being vital to our own psychological wellbeing and it's a key to having more friends.

How good are we as listeners? Listening ability is one communication skill that is relatively easy to measure and when researchers have measured it, the results have been astounding. Studies have found that the average listening efficiency in this culture is 25 percent. This dismal figure was first discovered in research with college students listening to a 10 minute lecture. While we may wish that the percentage was higher or even feel that we aren't as bad at listening as other people, the facts suggest that there is a great deal of room for improvement. To test out your own listening efficiency, ask yourself how often you repeat questions that have just previously been answered, ask someone to repeat something she said, write down the wrong information, or try to listen to someone while reading or watching television at the same time. None of us is perfect but when it comes to being a good listener, most of us don't even come close! The logical question to ask is, "Well, if we're such poor listeners, how did we get that way and what's keeping us from being better?" Before dealing with these two questions, let's consider the different kinds of listening that are possible.

TYPES OF LISTENING

Listening is not just a single activity, rather it is a series of steps relating to a specific goal—what we wish to pay attention to. Just as there is more than one thing to which we can pay attention, there is more than one type of listening. For our purposes, listening can be classified into the following five types:

1. Listening for enjoyment
2. Listening for details
3. Listening for main ideas
4. Listening for overall understanding
5. Listening for emotional undertones

Listening for enjoyment is probably the easiest type of listening we are involved with because, rather than paying attention to someone else, we simply tune into our own emotional response to what we are listening to. This is the type of listening we do when we listen to our favorite radio station or a favorite tune. We enjoy the music for what it does to us, how it makes us feel.

Listening for details is one of the types most closely associated with school. This is the type we use when we are listening for the detailed information in a teacher's lecture. Here we are trying to pay attention to specific factual information which the speaker is trying to relate.

Listening for main ideas is also closely allied with the classroom. However, in this situation we are trying to identify the speaker's main point. What is he driving at? What is the point he is attempting to make? In this type of listening, we must pay more attention and attempt to tune in to the general main ideas.

Listening for overall understanding is even more difficult than the types previously mentioned. In this situation we are trying to piece together all of the speaker's information in an effort to get at the overall meaning in the message. What is the bottom line? In order to do this type of listening, we must attend to much more of the message and try to assemble it in much the same way that a child might assemble a puzzle in order to see the entire picture.

Yet another type of listening is **listening for emotional undertones.** This is probably the most difficult of all because it requires the most attention and effort. In this type of listening, we shift our focus from what is being said to how the speaker is *feeling*. We are attempting to understand what is going on inside of her. Unlike listening for enjoyment where we were concerned with tuning in to our emotions, in this situation we are concerned with the emotions of the other person. This is particularly difficult since emotions are often hidden beneath layer upon layer of verbal camouflage. Often the speaker may not be in touch with her own feelings. Here, great attentiveness to the emotion-laden words is vital along with the discipline to keep our own thoughts and comments quiet.

These, then, are the major types of listening. As we can see, this seemingly simple task is far more complicated than may have previously been thought. But why are we such bad listeners on the average? What keeps us from achieving our goal?

The word "listen" contains the same letters as the word "silent." —*A. Brendel*

BARRIERS TO LISTENING

What are the major causes of the problem? While there are probably many causes to poor listening, four major factors can be identified which contribute in large part to the problem.

PHYSIOLOGICAL FACTORS

The first major factor is physiological in nature and, as such, is one we must learn to live with. That is the difference between the thinking and speaking rates. In essence, the brain works much faster than the mouth. Although the average speaking rate in our culture is about 125 words per minute, the brain processes language at the rate of approximately 800 words per minute. Since we can't slow the brain down, this gives us approximately 675 words per minute "free time" in our brain. So how do we use this "free time?" Well, we could use it to reinforce the message we are listening to, or we could use it to identify and organize the speaker's main points and supporting ideas. Unfortunately, most of us don't do this. Instead, we use this time to evaluate or criticize the speaker or message, prepare our rebuttal or just daydream about a million things totally unrelated to the message. In short, we tune in to our own internal dialogue rather than tuning in to the speaker's message.

Some researchers have approached this problem from the other side. If we can't slow down the brain, perhaps we can speed up the message. Speech "compressors," which increase the rate without distorting the tone, have been developed and tested on subjects. Results have shown that it is possible to listen to rates two to three times normal without significant loss of comprehension. In fact, in some instances comprehension has been improved. Perhaps this is due to having less "free time" to allow distractions to creep in and divert the listener's attention. However, even though it sounds promising, "speed listening" is not practical in our day to day lives, so we must develop skill that enables us to use this "free time" constructively or we will surely continue to use it destructively.

PSYCHOLOGICAL FACTORS

The second major factor for poor listening is psychological. This is the tendency to treat listening as a passive, automatic activity. In other words, we confuse listening with hearing. Hearing is a physical process involving the reception of sound waves. It is passive and automatic. Listening, on the other hand, is an extremely active psychological process requiring attention and interpretation and involving skills which must be learned. As we have seen, there is more than one kind of listening and each involves a different set of skills suited to different needs or situations.

When we are actively involved in listening, our blood pressure and pulse rate increase and our palms tend to perspire. We actually burn more calories when we listen. (It might even be possible, but not too practical, to go on a listening diet.) Obviously, therefore, if listening takes work, it is important that we get our bodies ready to work in order to be better listeners and that we employ the proper skills.

EDUCATIONAL FACTORS

The third major factor causing poor listening is educational. To understand this factor we must remember two concepts mentioned earlier: listening is the largest part of our daily communication and listening is an active process. Yet in all the formal education which we have received, we have spent major amounts of time learning how to read and write, two skills which total only 25 percent of our daily communication, little if any time learning how to speak in a formal way and, for the vast majority of us, no time learning how to listen effectively. This is not to suggest reading and writing should not be taught, but when you consider the lack of emphasis which listening skills have received in our formal education, it is no wonder why our average listening efficiency is only 25 percent.

Some private corporations have come to realize the importance of teaching listening skills and have developed their own listening programs. As the educational community increases its focus on the importance of listening education and more of us are taught proper listening skills, we will hope to see improvement in that 25 percent efficiency rate.

The last major factor relates to the previous one. Since we have not been taught how to listen effectively, *we often choose the wrong type of listening to do.* Have you ever found yourself tuning in to your own internal dialogue or emotions rather than trying to understand the meaning or emotion in the other person? Have you ever found yourself getting nice and comfortable, as if you were listening for enjoyment, when you were about to listen to a classroom lecture? Clearly, you may have wanted to listen, but you were doing the wrong type of listening.

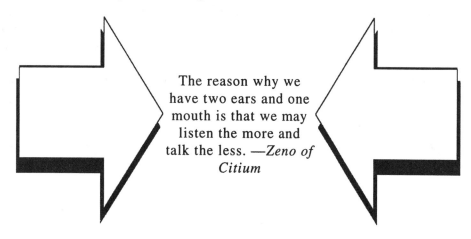

The reason why we have two ears and one mouth is that we may listen the more and talk the less. —*Zeno of Citium*

Listening Is a Lost Art Until Someone Needs You

Erma Bombeck*

It was one of those days when I wanted my own apartment . . . unlisted. My son was telling me in complete detail about a movie he had just seen, punctuated by 3,000 "You know's?" My teeth were falling asleep. There were three phone calls—strike that—three monologues that could have been answered by a recording. I fought the urge to say, "It's been nice listening to you."

In the cab from home to the airport, I got another assault on my ear, this time by a cab driver who was rambling on about his son whom he supported in college, and was in his last year, who put a P.S. on his letter saying "I got married. Her name is Diane." He asked me, "What do you think of that?" and proceeded to answer the question himself.

There were 30 whole beautiful minutes before my plane took off . . . time for me to be alone with my own thoughts, to open a book and let my mind wander. A voice next to me belonging to an elderly woman said, "I'll bet it's cold in Chicago."

Stone-faced I answered. "It's likely."

"I haven't been to Chicago in nearly three years," she persisted. "My son lives there."

"That's nice," I said, my eyes intent on the printed page of the book.

"My husband's body is on this plane. We've been married for 53 years. I don't drive, you know, and when he died a nun drove me from the hospital. We aren't even Catholic. The funeral director let me come to the airport with him."

I don't think I have ever detested myself more than I did at that moment. Another human being was screaming to be heard and in desperation had turned to a cold stranger who was more interested in a novel than the real-life drama at her elbow.

All she needed was a listener . . . no advice, wisdom, experience, money, assistance, expertise or even compassion . . . but just a minute or two to listen.

It seemed rather incongruous that in a society of super-sophisticated communication, we often suffer from a shortage of listeners. She talked numbly and steadily until we boarded the plane, then found her seat in another section. As I hung up my coat, I heard her plaintive voice say to her companion, "I'll bet it's cold in Chicago."

I prayed, "Please God, let her listen."

Why am I telling you this? To make me feel better. It won't help, though.

STEPS TO BETTER LISTENING

How then can we overcome these barriers and improve our listening? As was mentioned earlier, listening actually consists of sets of skills which can be employed in different situations to meet different needs. However, there are six steps which actually underlie all the different types of listening skills.

1. Decide to listen. Obviously, the commitment to listen is at the heart of being a better listener.
2. Get your body ready to work. Remember that listening is work. So it's important to get ready to do work by having an erect posture, being located close to the speaker and creating some inner tension to combat the tendency to relax and daydream.
3. Create a supportive climate. Reduce or eliminate environmental distractions. Avoid statements or actions likely to create defensiveness.
4. Put the other person first. Focus on understanding what he/she has to say and use your brain's "free time" to that end.
5. Select the appropriate type of listening. Determine what your goal should be and focus on the appropriate part of the other person's message. Is the most important element your own feelings, the other person's details, main ideas, overall meaning or underlying emotions?
6. Communicate that you are listening. Being a better listener is only half the job; you must also let the other person know that you are listening through eye contact, facial expressions, body posture and feedback.

Since listening is a learned skill, changes won't occur overnight. As with any skill, "practice makes perfect." With the desire to become a better listener, knowledge of listening skills and a willingness to work, major improvements can be made. Then, no one will say to you, "You never listen to me!"

 Listening Quiz

PURPOSE:

This quiz is designed to get you thinking about the topic of listening and to expose popular conceptions and misconceptions about listening. To the left of each statement indicate whether you think that the statement is true or false by placing a T or F in the blank. Please answer honestly and don't try to "psych-out" the quiz.

True or False

_____ 1. Most people are pretty good listeners.

_____ 2. Listening is an easy, natural, passive behavior.

_____ 3. While listening, it is possible to learn how to pay attention to some other idea, person, event, etc. in our environment at the same time.

_____ 4. There is no way you can "make" someone listen to you.

True or False

_____ 5. To be an effective listener we must focus only on what the other person is saying and avoid being distracted by nonverbal cues.

_____ 6. There is basically only one type of listening we can utilize in our day to day lives.

_____ 7. When listening to someone with a problem, it's a good idea to offer sympathy or advice when possible.

_____ 8. Good listeners are better liked than bad listeners.

_____ 9. Hearing and listening are essentially the same thing.

_____ 10. Good listeners are born not made.

_____ 11. Being a better listener simply means taking in more information from the other person.

_____ 12. When we are listening, we are also communicating to the other person at the same time.

_____ 13. To be a really good listener, you have to be a mindreader.

_____ 14. Using feedback is an important part of listening.

_____ 15. Sometimes when listening, the words get in the way.

_____ 16. The single most neglected communication skill is listening.

_____ 17. There are ways to tell when a person is probably not listening.

_____ 18. We spend about 25 percent of our awake time listening.

_____ 19. No matter how good a listener a person may be, he/she will always misunderstand part of what is being communicated.

_____ 20. When people listen to each other more, there is less chance that they will disagree.

_____ 21. The average listening efficiency of this culture is about 60 percent.

_____ 22. Pretending to listen is better than admitting that we're not interested or don't have the time.

_____ 23. The major cause of poor listening is physical rather than psychological.

_____ 24. Good listeners get sweaty palms.

_____ 25. Most people are more interested in "telling their own story" than in listening to anyone else.

DISCUSSION:

As a class (or in small groups) discuss each question and its implications.

Communication: Its Blocking and Its Facilitation

Carl R. Rogers[*]

Note to the Reader: These excerpts from the following article provide foundational material in the field of communication. As the father of Humanistic Psychology, Dr. Rogers developed the major theories and practice of Active/Empathic Listening. These techniques continue to be widely used in counseling, business and other communication-related fields today.

The whole task of psychotherapy is the task of dealing with a failure in communication. The emotionally maladjusted person, the "neurotic," is in difficulty first because communication within himself has broken down, and second because as a result of this, his communication with others has been damaged. As long as this is true, there are distortions in the way he communicates himself to others, and so he suffers both within himself, and in his interpersonal relations. The task of psychotherapy is to help the person achieve, through a special relationship with a therapist, good communication within himself. Once this is achieved he can communicate more freely and more effectively with others. We may say then that psychotherapy is good communication, within and between men. We may also turn that statement around and it will still be true. Good communication, free communication, within or between men, is always therapeutic.

It is, then, from a background of experience with communication in counseling and psychotherapy that I want to present here two ideas. I wish to state what I believe is one of the major factors in or impeding communication, and then I wish to present what in our experience has proven to be a very important way of improving or facilitating communication.

I would like to propose, as a hypothesis for consideration, that the major barrier to mutual interpersonal communication is our very natural tendency to judge, to evaluate, to approve or disapprove, the statement of the other person, or the other group. Let me illustrate my meaning with some very simple examples. As you leave a lecture meeting, one of the statements you are likely to hear is, "I didn't like that man's talk." Now what do you respond? Almost invariably your reply will be either approval or disapproval of the attitude expressed. Either you respond, "I didn't either. I thought it was terrible," or else you tend to reply, "Oh, I thought it was really good." In other words, your primary reaction is to evaluate what has just been said to you, to evaluate it from your point of view, your own frame of reference.

This brings in another element connected with my hypothesis. Although the tendency to make evaluations is common in almost all interchange of language, it is very much heightened in those situations where feelings and

* By permission, Carl R. Rogers, *Northwestern University Information*, 1952, 20, 9–15.

emotions are deeply involved. So the stronger our feelings, the more likely it is that there will be no mutual element in the communication. I'm sure you recognize this from your own experience. When you have not been emotionally involved yourself, and have listened to a heated discussion, you often go away thinking, "Well, they actually weren't talking about the same thing." And they were not. Each was making a judgment, an evaluation, from his own frame of reference. There was really nothing which could be called communication in any genuine sense. This tendency to react to any emotionally meaningful statement by forming an evaluation of it from our own point of view is, I repeat, the major barrier to interpersonal communication.

But is there any way of solving this problem, of avoiding this barrier? Real communication occurs, and this evaluative tendency is avoided, when we listen with understanding. What does this mean? It means to *see the expressed idea and attitude from the other person's point of view, to sense how it feels to him, to achieve his frame of reference in regard to the thing he is talking about.*

Stated so briefly, this may sound absurdly simple, but it is not. It is an approach which we have found extremely potent in the field of psychotherapy. It is the most effective agent we know for altering the basic personality structure of an individual and improving his relationships and his communications with others. If I can listen to what he can tell me, if I can understand how it seems to him, if I can see its personal meaning for him, if I can sense the emotional flavor which it has for him, then I will be releasing potent forces of change in him. We know from our research that such empathic understanding—understanding *with* a person, not *about* him—is such an effective approach that it can bring about major changes in personality.

Some of you may be feeling that you listen well to people, and that you have never seen such results. The chances are very great indeed that your listening has not been of the type I have described. Fortunately, I can suggest a little laboratory experiment which you can try to test the quality of your understanding. The next time you get into an argument with your wife, or your friend, or with a small group of friends, just stop the discussion a moment and for an experiment, institute this test. Each person can speak up for himself only when he has first restated the ideas and feelings of the previous speaker accurately, and to that speaker's satisfaction. You see what this would mean. It would simply mean that before presenting your own point of view, it would be necessary for you to really achieve the other speaker's frame of reference— to understand his thoughts and feelings so well that you could summarize them for him. Sounds simple, doesn't it? But if you try it you will discover it is one of the most difficult things you have ever tried to do. However, once you have been able to see the other's point of view, your own comments will have to be drastically revised. You will also find the emotion going out of the discussion, the differences being reduced, and those differences which remain being of a rational and understandable sort.

If, then, this way of approach is an effective avenue to good communication and good relationships, why is it not more widely tried and used? I will try to list the difficulties which keep it from being utilized.

In the first place it takes courage, a quality which is not too widespread. I am indebted to Dr. S. I. Hayakawa, the semanticist, for pointing out that to carry on psychotherapy in this fashion is to take a very real risk, and that courage is required. If you really understand another person in this way, if you are willing to enter his private world and see the way life appears to him without any attempt to make evaluative judgments, you run the risk of being changed yourself. You might see it his way, you might find yourself influenced in your attitudes or your personality. This risk of being changed is one of the most frightening prospects most of us can face.

But there is a second obstacle. It is just when emotions are strongest that it is most difficult to achieve the frame of reference of the other person or group. Yet it is the time the attitude is most needed, if communication is to be established. We have not found this to be an insuperable obstacle in our experience in psychotherapy. A third party, who is able to lay aside his own feelings and evaluations, can assist greatly by listening with understanding to each person or group and clarifying the views and attitudes each holds. We have found this very effective in small groups in which contradictory or antagonistic attitudes exist. When the parties to a dispute realize that they are being understood, that someone sees how the situation seems to them, the statements grow less exaggerated and less defensive, and it is no longer necessary to maintain the attitude, "I am 100 percent right and you are 100 percent wrong." The influence of such an understanding catalyst in the group permits the members to come closer and closer to the objective truth involved in the relationship. In this way mutual communication is established and some type of agreement becomes much more possible.

In closing, I would like to summarize this small-scale solution to the problem of barriers in communication, and to point out certain of its characteristics.

I have said that our research and experience to date would make it appear that breakdowns in communication, and the evaluative tendency which is the major barrier to communication, can be avoided. The solution is provided by creating a situation in which each of the different parties comes to understand the other from the *other's* point of view. This has been achieved, in practice, even when feelings run high, by the influence of a person who is willing to understand each point of view empathically, and who thus acts as a catalyst to precipitate further understanding.

This procedure has important characteristics. It can be initiated by one party, without waiting for the other to be ready. It can even be initiated by a neutral person, providing he can gain a minimum of cooperation from one of the parties.

This procedure can deal with the insincerities, the defensive exaggerations, the lies, the "false fronts" which characterize almost every failure in communication. These defensive distortions drop away with astonishing speed as people find that the only intent is to understand, not judge.

This approach leads steadily and rapidly toward the discovery of the truth, toward a realistic appraisal of the objective barriers to communication. The dropping of some defensiveness by one party leads to further dropping of defensiveness by the other party, and truth is thus approached.

This procedure gradually achieves mutual communication. Mutual communication tends to be pointed toward solving a problem rather than toward attacking a person or group. It leads to a situation in which I see how the problem appears to you, as well as to me, and you see how it appears to me, as well as to you. Thus accurately and realistically defined, the problem is almost certain to yield to intelligent attack, or if it is in part insoluble, it will be comfortably accepted as such.

Listening Skill Exercise

PURPOSE:

To practice the "Rogerian" Listening Technique in order to improve listening skills.

PROCEDURE:

1. Form listening triads and designate each participant A, B or C. In each group, one person will act as referee (observer) and the other two will have a discussion, each alternating between being the listener and the speaker.
2. The discussion is to be unstructured, except that before each participant speaks she must summarize, in her own words and without notes, what has been said previously. If the summary is thought to be incorrect, the others are free to interrupt and clarify the misunderstanding. After about seven minutes, the participants switch roles and continue the process. The following topics may be used:

    a. nuclear energy
    b. internet regulation
    c. immigration
    d. smoker's vs. nonsmoker's rights
    e. pollution
    f. Affirmative Action
    g. death penalty
    h. crime/criminals
    i. gun control
    j. drug abuse
    k. violence in media
    l. abortion
    m. Education Standards
    n. political parties
    o. _____

DISCUSSION:

1. Do we usually listen to all that the other person is saying?
2. Did you find that you had difficulty formulating your own thoughts and listening at the same time?
3. Were you forgetting what you were going to say? Not listening to others? Rehearsing your response?
4. When others paraphrased your remarks, did they do it in a more concise way?
5. How important is it to *check out* with the other person what you thought you heard her say?
6. Was the other's manner of presentation affecting your listening ability?
7. Does the way another person listens to you affect *your* self-concept? How?
8. Does the way a person listens to you affect your perception of *that person's* intelligence and personality? How?

9. What are some guidelines for good listening?
   a.
   b.
   c.
   d.

NOTE:

The preceding article entitled "Communication: Its Blocking and Facilitation" by Carl Rogers explains Rogers' feelings about the value of the above method.

Listen

(anonymous)

When I ask you to listen to me and you start giving advice,
you have not done what I asked.
When I ask you to listen to me and you begin to tell me
why I shouldn't feel that way,
you are trampling my feelings.
When I ask you to listen to me and you feel you have to
do something to solve my problems, you have failed me,
strange as that may seem.
So please, just listen and hear me. And if you want to talk,
wait a few minutes for your turn and I promise I'll listen
to you.

It is the providence of knowledge to
speak and it is the privilege of wisdom to listen. —*O. W. Holmes*

Listening Questionnaire

1. Think about 3 people whom you consider to be good listeners.

    a. What is it about them that makes them good listeners? How do they act, what do they do, what do they say?—Be as specific as possible.

    b. What is your attitude about these people?

2. Do you consider yourself a good listener? Why/why not?

    a. When do you have the greatest difficulty listening?

    b. When do you have the least?

3. Why would you want to improve your listening?

    a. When do you consider it important for you to listen?

    b. What do you want to gain from studying listening techniques? In what ways do you want to improve your listening? (Be as specific as possible since these will be your personal objectives for this unit.)

Analysis of My Listening Effectiveness

This form is designed to give you an opportunity to evaluate your own listening effectiveness and another to evaluate you. Ask another to complete it and return it to you within two days. The information provided will enable you to gain some important insight into your strengths and areas for improvement as a listener.

PART 1—OVERALL ESTIMATE OF MY LISTENING ABILITY

Please rate my overall ability as a listener according to the following scale:

POOR   FAIR   AVERAGE   GOOD   EXCELLENT

PART 2—ASSESSMENT OF SPECIFIC LISTENING SKILLS

Section A—For each of the following items, please indicate to the left of each item the frequency with which I demonstrate, to you, the behaviors indicated based upon the following scale:

0	1	2	3	4
never				always

_____ 1.   Appear interested and concerned about what I have to say.

_____ 2.   Appear energetic and anxious to listen.

_____ 3.   Encourage me to continue communicating.

_____ 4.   Indicate if you are confused or don't understand what I am saying.

_____ 5.   Respond to what I am saying in a non-evaluative and non-judgmental way.

_____ 6.   Avoid interrupting me while I am speaking.

_____ 7.   Look at me when I am speaking to you.

_____ 8.   Don't try to change my mind when it's your turn to speak.

Section B—In your own words complete the following two items:

1.   My main strength as a listener is:

2.   The area I most need to work on as a listener is:

Listening Activity

PURPOSE:

To demonstrate how vital listening is to memorization.

PROCEDURE:

1. Break into dyads.
2. Have one person in each pair read the following list to the other. The reader should first read item one, then items one and two, and so on through ten. The listener should try to repeat what she heard after each reading.
3. Read the following as directed:

   One pig.
   Two jaws.
   Three orange VWs.
   Four lively pacifiers.
   Five squelching jackasses.
   Six marinated chicks, prepared to perfection.
   Seven fox-trotters from Amazon County, New Delhi.
   Eight rusty outhouse seats unearthed from the tomb of King Tut.
   Nine dirty men, wearing purple tennis shoes, jogging to Lucretia's massage parlor in back of Mr. Yee's gas station.
   Ten amphibious, blubbery octopi legs from the northeast corner of the westernmost island of Mungula-Stikwee, two-stepping to "I Wanna Hug You All Night Long."
4. Get into a circle and see how many can repeat all ten lines.

DISCUSSION:

1. What problems did you encounter as you got into this activity? Why?
2. How important is concentration to effective listening?
3. What part can verbal repetition play in acquiring good listening-memory skills?
4. Does the quality of the source's message affect receiver listening?

DILBERT by Scott Adams

DILBERT reprinted by permission of United Feature Syndicate, Inc.

SUGGESTIONS ABOUT LISTENING HABITS

10 Bad Listening Habits	10 Good Listening Habits
1. Calling subject "uninteresting."	1. Tuning in the speaker to see if there is anything you can use.
2. Criticizing speaker's delivery, personal appearance, etc.	2. Getting the speaker's message which is probably more important.
3. Getting overexcited and preparing rebuttal.	3. Hearing the person out before you judge her.
4. Listening only for facts.	4. Listening also for main ideas, principles and concepts.
5. Trying to make an outline of everything you hear.	5. Listening a couple of minutes before taking notes.
6. Faking attention to the speaker.	6. Good listening is not totally relaxed. There is a collection of tensions inside.
7. Tolerating distractions.	7. Doing something about the distractions, closing a door, requesting a person to speak louder, etc.
8. Avoiding difficult material.	8. Learning to listen to difficult material.
9. Letting emotion-laden words affect listening.	9. Trying to understand your reaction to emotion-laden words which might cause barriers.
10. Wasting difference between speech speed (words per minute) and thought speed (words per minute).	10. Making thought speed an asset instead of a liability by: a. Anticipating the next point to be made. b. Mentally summarizing.

By permission Ralph Nichols and Leonard Stevens; *Are You Listening?*

Test for Listening Power

PURPOSE:

To carefully examine your listening habits and identify those that might be improved.

PROCEDURE:

Imagine yourself in a classroom or meeting where you are not the most important individual, but a participating member. Score yourself on these 10 worst listening habits:

Rating Scale	
1	always guilty
2	almost always
4	frequently
6	infrequently
8	almost never
10	never

Score

_____ 1. Calling the subject uninteresting. When the subject is a little remote, do you take the first opportunity to "tune out"?

_____ 2. Reacting to externals. Do you let the speaker's facial expression, accent or dress interfere?

_____ 3. Getting overstimulated. Are you easily aroused to anger or unbridled enthusiasm?

_____ 4. Listening for specifics only. Do you listen to words rather than for themes?

_____ 5. Writing too little or too much. Do you think you will remember everything without abbreviated notes? Or, equally bad, are you a compulsive note taker?

_____ 6. Faking attention. Do you smile and nod your head in the speaker's direction? (No extra points for doing it because you think it's polite.)

_____ 7. Tolerating or creating distractions. Do you let noises outside the room interfere? Do you chat, doodle, play with paper?

_____ 8. Avoiding difficult material. Are you only attracted to material of general interest?

_____ 9. Letting personal prejudice or bias interfere. Do personal biases clog your listening?

_____ 10. Wasting the thought-speech ratio. Do you tell yourself you can follow the speech and still do some private blue-skying?

_____ Total Score

Score	
90+	Superior
	(A psychiatrist or personnel interviewer might score this high)
80–90	Excellent
70–80	Good
–70	Needs improvement

DISCUSSION:

1. Were you surprised by your score? Identify your worst habits and how to improve them.

One of the best ways to persuade others
is with your ears—by listening . . . —D. Rusk

R E A C T I O N S

Name _____
Date _____

Your professor may require this exercise to be handed in.

1. Why is listening such an important communicating skill?

2. Why is it that we have a tendency to evaluate what a person says rather than listening with understanding?

3. Explain why we don't need training to hear, but we do need training to become better listeners.

4. What kinds of verbal and nonverbal feedback can we use to let a person know we are listening?

5. Select a specific listening experience where you blocked out what the person was saying. What are some ways you plan to overcome this bad listening habit?

6. Where do you plan to practice empathic or active listening? How do you expect it to improve your communication?

Perception

DEFINITIONS

We spend our entire lives communicating our perceptions of what we think our world is like, what is happening in it and what we are doing about it.

Thus, what and how we perceive constitutes a critical element in our study of communication.

✳ Perception

Definitions:

- The manner in which we assign meaning, value, significance and usefulness to elements in our environment
- The sensing, processing, organizing and interpreting of our reality

Examples:

Consider the following situations. Your *perception of* the central figure in each will determine your *reaction to* it.

As you are casually strolling through your own neighborhood, you observe a female black kitten on the sidewalk in front of you. Do you:

- Want to lift, cuddle and talk to her because she is soft, loving and vulnerable?
- Step around but otherwise ignore her because you are simply not interested in cats?
- Avoid even looking at her, crossing to the other side of the street, because in your mind she is associated with the devil and bad luck?

As you continue through this chapter, you will become more aware of the importance of perception in everyday communication.

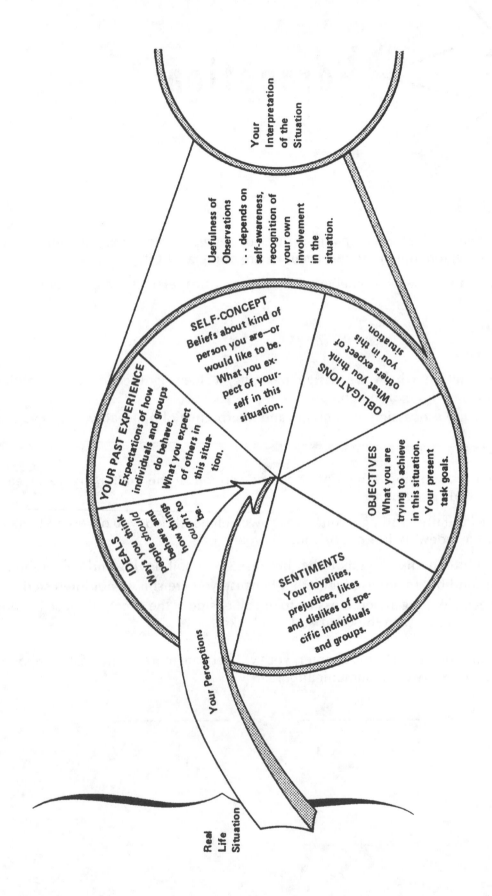

SELF-CONCEPT
Beliefs about kind of person you are—or would like to be. What you expect of yourself in this situation.

YOUR PAST EXPERIENCE
Expectations of how individuals and groups do behave. What you expect of others in this situation.

IDEALS
Ways you think people should behave and how things ought to be.

OBLIGATIONS
What you think others expect of you in this situation.

OBJECTIVES
What you are trying to achieve in this situation. Your present task goals.

SENTIMENTS
Your loyalites, prejudices, likes and dislikes of specific individuals and groups.

Usefulness of Observations . . . depends on self-awareness, recognition of your own involvement in the situation.

Your Interpretation of the Situation

Your Perceptions

Real Life Situation

Factors affecting your interpretation of a situation. By permission, Dr. Robert L. Katz, *Developing Human Skill*; © 1955, Amos Tuck School of Business Administration, Dartmouth College.

THE IMPORTANCE OF PERCEPTUAL AWARENESS

If you were in a shoe store and asked the sales person for a pair of black cowboy boots in size 8, and the individual returned with a pair of calf-skin loafers in size 9, you might think that the salesperson was not listening. It may be that he did hear you but flashed on calfskin when you said cowboy, perceived you as preferring loafers, and thought that a size 9 might be a more comfortable fit for you. This kind of misperception occurs often in our interactions with others. It happens because we think that everyone sees the world the same way that we do. But they don't. Just as each of us has different fingerprints or a unique voice print, a person's perceptions likewise carry a unique code. We will examine four key factors that are responsible for our individual perceptions of the world. These four factors determine how we select, organize and interpret our experiences into a meaningful picture of the world around us.

THE FOUR P'S OF PERCEPTION

Effective communication skills can help us bridge our innate differences. But, we can only share perceptions in so far as we are able to see the other person's perspective. When we communicate we share our *perception* of the world, not necessarily the *truth*. Some reasons for the differences in the perceptual process include: (1) physiological factors, (2) psychological factors, (3) position in space and (4) past experiences. Taking each of the four in turn, it is interesting to consider the odds against effective communication.

Physiological factors include what we are able to perceive; i.e., what capacity we possess with our senses of sight, touch, hearing, taste and smell. You might try wearing someone else's eye glasses just long enough to experience how different that person's world must appear to him or her. Compound that difference by putting cotton in your ears to reduce your ability to hear or wear cotton gloves to reduce sensitivity of your touch. You might notice how different the world appears if you wear a 25-pound weight belt

around all day. It is difficult to imagine that the world that we experience is not the same world that every other person experiences.

Psychological factors encompass what we need to perceive and, therefore, do. We all differ in immediate needs, desires, interests and motives. Thus, we tend to pay attention to only—or especially—those things which interest us. The continual barrage of external stimuli necessitates that we attend to limited aspects of our environment; however, we make choices not randomly but with our psychological drives as a primary motive. For example, two friends are riding together in a car. If one is looking for entertainment or a good time, he is more likely to see the theaters and bars; the other, who happens to be tired after a long day at work, may fail to see any of those. The less energetic of the two may, in fact, tend to focus on relaxation-oriented stimuli. Most of us are so good at paying attention only to what interests us that we even distort external events and things to make them fit what we want to perceive. The need for beauty, for example, can be strong enough that someone can find it in rubble. An intense need for security may cause someone to sense trouble where it does not exist. An unsatisfied need for love or friendship might cause one to recognize a reciprocal desire in another person where it may not merit this perception.

Position in space of a person certainly adjusts what can be seen. We are limited in what we perceive by angle, height, and location in time and space. How different a parade must appear to a small child who is perched on her dad's shoulders compared to a little boy who is standing on the ground.

Past experience is our last stop in this sequence of P's. People tend to perceive according to what they've learned to perceive. Call it expectation or even anticipation, but regardless of terminology, it is the knee jerk of familiarity. Our familiarity with something helps us to accept, as well as recognize it. Our past experiences accompany us in each perception we have.

CUE SENSITIVITY

The P's of Perception are four in number; the cues are innumerable. Cue sensitivity is still another way of understanding the selectivity of perception. The cues are external to oneself out there in the world of stimuli; the sensitivity is internal and quite individualized. The sensitivity or lack of it on the part of the individual is not uniform or equivalent by any stretch of the imagination. The following list indicates some reasons why we might overlook some of the cues that exist.

Familiarity We often ignore what we take for granted. The "a's" and "the's" on this page were probably not even seen by you, yet they are indeed printed. A gate passed through daily is not there consciously. A frequently heard sound disappears, but only in your perception. A spouse's repeated question is simply not heard. Such cues may not seem important until demand or change forces recognition—bringing with it a degree of consequence, too *often* negative in nature.

Complacency Our very contentment can serve to disarm us and render lessened degrees of sensitivity. A relaxed state of body and/or mind can diminish our awareness. Trained states of relaxed awareness such as meditation can overcome this; however, on a daily scale of activity we become numb as our needs are satisfied.

Lack of experience or knowledge If something is not familiar at all, a signal for danger

for example, no capacity for sensitivity is yet developed for one's own protection. A child soon learns the hazard of a hot stove. Any noise, smell or sight is not an understood cue for the untried perceiver. New ideas or values could be included here also.

Problem Paralysis The person who is experiencing problem overload or sensory overkill and is burdened from within is likely to miss that which is outside. There simply is no room for one more thing.

Singularity Thoughts or concerns which are near-obsessive tend to override other stimuli. The task-oriented, Task A personality attempting to succeed in a given assignment may block not only distractions but also helpful cues as well. Many generals have, indeed, won the battle but lost the war.

Having examined cue sensitivity from the standpoint of reasons for overlooking important cues, a brief summary of why we see particular cues might be illuminating. Our degree of awareness,—our internal sensitivity—stems from knowledge, sensing selectivity, vigilance, vocabulary, topic interest, open-mindedness, experience, and even practice.

Because of the P's and cues, we tend to individually select from a myriad of cues, organize in a way that makes sense to us, and interpret based on our unique experiences. It is important to keep in mind that no one else sees the same world that we see.

BARRIERS TO PERCEPTION

Let's summarize some of the problems we have communicating with others because of our perceptions. We tend to perceive the world in terms of our own needs, wants, experiences, culture, expectations and physical abilities or limitations regardless of what external reality might be. Since our perception process is unique to each of us, we often perceive the world very differently from those around us.

We have trouble communicating with others when we fail to be aware that we perceive the external world through our senses (an internal process) and we can be fooled. Even the symbols (both verbal and nonverbal) we use to communicate our perceptions to others may have meanings which are considerably different from what we intend our receiver to understand.

THE PERCEPTUAL PROCESS

The perceptual process can cause confusion about what is going on in the real world. We believe what we perceive; we treat it as truth. On the other hand, another person with whom we are communicating believes that what he/she perceives is what is going on in the real world and treats it as truth. What is it about the perceptual process that allows such unique selectivity to occur?

We believe that our world of experience has structure.

The question here is how do our senses interact with the real world? Many people assume that our eyes, ears, nose and fingers impassively connect with the world the way a video camera does—passively. If that were the case, our senses would record everything that was happening to us and then we would sort it out at the cognitive level. That is, we would interpret it later. What actually happens is that the very act of sensing is also one of creating. We perceive the world that we are prepared to perceive. An example of this can be seen by doing a little experiment. Use figure 3.1. Have one or more people first look only at drawing (a), then have one or more people look only at drawing (c). Then have all of the people look at drawing (b) and ask them if they see the old lady or the young lady.

(a)   (b)   (c)

Chances are, they will see the person similar to the one that they saw first. The people whom you asked to look at the pictures had been preconditioned to process the input stimuli in a certain way, and they created a structure consistent with that mind-set. In this categorizing process, a person extracts stimuli from the world and forces that stimuli into a set of categories. The categories we use are derived from our past history, so for each of us we create a world of structure.

Our world of experience has stability.

When we open our eyes and look at a scene, we are not aware of the constant shifts in the picture as our eyes and our attention wander. There is an enduring aspect to our experience. We select certain facets of the situation and stick with them. Check this statement against your own experience with the ambiguous picture in Fig. 3.1. If it was like the experience of most people, your first perception of the picture, whether it was the old lady or the young woman, continued to demand your attention. In order to understand the world we experience, it is easier for us to give it stability.

Our world of experience is meaningful.

Can you conceive of a world in which everything was random, with no apparent causal relationships? Nothing would seem familiar. The general experience would be one of chaos. Such a state of affairs is so alien to our everyday-life experience that it is extremely difficult to imagine.

We make our experiences meaningful so that they are related and seem familiar. In a way, that is what we do when we look at a cloud in the sky and imagine that it is an elephant or a rabbit. We constantly do this with every aspect of our daily lives. We force two or more nonrelated events into a meaningful relationship. And we do it differently than anyone else. This means that everyone else will create a different meaning from life experiences than we do.

In order to give the world of our perceptions structure, stability and meaning, we must organize it. The way we do this causes our perceptions to differ from everyone else's.

PERCEPTION: AGREE/DISAGREE

PURPOSE:	To test your understanding of basic perception principles.
PROCEDURE:	1. Read each statement carefully.
	2. If you believe it to be true, check the Agree column under Individual. If you believe it, or any part of it, to be false, check the Disagree column under Individual.
	3. For each of the following statements, check if you agree or disagree.

Individual				Group	
Agree	Disagree			Agree	Disagree
		1.	The perception of a physical object or event depends more upon the object or event than upon the mind of the observer.		
		2.	Perception is primarily an interpersonal phenomenon.		
		3.	The fact that hallucinations and dreams may seem as real as waking perception indicates that perception depends very little upon external reality.		
		4.	The reaction we have to what we see generally depends upon learning and culture.		
		5.	We tend to see what we wish to see or are expecting to see regardless of what reality is.		
		6.	We can eliminate all distortion in our perception by careful, scientific observation.		
		7.	Scientific instruments, though they extend the limits of our perception, do not make perception any more real.		
		8.	What we perceive is no more than a representation of what is.		
		9.	Perception is a physical response to a physical reality. It is only when we begin talking about our perceptions that we begin to distort them.		
		10.	If we are careful, we can see the world as it really is.		
		11.	We react to our environment on the basis of what we perceive that environment to be like and not on what the environment is really like.		
DISCUSSION:			Your instructor will lead a discussion, comparing Individual and Group responses.		

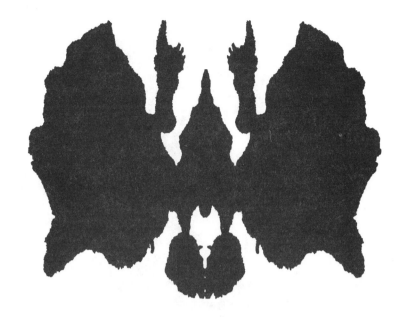

Rorschach ink-blot
What do you perceive?

"Black Signature" by Magritte
What do you perceive?

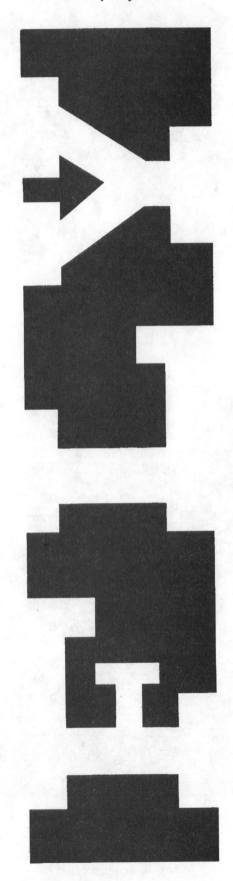

What do you perceive?

 **Check Your Perception**

PURPOSE:

To give you a chance to check your perception.

PROCEDURE:

1. Read the following aloud.

Paris
in the
the Springtime

Bird
in the
the Hand

Once
in a
a lifetime

2. How many times does the letter F appear in the box below?

> Finished Files are the Result
> of Years of Scientific Study
> Combined with the Experience
> of Many Years

What do you perceive?

What do you perceive?

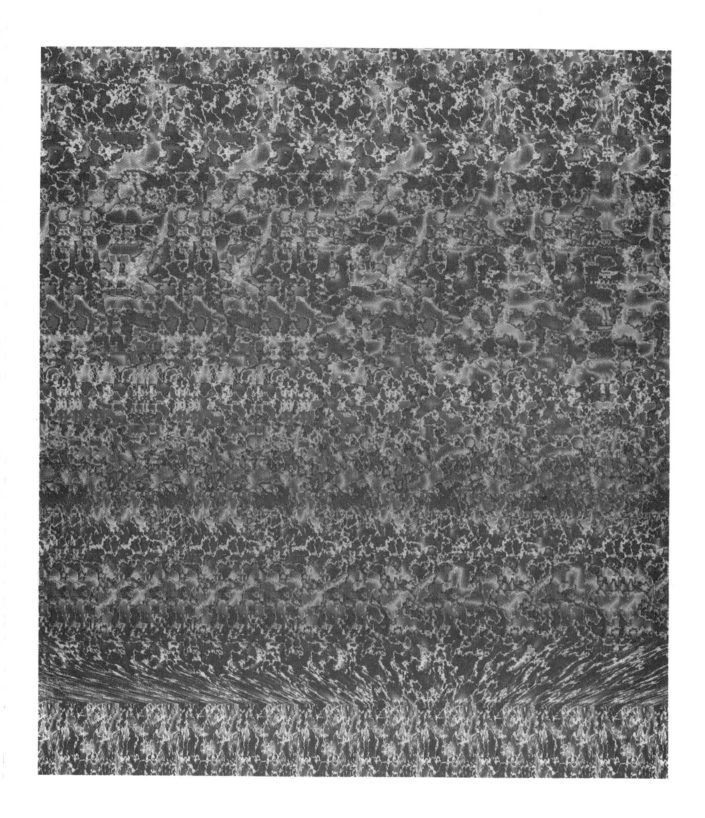

From *Hidden Dimensions* by Dan Dyckman. Copyright © 1994 by Dan Dyckman. Reprinted by permission of Harmony Books, a division of Crown Publishers, Inc.

The Author at Work
What do you perceive?

Quiz—Common Perception

PURPOSE:

To understand how accurately we perceive our commonplace world.

PROCEDURE:

This is a timed test (10 minutes). Place your answer to the left of the number; you are encouraged to guess.

_____ 1.   On a standard traffic light, is the green on top or bottom?

_____ 2.   The stripes of a man's tie usually slant down in what direction from the wearer's view (left, right, both)?

_____ 3.   In which hand is the Statue of Liberty's torch?

_____ 4.   Name the six colors in the Campbell's soup label.

_____ 5.   What two letters of the alphabet do not appear on a telephone dial?

_____ 6.   What two digits on a telephone dial are not accompanied by letters?

_____ 7.   When you walk, does your right arm swing with your right leg or your left leg?

_____ 8.   How many matches are in a standard pack?

_____ 9.   On the American flag, is the upper-most stripe red or white?

_____ 10. What is the lowest <u>number</u> on an FM radio dial?

_____ 11. On a standard computer, over which number is the "%" symbol? (percent)

_____ 12. Which way does the red diagonal slash go in the international "no parking" or "no smoking" signs?

_____ 13. How many channels on a standard VHF television dial?

_____ 14. Which side of a woman's blouse has the button holes?

_____ 15. On the California license plate, is the state name at the top or the bottom?

_____ 16. Which direction do the blades on a fan rotate?

_____ 17. Whose face is on a dime?

_____ 18. How many sides does a stop sign have?

_____ 19. Do books have their even-numbered pages on the left or the right?

_____ 20. How many lug nuts are on a standard American car wheel?

_____ 21. How many sides are there on a standard pencil?

_____ 22. Sleepy, Happy, Sneezy, Grumpy, Dopey and Doc. Name the seventh dwarf.

_____ 23. How many hot dog buns are in a standard package?

_____ 25. On which card in the deck is the cardmaker's trademark?

_____ 26. On which side of a standard venetian-blind is the cord that adjusts the opening between the slats?

_____ 27. On the back of a $5 bill is the Lincoln Memorial. What's in the center of the backside of a $1 bill?

_____ 28. There are 12 buttons on a touch-tone telephone. What symbols are on the two buttons that bear no digits?

_____ 29. How many curves in a standard paper clip?

_____ 30. Does a merry-go-round turn clockwise or counterclockwise?

Score	
28–30	Excellent
25–27	Good
20–24	Okay
16–19	Fair

DISCUSSION:

1. What are some reasons you may fail to perceive, or perceive incorrectly, your commonplace world?
2. How much of our perception comes from experiences stored in our subconscious (those items at which you guessed)?
3. Is it important to perceive our immediate environment/surroundings accurately? Objectively? Why? Why not?

The Way I See Things

PURPOSE:

To help you understand that recent events in your life affect the way you perceive the world.

PROCEDURE:

1. In the space below, write about an event which has occurred within a recent time period which has affected the way you perceive the present and, thus, your intra/interpersonal communication with others. For example, it might be a new job, a change of schools, a birth or death, a relationship, experience, accomplishment, decision, etc. Be very specific in your description.

2. Describe the ways this event has affected your perception, your communication, your opinion about yourself and your values.
3. In what ways has this event caused you to alter your behavior? Explain.
4. Form small groups and discuss what each has written. Also discuss the following questions.

DISCUSSION:

1. How does the way you see the world affect your communication on both the intrapersonal and interpersonal levels?
2. How can you relate this knowledge and insight to your personal, professional and social lives?
3. Are you likely to let this event have a lasting effect or will you soon forget it?

Count the Squares

PURPOSE:

To compare your perception with the perception of others and to see how others can teach you to perceive.

PROCEDURE:

1. Count the number of squares in the diagram below. How many squares are there?
2. Join a triad, recount the squares and enter the total number of squares you see.

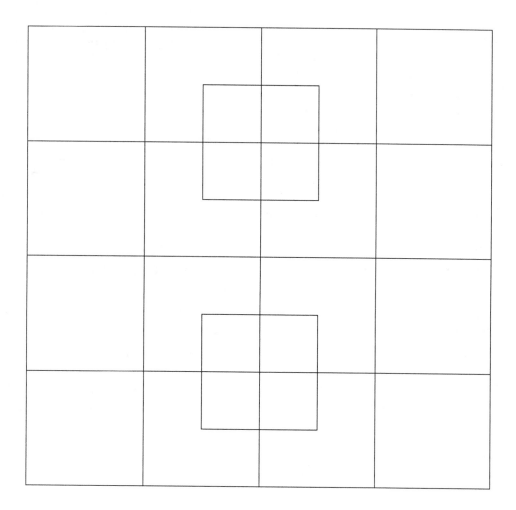

DISCUSSION:

How does communicating with others affect our perception?

In order to objectify our perceptions of the real world so that they are in alignment with what really is rather than the way we perceive them to be, we have to be aware. Such awareness is not easy. Constant awareness is probably impossible. Jon Kabat-Zinn in his book *Wherever You Go There You Are,* writes about being "mindful" in our daily activities.

You might begin your journey toward awareness by taking some small steps. Set aside a brief time each day in which you plan to observe what is going on without having any expectations or making any judgments about what occurs. Gradually increase the number of times each day that you do this. You might then extend this process to an interaction that you plan with another individual. After you have spent some time on this technique, you might ask others to share their perceptions with you of some things that you have both observed. Stay open to just listening to what they have to say. From such a simple start, you will soon find yourself being more objective, and more open to what is really happening in the world.

Perception Checking

One specific approach to be more objective that we can begin today is described in the following activity. It is an approach to check out the difference between what another person means by a specific behavior and the meaning that we attach to it. This activity is one that you can do anytime you are confused by another person's words or behavior.

First step: Describe the behavior to the other person in objective, neutral language.

Second step: Indicate two possible explanations that you have made about the behavior.

Third step: Ask the person to tell you which explanation is correct.

Example: The situation might look like this:

Your friend said that she would meet you in front of the library at 9:00 A.M. today to study for the exam that you will both take tomorrow. But she failed to show. At 3:00 P.M. you ran into her in the cafeteria and she acted like you never had an appointment.

First step: (Describe the event objectively) "Hi Karen, we had planned yesterday in Bio to meet today in front of the library at 9:00 A.M. I was there from 8:55 until 9:10, but you never showed up."

Second step: (Offer two possible explanations of her behavior) "Either you misunderstood our plans or you had something else come up."

Third step: (Ask which explanation is correct) "Which was it?"

Such perception checking does not reverse the failed 9:00 A.M. appointment but it lets your friend know what you are thinking, and it allows her to explain her behavior. This takes the guessing out of her motives and allows you to communicate accurately about what occurred.

The Whole Truth

PURPOSE:

In this exercise, you are to examine your emotional responses to the following situations. How well are you able to project yourself into these situations and describe how you would actually respond? There is a tendency for us to be logical and describe how we would like to act, or how nobly we are supposed to act, but the test is to determine if we can accurately and honestly describe our first feelings—our emotional reactions to these situations.

PROCEDURE:

Read about each situation and briefly describe your first reaction to each one in the space provided.

1. You are in a hurry. You drive to a school supply store to pick up some items for a quiz. You look for a parking place close to the store. The lot is full. But there are two parking places directly in front of the store that are occupied by just one car. The driver has left the car at an angle with part of it in both places. The parking stalls are clearly marked. There is no reason the car could not be parked so that another driver could use the valuable parking space.

    Was the driver being considerate of others? What are your feelings when you see something like this? What is your attitude toward the driver?

2. You are terribly busy at work. You stop long enough to dash across the street to pick up something at the store. You stand at the counter waiting. Behind the counter is a young girl reading a book. She apparently ignores you. You stand there for several minutes before you finally go to another checkout stand.

    What are your reactions and your feelings? What is your attitude toward the girl?

3. You are walking through a run-down section of a city. Lying against the wall of a building is a man with messed-up clothing and an empty wine bottle beside him. He is mumbling to himself.

    What are your feelings? What is your attitude toward him?

DISCUSSION:

In small groups, compare your reactions with others and determine what caused each of you to react as you did.

Now the Rest of the Truth (A follow-up activity)

PURPOSE:

Now that you have had an opportunity to express your feelings about each of these situations, let's go a step further and see how the stories ended. These are based on true instances so they aren't as unusual as they might sound. Your task is to see how your feelings change once you gain a different perspective.

PROCEDURE:

After reading the additional information about each situation below, write how your feelings or attitudes have changed.

1. You finally park your car. You are about to enter the store and see the driver of the car parked in two places run out, jump in the car and drive away. Inside the store, the clerk tells you that there has just been a bad accident a mile away. The driver of the car who parked carelessly taking up two spaces had driven to the store to telephone the ambulance and the police. In his rush to get to a phone, he was not aware of the way he had parked.

    Any change in feeling now? How about your attitude toward the driver?

2. As you prepare to leave the store, the owner approaches the girl who had ignored you. After speaking a few words to her in French, he introduces her to the clerk who checked you out as a foreign student who will be living with his family during the next school year. The student was just waiting for a ride to the owner's home.

    Any change in feeling now? How about your attitude toward the girl?

3. A police ambulance pulls up. You learn that the man, a banker, was just hit on the head with the wine bottle and robbed.

    Describe your feelings now. Any changes in attitude?

DISCUSSION:

Return to your small groups and discuss how your attitudes or feelings changed after learning the additional facts.

What disturbs men's minds is not events but their judgments on events. —*Epictetus*

Increasing Perceptual Understanding

PURPOSE:

To allow the students an opportunity to practice perception checking.

PROCEDURE:

1. Divide into small groups
2. Have each group member describe a situation when he/she was not clear about the meaning of another person's behavior.
3. Have each group member now offer a 3-step perception checking response to each situation.

DISCUSSION:

1. How does the first step of the process take the threat out of talking to the other person?
2. How does offering two possible explanations allow the other person to understand your perceptions?
3. How does asking a question at the end clarify what you want from the other?

Changing Course

Two battleships assigned to the training squadron had been at sea on maneuvers in heavy weather for several days. I was serving on the lead battleship and was on watch on the bridge as night fell. The visibility was poor with patchy fog, so the captain remained on the bridge keeping an eye on all activities.

Shortly after dark, the lookout on the wing of the bridge reported, "Light, bearing on the starboard bow."

"Is it steady or moving astern?" the captain called out.

Lookout replied, "Steady, captain," which meant we were on a dangerous collision course with that ship.

The captain then called to the signalman, "Signal that ship: We are on a collision course, advise you change course 20 degrees."

Back came the signal, "Advisable for you to change course 20 degrees."

The captain said, "Send, I'm a captain, change course 20 degrees."

"I'm a seaman second class," came the reply. "You had better change course 20 degrees."

By that time, the captain was furious. He spat out, "Send, I'm a battleship. Change course 20 degrees."

Back came the flashing light, "I'm a lighthouse."

We changed course.

R E A C T I O N S

Name _____

Date _____

Your professor may require this exercise to be handed in.

1. List at least five reasons you perceive differently from everyone else.

2. Why do we study perception in a Speech Communication class?

3. How will your new knowledge of perception help you to be a better communicator? Give an example using a specific person from your job, family, friends or other relationships.

4. What are at least four things we can do to increase fidelity when we find that the persons with whom we are communicating have perceptions different from our own?

5. Indicate a recent event in which you might have used the perception checking technique. How might the results have been different?

Nonverbal Communication

DEFINITIONS

Nonverbal communication consists of relaying message units to augment, contradict or replace verbal communication. In other words, nonverbal communication:

✳ **Nonverbal Communication**

General Definitions:

Relays messages from individual to individual or from object to individual.

Example: Husband smiles at his wife.
Red light signals vehicles to stop.

Can augment verbal communication.

Example: A mother can shout at her child and simultaneously stamp her foot. Both her vocal utterance and physical gesture convey similar meanings.

Can contradict verbal communication.

Example: A man can tell a woman that he loves her while unconsciously he is backing away from her.

Can replace verbal communication.

Example: Visitors in foreign countries have often asked for and received directions through gesture.

THE IMPORTANCE OF NONVERBAL COMMUNICATION

Most of us already know a great deal about nonverbal communication. After all, we've been doing it since the instant we were born. We already know (or think we do) when someone's verbal message is contradicted by the nonverbal signals. And we almost always subconsciously choose the nonverbal message over the verbal!

Depending on which set of definitions we use, from 75–95 percent of all the communication that we do is nonverbal. With these two facts in mind (we already know much about nonverbal communication and we do an enormous amount about it), let's ask one more question: How good are we at communicating nonverbally?

If we are honest with ourselves, we may have to admit that we are not very effective at it. Many of our misunderstandings and our communication failures result from the errors we make in "reading" nonverbal communication.

And that is what this chapter is all about. Taking the knowledge you already have, let's learn how to make our own nonverbal communication more effective and how to do a better job of interpreting the nonverbal language of others.

Some very basic definitions follow and are in the articles by Gelman. Reasons that nonverbal communication is really important are in the next five articles.

BARRIERS TO NONVERBAL COMMUNICATION

Since nonverbal communication is so important, you would think that people would be more aware of how to make effective use of it in their conversations, but they don't. Why don't they? We think that at least three barriers get in the way: 1. A lack of awareness of our own nonverbal messages. 2. A lack of knowledge and training about nonverbal communication. 3. A tendency to assume that we understand each other's nonverbal communication.

LACK OF AWARENESS

A lack of awareness of our own nonverbal messages. Most of us tend to be unaware that we are always communicating nonverbally with everyone who can see or hear us. As soon as other persons notice us, they attach some meaning to what they see or hear. If they like what they hear or see, they attach positive value to us. If we seem similar to someone they like, they think well of us. The opposite can also occur if they don't like what they see. Much of our talking is an attempt to make sure that others see us as we want them to, not as they do.

In addition to the passive messages that we send to others, we also actively send messages to others about how we feel about them every time that we communicate with them. For example, when I tell the person behind the ice cream counter that I want a vanilla ice cream cone, my nonverbal message will let the person know how I feel about her. Are we equal as people or is she my servant for the moment?

We may spend a lot of time carefully planning the words that we are going to say but our nonverbal messages may totally invalidate everything that we had intended.

LACK OF KNOWLEDGE AND TRAINING

A lack of knowledge and training about nonverbal communication. The elocutionists of the 18th and 19th centuries were very much aware of the impact that their gestures, posture and use of their voices had on audiences and they received careful training to perfect those skills. With the more conversational style of modern speakers, we left behind the grand style of earlier speakers and we also forgot the understanding on which it was all built. Recently, communication experts have popularized nonverbal communication as a way of learning about others' behavior. Few, however, have indicated the need to be aware of and to understand our own nonverbal actions.

Although many courses are available for teaching how to speak and fewer courses and seminars are designed to help people to listen better, there is still little opportunity to learn how to more effectively use nonverbal communication.

OUR TENDENCY TO ASSUME

A tendency to assume that we understand each others' nonverbal communication. If you have already read about verbal communication (sending audio messages), you should be able to see the similar pattern with nonverbal communication. When others send messages, whether they are sent verbally or nonverbally, our tendency is to respond to them from our frame of reference. That means that we guess what they are saying and respond based on our guesses. For example, if we guess correctly that our friend's crossed arms mean that she is upset, we would respond correctly by quietly talking about what is bothering her. However, those symbols of crossed arms may merely mean that she is cold.

It is difficult not to see others as we see ourselves. Yet to be effective communicators, we need to know that we are all very different from each other and that the purpose of communication is to discover our differences and similarities.

Nonverbal Aspects of Communication: Notable Quotes

"Americans are characteristically illiterate in the area of gesture language."
  Weston LaBarre

"Watch out for the man whose stomach doesn't move when he laughs."
  Cantonese Proverb

"The eyes of men converse as much as their tongues, with the advantage that the ocular dialect needs no dictionary, but is understood the world over."
  Ralph Waldo Emerson

"Man is a multisensorial being. Obviously he verbalizes."
  Ray Birdwhistell

"Silence, the instrument of isolation, can create community."
  J. Vernon Jensen

"Words can mean that I want to make you into a friend and silence can mean that I accept you already being one."
  Hugh Prather

I learn a great deal by merely observing you, and letting you talk as long as you please, and taking note of what you do not say. —*T. S. Eliot*

You Don't Say

Y ou arrive at work and a message awaits you at your desk. The boss wants to see you. You enter the grey walled office of your boss. He stands . . . arms folded, behind a large rectangular desk. He motions you to sit. He peers at you with a direct, unwavering stare.

The term "nonverbal" is commonly used to describe human and animal communication excepting those of spoken or written words. Our "nonverbal" communication, which is our manner of speaking without words, is partly taught, partly imitative and partly instinctive. These "nonverbal" messages may repeat, contradict, compliment, accent or regulate that which we actually "say."

Let us look at the fact situation above. What would be your reaction? "Why is he staring at me?" "His arms are folded, why is he angry?" The direct stare is seen by many in this culture as a form of threat. However, while not unique, this is characteristic of our culture specifically. Staring, in addition, is considered a threat in many species of animals. Now, let us change slightly the fact situation above. Now, your boss stares, but also smiles and nods suggestively. What does he mean now? He may be expressing emotion, a possible raise, even sexual interest by the same stare when coupled by other nonverbal messages.

Nonverbal communication is quite possibly the most important part of the communicative process, for researchers now know that our actual words carry far less meaning than nonverbal cues. For example, repeat many times the following sentence, emphasizing different words in the sentence each time you do so: "I beat my spouse last night." Does not the meaning of the sentence change? The words themselves carry many meanings depending upon nonverbal cues, in this case, inflection. Essentially, the study of nonverbal communication is broken down to (1) environmental clues; (2) spatial study; (3) physical appearance; (4) behavioral cues; (5) vocal qualities; and (6) body motion or kinesics.

KINESICS—EYE CONTACT AND FACIAL EXPRESSION

A great deal is conveyed through our eyes and facial expression. However, we cannot isolate this study without considering all other bodily and environmental cues. Facial expression is probably the most communicative of our body. Researchers have only recently discovered that the facial expressions made are extremely rapid and may not be consciously noticed in normal communication. They are, however, picked up by our subconscious or faculties in giving meaning to the words used. By careful study, one can learn to notice expressions of affective states and be accurate in identifying facial expressions.

Of all facial cues, eye contact has found the most interest by researchers. Years of study have gone into characterizing and identifying pupil dilation. We know, for instance, that continued eye contact may signal arousal, interest or attentiveness. However, we do not as yet know the full extent of cultural aspects of such eye contact. As an example, in our culture when we feel physically uncomfortable due to the proximity of others, we lower our eyes traditionally though not always. We feel awkward or somehow invaded if someone stares intently at us. It is deemed a threat. Eye contact may differ from age to age and between sexes. Researchers are, however, not sure to what degree. It remains an open field for research and investigation.

THE ENVIRONMENT

There is little doubt that the environment in which one speaks may contribute to the overall communicative process. Ponder for a moment how the size of the room, furniture arrangements, temperature, lighting, color of the walls and even the space between persons may affect our desire to communicate or the openness of the communication.

High in the study of environmental clues is the study of "proxemics," or the investigation of how space between individuals may affect the communicative process between them. It appears that we culturally and instinctively maintain a protective perimeter of space between us and the outside world. While this space may differ from culture to culture, it may have its base in the protective instincts of our animalistic past. Researchers have isolated several distances and attached to them levels of communication. Between zero and 18 inches, we traditionally allow our most intimate friends. We communicate on a "personal" level with those persons within 18 inches to four feet. This personal level is usually reserved to classmates or other persons at a party or meeting. A "social" distance is considered somewhere between four feet and twelve feet, this level being reserved to guests in living rooms, etc. Finally, there appears a "public" distance, which does not seem to generate communication. These distances are not hard and fast but seem to differ with cultural, even physical differences between individuals.

KINESICS—BEHAVIOR AND GESTURES

When we speak of gestures and body language, we deal with the heart of the study of nonverbal behavior. As in all nonverbal study, we note that such behavior is contextual and must not be isolated from the study of other "cues." We also note that the field of body language or kinesics is still ripe for eager and youthful research.

For the most part, body language seems to reinforce facial communication. For instance, while our face may indicate what emotion we feel, the body gestures may indicate the intensity of that emotion. Think of the small child that frowns and stamps her foot. This body gesture study and body language itself seems to parallel elementary spoken language without the complexity of grammar, punctuation or the like. Consider the way other individuals and ourselves stand. Do we point our body, so to speak, toward the source of a verbal message, or do we seem to lean away from the source? Do we cross both our arms and legs when faced with unwished vocality?

What message is portrayed by an individual who slouches in his chair? Generally, he appears to lack interest in the conversation. He may, in fact, be intensely interested but his body language contradicts his motivation. Those communicating with him perceive this lack of interest and adjust accordingly, many times negatively to the communicative process. However, what message is portrayed by an individual who leans forward, nodding occasionally?

When we speak of gestures, we usually speak of hand gestures, although other body parts may, in fact, gesture equally as well. In fact, some hand gestures may be used instead of words such as the language of the deaf. Hand gestures may also indicate the intensity of the emotion felt.

PHYSICAL APPEARANCE AND DRESS

Here, as in most of the nonverbal communication studies, while researchers are aware of the power of physical appearance and dress on communication, they are yet unsure of the full role it plays. We know, for example, that appearance plays a part in the process as it influences responses to vocal messages. Appearance can be the determinative feature of our message and may signal messages to others as to our own personality. To deny this importance is to deny the millions of dollars spent each year on perfumes, creams, oils, hair ornaments, contact lenses, beards, eye shadow, suits, clothes, toothpaste, mouthwash, deodorant. These physical messages we give are many times called "Thing Communication" or "Object Language."

Our clothing often determines the credibility of our message as does our physical make-up. If we are going to speak to a business group, we dress conservatively, less comfortably to show confidence and personality. For example, how do we perceive the personality or individual who is dressed in a military uniform? How is that military person perceived differently from the judge in a black robe? Consider the length of someone's hair, whether the beard or hair is unkempt or neatly trimmed.

PARALANGUAGE (VOCAL CUES)

The last nonverbal cue to be discussed here, while certainly not the end of the study of nonverbal messages, is the area of vocal cues or paralanguage. These vocal cues play a major role in assisting the listener in determining meaning. A vocal cue can be defined as an audible stimulus to a message that, while not using actual words, conveys a type of meaning. For example, consider the nervous man who speaks too fast . . . the angry person who begins speaking louder and louder. As we discussed before, the simple inflection in a sentence can greatly change the meaning of the message.

NONVERBAL COMMUNICATION

The most important aspect of message delivery is still wide open for scrutiny and research. Investigators have only reached the surface of a vastly interesting and meaningful study.

Policemen's "Body Language" Speaks Louder Than Words

Doug Smith[*]

If you should be stopped by a policeman and go away thinking him rude, impersonal and hostile but unable to say exactly why, Lt. Ken Hickman, community relations officer for the West Los Angeles Division, has an answer.

He's just hit you with an assault of policeman's "body language."

Policemen, like everyone else, have an unconscious silent language, says Hickman, but the nature of it, unfortunately, rubs against deeply ingrained social standards of dignity, privacy and territorial security.

In a research report prepared for a public administration class at USC, Hickman describes how policemen use visual and body intrusion under stress conditions to gain physical and psychological superiority over subjects who might be dangerous.

After patroling for a month on his off-time with fellow policemen to watch them at work, Hickman has compiled a statistical composite of how policemen acted in 123 one-to-one contacts with persons under stress and nonstress conditions.

In effect it shows the policeman zeroing in on the subject, looking him over like an inanimate object, moving with hands in a ready position, stepping up to what behavioralists describe as an intimate distance and then leaning even a little closer.

The aggressive "body language" subsides as soon as the policeman feels that the subject does not represent a threat to him, but not before that person has suffered a decidedly negative experience with the police.

In this conflict between the citizen's right to privacy and dignity and the policeman's need to protect himself, Hickman feels that the use of aggressive "body language" is justified when it is necessary and effective, but that "the frightening aspect of 'body language' and its impact on police-citizen relationships is the fact that neither party is usually aware of what is happening."

Hickman got into his research to test a theory he developed over 10 years with the Los Angeles Police Department.

"As one who has had considerable experience as a police officer and who has spent several years listening to citizen complaints against police officers," Hickman wrote, "I am convinced that much of the negative response voiced by citizens stems from nonverbal sources and that during in-field stress contacts with citizens, police officers unconsciously use body movements, body

---

space violations and visual intrusion to effect psychological and physical control over the subject."

His findings, after one month of watching West Los Angeles policemen in action, clearly support that theory, he said.

The following is a summary of what he saw: In most of the 82 stress encounters, Hickman noted that the officers' "heads were tilted back slightly, causing their chins to tilt upward somewhat," and that "once the officers exited their vehicles and assumed their basic approach posture, the head, neck, and trunk did not change position appreciably."

This conveyed the impression that the officer had zeroed in on a target by sighting down his nose and was making a deliberate and unwavering approach toward contact.

ZEROED IN

"There was often an apparent build-up of anxiety on the part of the citizen as he watched the officer approach. This was even observable on the part of some citizens who had called for police assistance and were not, themselves, the subject of police inquiry."

In making contact it was almost always the officer who established the conversation distance by stepping to within 18 inches of the citizen and maintaining that distance even when the citizen backed off. In 36 specific cases the officer closed that distance to as little as eight inches.

"The significance of those 36 instances is that relations between the officers and the citizens more often than not remained strained through the encounter," said Hickman. "Two of these contacts ended in minor altercations and a total of 12 with the arrest of the citizen."

STRAINED RELATIONS

While approaching the subjects, "not one officer walked with his arms swinging naturally at his side. Every officer had at least one hand resting somewhere along the front portion of his equipment belt," a gesture that suggests defensive readiness, Hickman said.

In all "negative" contacts, the officer's arms and hands moved considerably but "never hung at the sides or moved away from the front portion of his body," and in "positive" contacts only when the original tension subsided.

Finally, Hickman said, "policemen observed during stress contacts did not 'look at' the citizens to whom they spoke; they 'watched' them, 'measured' them and visually digested them."

The eye intrusion was of the type normally reserved for someone who is looking at an inanimate object such as a statue or painting, showing "purposeful but casual watching rather than eye to eye confrontation."

Although Hickman's observations all took place within the West Los Angeles Division, the stress encounters included almost all the major or possibilities. Thirty-six occurred during the daytime, 42 at night.

Of 34 contacts in which the officer stopped a pedestrian to investigate suspicious conduct, 12 were blacks, 6 Mexican-American and 16 Anglo, ranging from teenage to middle-age. The suspicions included curfew violations, narcotics, burglary, robbery and theft.

PERSONS INVOLVED

The 17 vehicle stops in stress conditions involved 13 males and four females suspected of car theft, intoxicated driving and robbery. By contrast, Hickman noted only four cases out of 41 nonstress encounters in the Police Station and at Basic Car Plan meetings in which an officer changed from a casual and polite demeanor.

Three times he noticed an officer "assume a greater degree of muscle tone around the torso" when talking to exceptionally attractive females and once, when a middle-aged woman abruptly asked an officer "when are you going to do something about the speeders in Beverly Glen?" the officer "moved from a relaxed posture to the common stress mode of back-tilted head, raised chin and vertical trunk."

Characteristically, in these encounters it was the citizens who set the conversation distance by moving up closer after the officer was standing still.

The significance of the intrusive police conduct Hickman observed under stress is immediately obvious, but becomes even more so in the context of the research that has recently been conducted on the effects of "body language."

BODY ZONE

"Researchers in the field of proxemics (body space) have generally concluded that the average American maintains an invisible bubble, or body zone, of about two and a half feet around his body," Hickman said.

Dr. August F. Kinzel of the New York Psychiatric Institute has found that people tend to react in quite negative fashions when unwanted intrusions of this personal body zone occur. The reactions may range from an attempt to move away from the intruder as unobtrusively as possible to violent physical attack.

Other studies have concluded that one of the most common methods used by one person to dominate another is to covertly signal an aggressive readiness by leaning toward the person and moving into an intimacy distance of about 13 inches.

VISUAL INTRUSION

It is the prolonged visual intrusion which Hickman found the most dehumanizing aspect of nonverbal police communication, however.

As a result of his research, Hickman believes that the need for greater research into the nature of police body language is clear and that police basic training in Los Angeles should certainly include far greater emphasis on nonverbal communication and its effects both for the safety of officers and for the improvement of community relations.

The Los Angeles Police Academy does not teach recruits anything about the significance of body zones or nonverbal communication in stress situations, Hickman said.

LITTLE TRAINING

Ironically, the academy teaches them to maintain slightly more than the suspect's arm reach to avoid being grabbed, a practice which policemen obviously teach themselves not to follow.

"It is commonly accepted by lawmen, criminologists and legal experts all over the world that 'reading' people is the key to successful interrogation, investigation and police community relations," Hickman said. "Yet, there is little training given to police officers in this country to teach them this skill.

"It is generally left to the individual policeman to develop these skills in the field. While he is learning, if he ever does, who can guess how many cases he loses or how many confessions he does not get or how many people he angers, all because he hasn't learned the significance of body language.

"Even those officers who excel in the ability to read nonverbal messages cannot usually describe their observations. They refer vaguely to a 'hunch' or, as the courts have recently called it, 'a policeman's sixth sense.'"

"Unfortunately, too many cases are lost in court today because officers have seemed to rely on hunches and sixth senses, abstract terms that fail to meet constitutional requirements," says Hickman.

Because the aggressive investigation of unusual or suspicious conduct is accepted as a superior method of crime prevention, Hickman does not propose that policemen discard the use of intrusive "body language," which generally provides the protection for which it is developed.

What he suggests is greater training so that policemen will be aware of their body intrusions and know when to use them and when to avoid them.

To communicate through silence is a link between the thoughts of man. —*M. Marceau*

Please Touch! How to
Combat Skin Hunger in Our Schools

Sidney B. Simon[*]

You can see them in any junior high school. They're the ones who shove and push. They knock one another down the stairwell and slam the locker door on each other's head. And behind every push and shove, they are crying out their skin-hunger needs.

The shovers and trippers aren't your disruptive discipline problems. They're not the window breakers, either. The ones I have in mind are your nice kids from nice families. They abound in those suburban orthodontia belts ringing our major cities.

They are kids with a severe form of malnutrition—a malnutrition of the skin. Their disease is called skin hunger, and it has reached almost epidemic proportions in all of our schools.

It is shocking that we have allowed this disease to persist despite research which shows that infants who weren't touched and handled and fondled when they were fed by their orphanage attendants simply withered up and died. Today, no orphanage or child-care agency would think of putting a baby down with a bottle propped up to work on gravity feed.

There are dozens of animal studies which support what so many of us instinctively know. Researchers found that laboratory rats from the cages of certain keepers were smarter than other rats. What was the difference? The smarter rats had keepers who fondled them, stroked them, or touched them when they cleaned their cages or fed them. Not only were the rats smarter, they were less vicious, had larger and healthier litters, and took care of their young with much more tenderness and warmth. The research was overwhelmingly clear: when we touch and caress and stroke, life is better for rats.

There are enormous implications here for people: Touch! But don't do it in school. No way. There, the rules are clear. *No* one touches anyone else. No hand holding. No hugging. No recognition that touching and being touched are vital to the well-being of all of us.

Woe to the teacher who should dare break the icebound tradition. You can predict the responses—"Say, what are you? A dirty old woman?" (Or a dirty old man?) "Hey, aren't you getting enough at home?" Schools have people memorize research but act as if they don't believe that research since they don't apply it.

Oh, there are exceptions to the no-touch rule. Kindergarten children can be touched. And some first grade teachers might still hold kids on their laps and

* By permission; *Scholastic Teacher*, © 1974, Scholastic Magazines, Inc.

read to them. But by the end of the third grade, touching has just about dried up in most of our schools, replaced by the onward push of the college-entrance curriculum.

We have conveyed the message very clearly: Don't touch! There are some kids who even flinch when you reach out to them. They somehow have read us to say, "Touch is very dangerous. It can lead to sex." And in our schools, dominated by minds which are somehow third-sex neuters, we can't have any of that.

So, instead, we have the shovers and the pushers and the trippers. For some of these kids, violence becomes a way of getting the touching they need. Sometimes I think contact sports were invented to provide what a saner society would have supplied in a saner way. One wrestling coach told me, "My wrestlers don't have skin hunger. They get lots of touching, every day." In some ways, the coach is right. They do. But it is underground, not owned for what it is—a rather convoluted way of getting what we need naturally, daily and with open recognition of our need.

As you read this, you may be thinking: "What's all the furor about? I didn't need touching when I was in school, and these kids don't need it either. We've got other more important work to be done."

Well, I certainly hope you did get the touching you needed when you were younger and that because you did, you don't recall needing it in school. I do hope you came from a family which routinely gave each other back rubs and that hugging each other warmly and at some length was also a part of your family pattern. Clearly, there are thousands of adults roaming this pornographic society who were not touched by their families, and so they don't touch their own children, who will not touch their own children—and so on. Adults spread and dump onto children their own confusion and conflict about love and sex, touch and caring, and the difference between hands which touch to heal and hands which touch to turn someone on.

In this slightly cockeyed world, there doesn't seem to be provision for someone to get touched without having to go to bed with whomever does the touching. Think about that. We have mixed up simple, healing, warm touching with sexual advances. So much so, that there seems to be no middle road between, "Don't you dare touch me!" and, "Okay, you touched me, now let's make love."

Some of this confusion shows up in our high school kids today. In the spirit of the new freedom, many of them are experiencing intercourse years before they really are ready for it. Lovemaking involves such complex feelings and responses, requires so much more than merely being stroked; it's no wonder some youngsters remain baffled with the question, "You mean, that's all it is?" Of course it's a whole lot more. What many of these young kids really, truly want is simply to be held and rocked and stroked. They are suffering from skin hunger. And it is a need as strong as the need for water or food—and quite different from the need for sex. If touching were permitted—even tolerated—in our schools, how much less grief and anxiety and deep feelings of inadequacy we would find in our young people. How much less jumping into bed with the first person who strokes them gently.

I feel the schools should face this problem and begin to find ways to deal with the skin-hunger needs of the youth they serve. It is that simple. We are deeply involved these days in providing students with all kinds of help. We have budgets for helping students gain college entrance. We pour enormous resources into fostering athletic programs, preventing drug abuse, and aiding disabled children. But there is little attention paid to the children who are starving from skin malnutrition.

Since their skin-hunger needs are not being met in other ways, some students get pregnant, or cruise the highways at diabolical speeds—indifferent to life or start trafficking in drugs. Many of these cases are skin hunger related. The loss of human joy and potential is just too great for us to sit by and remain quiet while our students wither and die from skin starvation.

When you teach, you can see the difference. Children from homes which are well aware of skin-hunger needs tend to be more open and warm and less frenetic. Children at the other end of the continuum, those who rarely get touched at home, often seem more withdrawn, more fantasy ridden, or more aggressively hostile. I feel they tend to have a lesser sense of their own worth and beauty. In children who are getting lots of skin-hunger care and comfort, you can see clear eyes and energy which seems to flow effortlessly throughout their bodies. I feel I can always tell a child who is well-touched—the one with more brilliant eyes, looking out less afraid. Then there are the furtive eyes of those who don't get touched at all. Or the more glassy eyes of the ones who get touched a lot, but only for sex. The difference is marked.

Body Politics

Mills' law: Men and women in American culture speak a different body language. Corollary: Observable sex differences in nonverbal behavior influence male-female relations.

Gwen Rubinstein[*]

Professor Janet Mills has transformed the great urban pastime—and her great love—of people watching into a career. Primarily, she has observed, men speak a body language that is high in status, power and dominance, while women speak a language of submission, affiliation and passivity. These differences often create chaos in the workplace.

By realizing their differences and striving more toward blending the best of masculine and feminine traits, however, men and women can improve their organizations and themselves, Mills has contended in presentations to countless civic, professional and business groups, including the Ohio Hospital Association, Columbus, Altrusa International, Chicago and the Chamber of Commerce of the United States, Washington, D.C. On leave from her position as a professor of human relations at the University of Oklahoma, Norman, Mills has been a visiting professor of management at Northern Arizona University, Flagstaff, since last August.

Men and women learn their body languages unconsciously as they grow up, she says. So by the time they reach adulthood, they send and receive their signals relatively unconsciously. Only when someone breaks the unspoken rules do the differences—and the discord—rise to the surface of relationships.

Managerial and professional women face a particularly difficult struggle in their everyday communication, according to Mills. Expected to be feminine as women and powerful as managers, women simultaneously play two roles with different sets of often-contradictory rules.

Managerial and professional men are not exempt from the confusion, Mills adds. Expected to be the dominant and powerful protectors of women, many find themselves reporting to women executives and competing with women peers—the very women they were raised to protect.

Because one picture is supposed to be worth 1,000 words, Association Management offers this photographic essay for your education—and amusement. **Warning: By seeing traditional sex roles reversed in these poses, differences between men's and women's nonverbal behavior may become shockingly apparent.**

Women learn to sit with legs together, crossed at the ankles or knees, toes pointed in the same direction, feet tucked under the chair, as Mills demonstrates. Women also hold their arms close to their bodies, their hands together in their lap.

What's wrong with this picture? Volunteer model William D. Coughlan, CAE, executive vice president of the American Physical Therapy Association, Alexandria, Virginia, offers a man's interpretation of how a woman sits.

In what Mills calls the "power spread," men sit with legs in "broken four"—at a 5- to 15-degree angle and crossed ankle to knee—with their hands behind their head and their elbows away from the body.

How would you feel sitting across from this woman at a conference table, over lunch, or in your office? Notice that Mills leans back into the chair in her interpretation of this classic male pose.

In a typical office scene, ASAE Foundation Manager Eric Johnson portrays the dominant man—feet shoulder-width apart, hands in pockets, weight shifting side to side or back and forth, indirect gaze straight ahead.

In reverse, it's easy to notice how a man posing as a woman balances his weight on one hip, lowers his shoulders, and stands in a "bashful knee bend," with his hands "placed gingerly together."

Nonverbal Communication ☆ 79

In a typical scene from a convention general session: Between two men, a woman sits at attention, looking straight ahead, constricting her body and yielding her space to those around her.

In a mirror pose, Mills spreads out and intrudes on the space the two men have yielded to her. Notice the men have leaned their bodies tensely to the side; she is relaxed, "laid back," and comfortable.

Expected to be feminine as women and powerful as managers,
women play two roles with often-contradictory rules.

In an ordinary conversation with men or other women, whether in the workplace or somewhere else, women smile, open their eyes wide, arch their brows, lift and lower their heads, and nod more often than men.

Acting out a man's role in a one-on-one conversation, Mills sits back in her chair, sets her shoulders square, stares directly ahead, keeps her head erect and gestures forcefully.

To pick something up from the floor "femininely," women keep their knees together, their back straight, their arms close to their body and approach the object from the side.

To pick an object up from the floor "masculinely," men generally squat, keep their back flexible, extend their arms from their body and approach the object from the front.

Nonverbal Cafeteria Exercise

PURPOSE:

To demonstrate that nonverbal communication sends "clues, not facts."

PROCEDURE:

1. With the following worksheet, select an interesting looking individual (whom you do not know) to observe. Try to pick someone who does not seem ready to move on and station yourself far enough away so that you can *see* your subject but *not hear* what she is saying.
2. Observe the individual for as long as possible, remembering to be discreet, and record your impressions.
3. When the person looks as though she is getting ready to leave, approach her with a smile, confess your "spying" and check your observations. You'll be surprised how friendly a stranger can be when she discovers she's helping you with classwork.
4. When you return to class, compare your observations with your classmates.

NONVERBAL CAFETERIA OBSERVATION FORM

Basic Description	Appearance	Actual
Gender		
Age		
Major		
Bilingual		
Live with parents		
Political Party		
Sports		
Activities		
Veteran of military service		
Children		
Brothers, sisters		
Relationship to others at table		
Mood		
From out of state		
Type of car		
Name		
Type of employment		

Nonverbal Incongruity Activity

PURPOSE:

To learn how our nonverbal behavior might contradict or impede our verbal messages.

PROCEDURE:

Phase One

The class is divided into groups of four people according to the following diagram. A and B will discuss such a question as "What is my favorite movie?" C and D will observe as indicated. It is important that the observers watch their person both send and receive messages. The observers should take notes about ways in which the observee's nonverbal behavior denies or impairs the verbal message which was intended.

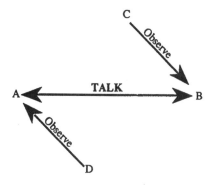

Phase Two

Same activity. This time the observers from Phase One become the observees.

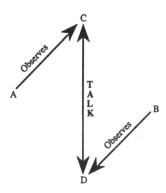

DISCUSSION:

Each of the observers, in turn, will describe how the person who was their observee behaved. The observers will share with the observees the results of their observation with the primary purpose of helping the observee to be more aware of the ways their nonverbal behavior may have negatively affected their message.

R E A C T I O N S

Name _____

Date _____

Your professor may require this exercise to be handed in.

1. Why is an understanding of nonverbal communication absolutely essential to high fidelity communication?

2. Which generally tells the truth of a message, verbal or nonverbal communication? Why?

3. What might be some of the reasons that a nonverbal signal might have different meanings for people in different situations?

5 Using Language

DEFINITIONS

As you have seen so far, our concern is to help you improve your interpersonal communication. This chapter shows the role that language plays in those encounters. Do you always understand what others are saying to you? Are you always understood by others? If you're like most of us, the answer to these two questions is an emphatic "No." When two people speak the same language, share the culture and experience similar incidents in their lives, why is it that one person can walk away confident that she has clearly communicated and the other stand in bewilderment wondering what was just said? In order to understand the problems that arise from taking our language abilities for granted, it will be necessary for us to first define a few concepts.

✳ **Language**

An established and accepted set of symbols and structure used for the transfer of meaning. (English, Spanish, Navajo, Farsi)

✳ **Denotation**

The commonly accepted definition of a word, as in the dictionary definition. (House = Dwelling)

✳ **Connotation**

The feeling and emotions that we associate with a word. (House = "Home")

✳ **Linguistics**

The study of language.

✳ **Semantics**

The study of meaning.

✳ **General Semantics**

The field of study that says language influences behavior.

———————— ✫ ✫ ✫ ————————

The Importance of Using Language Effectively

Language Is Power

The study of how people have used language must certainly bring us to the conclusion that the "pen is mightier than the sword." Books, newspapers and pamphlets have been so powerful that dictators waste no time banning and burning them and imprisoning those who seek freedom of the press.

What happens to you as you read, "The green, vile-looking pus oozed from the cut on the victim's arm?" How do you feel when someone calls you a dirty name? If you're like most of us, you can't help but react negatively and strongly.

We speak to be heard, to be listened to, to be understood. Our energies in sending symbols are spent in the presence of someone who can hear the results. We want something. Over 2,000 years ago the philosopher Aristotle said, "All speech is persuasive in nature." And so it is. We communicate to get our needs met. Whether that is strengthening a relationship, asking directions or arguing with a friend, sending information through symbols to another is a way of persuading, thus we say that language is purposeful.

It is difficult to deny the power of language. In this chapter, we will examine how we can use language intrapersonally and interpersonally. Additionally, we will examine the extent to which language influences and is influenced by our culture.

Intrapersonal Use of Language

Think for a moment about the last vacation that you took, the party that you attended or success that you had. What came to your mind? Did you close your eyes and see the entire experience played back as if you had just begun your video cassette player? A few people may have answered yes to those questions. For most of us, however, we probably began by saying to ourselves, "Let's see—that was when . . ." Whether you then actually saw pictures or continued to recall the experience based on words, your thinking was either in part or wholly influenced by your manipulation of language.

Thinking is dependent, for most of us, on the use of language. The more successful we are in using language, the more successful we are going to be in thinking.

One of the important aspects of thinking that requires effective use of language is our ability to reason. Reasoning involves at least two steps: observation and inference. When we begin our reasoning process, we begin with an observation or with a statement (assumption) based on someone else's observation. These observations can also be called facts and are subject to errors that we have already described in the chapter on perception.

The second step in reasoning is inferring. In this step, we use language to connect the observable fact to the unobservable conclusion. For example, you see your friend on April 15. You know that he went to see a tax advisor today. He looks sad and you hear him say that he doesn't know where he is going to come up with that much money. So far you have had a number of observable facts to deal with. You may infer that he has to pay more money for his income taxes. How did you come to that conclusion? You used language to relate the observable facts with outcomes related to each of those facts until you narrowed the probable outcomes to your best guess.

Our ability to use language gives us more choice in the number of outcomes we can match with the facts that we observe. It also gives us a way of discounting or eliminating outcomes which are not appropriate. In other words, the power of reasoning depends on effective use of language.

LANGUAGE IS SYMBOLIC

While this may seem to be quite apparent, it is of astonishing importance. Words do not have any meaning in and of themselves. They are void of meaning. The symbols D-O-G are not the animal that barks and answers to the name "Rover." The letters (symbols) represent the animal only when our culture/society agrees that they represent the reality. There is no living, breathing thing in the symbols themselves. There is only the meaning that we attach to them. This is why we say, "Words don't mean, people mean." Indeed, if we simply reverse the symbols D-O-G, we must form an entirely new concept in our minds. But notice, it isn't the word that has meaning, it's us. Some of our exercises in this chapter will point out the dangers of forgetting this important lesson.

LANGUAGE IS LEARNED

It is also important to realize that language is learned. Words, as symbols, must be learned in a context. While some are easily stored in our memory for future use (book, mother, day, food) many are so complex as to defy simply defining (is, to, be, the) and when you compound this with the idea that language (thus, words) is always changing, (bad, cool, gay, hip) it's no wonder that we often misunderstand another's intended "meaning." To further complicate matters, we have to consider the importance of how we learned the word. If you had a pleasurable experience when you learned the word "cat" (soft, purring, cute),

your image of "cat" will be forever influenced by that experience. However, if your experience was negative (scratches, biting, fleas, catbox), think how differently the symbol "cat" will affect you. Can a word that you assign meaning to affect you? For an answer to this question your instructor will have you participate in an exercise designed to show the difference between Connotation and Denotation.

GENERAL SEMANTICS

Perhaps there is a need to clarify General Semantics. Too often we hear, "Oh, we're only arguing semantics." Or, "Let's not get hung up on semantics." The implication is that the problem is a small one, but matters of meaning can have far-reaching implications. Those of us who study language will be the first to tell you that words affect behavior. For instance, would you care to stop by my house for a slice of dead cow? Probably not, but most of you have enjoyed a barbecued steak. Do the words make a difference? You bet they do. This is no small matter, this "semantics." It can determine our entire perception of "reality" and that leads us to a definition that will not only help us to understand General Semantics, but will set the stage for you to learn the importance of language in our daily communication. What I call something can cause you to perceive it differently. Semanticists carry this idea to the word to associate with it. Is it a thing without a name? This argument will be further developed in the chapter as you study the power of words.

> I know you believe you understand what you think I said, but I'm not sure you realize that what you heard is not what I meant.

BARRIERS TO USING LANGUAGE

Some people consider barriers to communication as roadblocks. That is, some obstacle that gets between what we intend to say and what is understood by the receiver. Language is much more complicated than the roadblock analogy. Many of the language barriers occur in our minds as we consider what we intend to say. These main barriers are described below:

CONFUSION BETWEEN LANGUAGE AND THE REAL WORLD

If I write that I plan to scratch my finger nails along the chalk board and you immediately feel a cold shiver down your spine, it is because you confused what I said for the reality of my doing it. Now such a reaction is not necessarily bad. As a matter of fact, if you were unable to react in such a manner, you probably would not enjoy reading a good book.

However, when we assume that the word we hear is exactly the same as the real-world counterpart that it describes, we are in trouble. To understand what we mean here, pretend that you are planning to hike up a mountain and have a trail map in front of you. You note that there is a moderate elevation gain and a small stream that you will have to ford. You consider that these representations on the map are exactly the way it will be and feel that you will have no difficulty on the hike. Once you set forth into the real world, however, you soon learn that the temperature is 92 degrees and the stream is 10 feet wide, five feet deep and is raging down the mountain. We very often make the same mistakes in the use of our language to describe the world around us.

An example of such confusion is found in the word "is." When you say, "He *is* a professional football player," what do you mean? To most people, the word "is" takes the place of "equals." Therefore, the meaning in the sentence is that "He equals professional football player." He is therefore not a father, brother, husband, student or anything else at the moment. Additionally, he "equals" professional football player as *you* see it to mean, which may be different from professional football player as *I* see it to mean.

Our language should be considered as a description of the real world the way maps are a description of the real world. Maps only tell us a small part of what really exists. Our language has the same limitation.

ALLNESS ATTITUDE

Just as maps are incapable of telling everything that there is to tell about the territory, language is incapable of telling everything that there is to tell about the way you feel about someone or how to do something that you have learned over many years of practice and effort. You can give us an idea through language of the broad boundaries. However, it is not possible for you to fill in every possible detail.

When people have an allness attitude, they act as though they have communicated everything that there is to say to another about a topic and then they expect that the other person will have exactly the same reaction to that topic that they have. When the other person fails to see it as they do, they blame the other person rather than recognizing that the other person only got part of the picture.

FROZEN EVALUATION

When we think about something the way that it was and describe it now as though it had never changed, we are guilty of frozen evaluation. Because language describes things, ideas and feelings, we often get hooked on the description and forget that everything in the real world constantly changes. So we run around with a lot of out-dated descriptions in our heads that we haven't recently checked out with reality.

People who are constantly talking about the way things should be (as in the "good old days") are unwilling to give up the old descriptions and look at what is happening now. If you think of the boy who was the eighth-grade clown as the same person you knew six or ten years ago, you are going to have problems talking to someone about him who sees him as he is today.

LABELING

Labeling is where the sender of a message stereotypes someone and rather than describe the behaviors, she merely takes the easy path and says "Oh, he's a _____." When the receiver hears this label, he becomes the victim of the sender's laziness. Rather than let the receiver find out for himself what the other person is like, the sender, by labeling, has already placed in the receiver's mind the idea of the label. Let's take the label "jock" for an example. As soon as you hear, "That new kid in my class is a jock," you've begun to form an image. This prejudging is extremely dangerous because even before you've met the new student, you've probably created an image that could well be wrong. He must be big, athletic, in school only for sports, doesn't care about classes and may not be too bright. What a terrible judgment to form based only on someone's careless use of language. You know full well that all athletes are not big. Look at wrestlers in the lightweight division or gymnasts or archers or golfers even. ChiChi Rodrigues is 5'6". You also know that all athletes are not in school just for sports. Many are involved in several extracurricular activities. Sports may be only one of several. You also know that many student athletes are outstanding scholars, earning excellent grades in even the most difficult classes. Many end up on the Dean's List for academic excellence and many receive scholastic scholarships. Pat Hayden (ex-professional football player) was a Rhodes Scholar. And did we say "he"? How careless of us, because student athletes can, of course, be women. Do you see what can happen when labels are used? They are convenient, handy and easy to use, but they are real road blocks to being an accurate communicator. In addition to labels, your instructor will show you the dangers inherent in confusing assumptions and judgments as "facts." Some of the activities that she may assign are: For Sexists Only, The Semantics of Prejudice, Hidden Assumptions Test and The Uncritical Inference Test.

POLARIZATION

This barrier occurs because of the nature of our language, English. Over the years English has evolved to a point where we have been forced to speak and think in extremes. The "middle ground" has been taken from us because we have few words to express the ideas that fall in the middle. Example: What word is the opposite of leader? Now, tell us what word is in-between? More difficult isn't it? Your instructor will have you participate in a brief activity called Polarization to further explain this barrier.

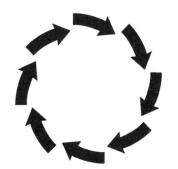

Language is the dress of thought. —*S. Johnson*

For Sexists Only

Why are forceful males referred to as charismatic while females are domineering?

When speaking about people who are talkative, why are men called articulate and women gabby?

Why are men who are forgetful called absentminded, when forgetful women are called scatterbrained?

Why are men who are interested in everything referred to as curious, but women are called nosy?

Why are angry men called outraged, while angry women are called hysterical?

Why are women who are ironic called bitter, while ironic men are called humorous?

Why are lighthearted men called easygoing, but the same type of women are called frivolous?

Why are devious men considered shrewd, when devious women are scheming?

Why are men who are thoughtful called considerate, while thoughtful women are called oversensitive?

Why are women who are dauntless considered brazen, when dauntless men are considered fearless?

Why is it that men of ordinary appearance are called pleasant looking, while ordinary women are homely?

"There's glory for you!"

"I don't know what you mean by 'glory,'" Alice said.

Humpty Dumpty smiled contemptuously. "Of course you don't—till I tell you. I meant, 'there's a nice knock-down argument for you!'"

"But 'glory' doesn't mean 'a nice, knock-down argument,'" Alice objected.

"When I use a word," Humpty Dumpty said, in rather a scornful tone, "it means just what I choose it to mean—neither more nor less."

"The question is," said Alice, "whether you *can* make words mean so many different things."

"The question is," said Humpty Dumpty, "who is to be master—that's all."

From *Alice in Wonderland* by Lewis Carroll.

Syd's Antics with Semantics

Sydney Harris[*]

- My witticism was "a well-turned phrase"; yours was a "wisecrack"; his was "a smart-aleck remark."
- My proposal is "some fresh thinking on the subject"; your alternative proposal is an "untried innovation."
- An "awful" man is one a woman has just met and is interested in; a "sweet" man is one she has known a long time and is no longer interested in.
- Readers complain about "sensationalism" in the newspaper, but they won't change to the opposition paper because it's "dull."
- He refuses to take a lie-detector test because "he must have something to hide;" I refuse to take one because "it has no legal status, and the machine violates my protection against self-incrimination."
- The extroverted club member I happen to like is "jolly and open"; the extroverted one I happen to dislike is "loud and pushy."
- He "goofed"; you made a "boo-boo"; but all I had was "a mental block."
- Male chauvinism reveals itself semantically even in the use of little prepositions: a promiscuous and unattached male is amiably referred to as a "man *about* town," but a woman of the same status and inclinations is disparagingly referred to as "*on* the town."
- The nations we currently favor have "governments"; the nations we are quarreling with have "regimes." (Notice how quickly after detente "Red China" turned into the "People's Republic.")
- I answered the awkward question with "polite evasion"; you answered with "double-talk"; he answered it with a "whopping lie."

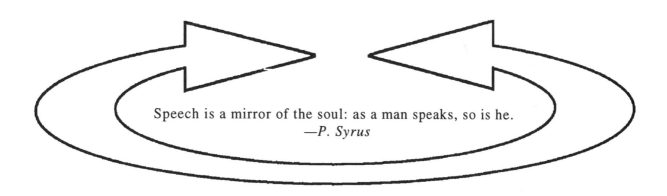

Speech is a mirror of the soul: as a man speaks, so is he.
—P. Syrus

---

[*] Reprinted by permission from Independent Press-Telegram.

Meaning Lift

The more specific your word choice, the more accurately others will receive your message.

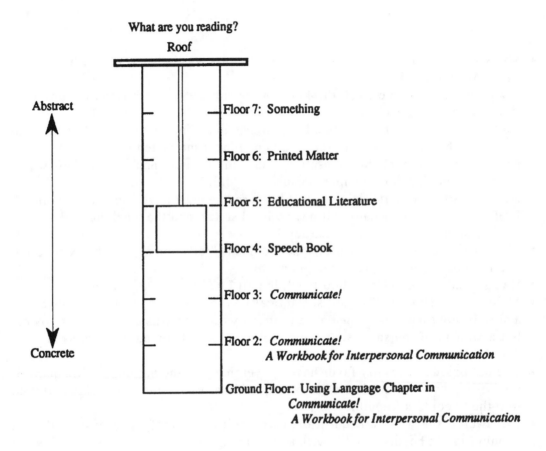

What are you reading?

Roof

Abstract

Floor 7: Something

Floor 6: Printed Matter

Floor 5: Educational Literature

Floor 4: Speech Book

Floor 3: *Communicate!*

Floor 2: *Communicate!*
A Workbook for Interpersonal Communication

Concrete

Ground Floor: Using Language Chapter in
Communicate!
A Workbook for Interpersonal Communication

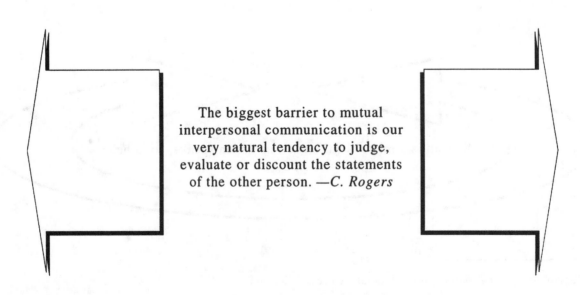

The biggest barrier to mutual interpersonal communication is our very natural tendency to judge, evaluate or discount the statements of the other person. —*C. Rogers*

The Semantics of Prejudice

In the following analysis, an expert in semantics analyzes the "language of prejudice." He shows that by choosing one word rather than another, we often structure the world into ingroups and outgroups and create unfavorable attitudes toward those we designate as "they."

Almost any human characteristic may be described either in honorific (favorable and approving) or in pejorative (unfavorable and disapproving) terms. If we examine the words used to describe particular human traits, we see that some are noncommittal and neutral, some favorable and *upgrading*, and others unfavorable or *downgrading*. For example, if we take a fairly neutral attitude toward a young man, we call him simply *young*. If we have an unfavorable attitude toward him and wish to *downgrade* him in the eyes of others, we say that he is *immature*. On the other hand, if we want to emphasize his vigor and freshness, we call the same person *youthful*. What word we use often depends upon some implicit value judgment we have made of a person and upon our desire to arouse the same attitude in others. The following list of the adjectives used to describe human traits shows how easy it is to create favorable or unfavorable attitudes toward the same behavior simply by a judicious use of language.

Favorable, Upgrading	In-Between, Neutral	Unfavorable, Downgrading
Discreet	Cautious	Cowardly
Loyal	Obedient	Slavish
Careful	Meticulous	Fussy
Devoted	Self-subordinating	Fanatical
Warmhearted	Sentimental	Mushy
Generous	Liberal	Spendthrift
Courageous	Bold	Reckless, foolhardy
Youthful	Young	Immature
Sound	Conservative	Reactionary
Open-minded	Liberal	Unsound
Realistic	Suspicious	Cynical
Humanitarian	Idealist	Do-gooder

Not only adjectives but nouns as well are used to express attitudes of approval and disapproval and to create them in others. Consider, for example, the varying connotations of respect or disrespect involved in choosing among the following ways of describing the position of a given individual.

Favorable, Upgrading	In-Between, Neutral	Unfavorable, Downgrading
Official	Office-holder	Bureaucrat
Statesman	Policymaker	Politician
Governess	Nursemaid	Servant
CEO	Employer	Boss
Financial leader	Banker	Moneylender
Pilgrim	Migrant, refugee, immigrant	Alien
Orator	Influential speaker	Rabble rouser

Verbs, too, fall on a value scale. The following list covers only a few of the key word-choices that, when applied to any controversial issue, may help us to identify the moral or political standpoint of the word-user and the direction in which he wishes to influence opinion, attitude and policy:

Favorable, Upgrading	In-Between, Neutral	Unfavorable, Downgrading
Discern	Think	Theorize
Demonstrate	Assert	Allege
Cooperate	Act in concert	Conspire
Assist	Aid	Abet
Clarify	Retract	Admit error
Advise	Urge	Demand
Serve	Control	Interfere
Administer	Manage	Manipulate
Enlighten	Report	Propagandize
Inspire	Motivate	Inflame

Semantic Reactions

PURPOSE:

To examine your own semantic reactions to terms and enable you to see how each of us experiences semantic noise.

PROCEDURE:

Following is a list of 20 terms. Beside each term place a checkmark which corresponds to your **immediate** reaction to that word according to the scale indicated. Remember that the intent of the activity is to allow you to examine your semantic reactions, so be as honest in marking your reaction as you can. Your immediate reaction is usually the most reliable.

Reaction	Highly Positive +2	Slightly Positive +1	Neutral or No Reaction 0	Slightly Negative -1	Highly Negative -2
1. patriotism					
2. breast					
3. pusilanimous					
4. love					
5. communism					
6. caucasian					
7. Mexican					
8. bureaucracy					
9. speech					
10. friendship					
11. chauvinist					
12. fox					
13. intercourse					
14. cancer					
15. exacerbate					
16. gay					

Reaction	Highly Positive +2	Slightly Positive +1	Neutral or No Reaction 0	Slightly Negative -1	Highly Negative -2
17. cum laude					
18. seersucker					
19. chicano					
20. whitey					
21.					
22.					
23.					

DISCUSSION:

Now that you have completed the list, you will have a chance to compare your reactions with another member of the class and discuss the following questions:

1. How do you react to the various words?
2. Why do you react as you do? On what is your reaction based?
3. How can reaction to words (semantic reactions) affect communication?
4. With respect to semantic reactions, what suggestions could you make to improve communication?
5. What variables—i.e., sex, race, religion, income, age—influence your responses?

For evil, then, as well as for good, words make us the human beings we actually are. Deprived of language, we should be dogs or monkeys. Possessing language, we are men and women able to persevere in crime no less than in heroic virtue, capable of intellectual achievements beyond the scope of any animal, but at the same time capable of systematic silliness and stupidity such as no dumb beast could ever dream of. —A. Huxley

Hidden Assumptions Test

PURPOSE:

To discover fallacies of thinking based on hidden assumptions and over-generalizations.

PROCEDURE:

1. This is a timed test. Answer the questions as quickly as possible.
2. Once you have answered, go on to the next question. **Do not go back to change any answers.**

1. Each country has its own "Independence Day." Do they have a 4th of July in England? _____
2. How many birthdays does the average man have? _____
3. Can a man living in Winston-Salem, North Carolina be buried west of the Mississippi? _____
4. If you only had one match and entered a room in which there was a Kerosene lamp, an oil heater and wood burning stove, which would you light first? _____
5. Some months have 30 days, some have 31. How many have 28? _____
6. If a doctor gave you three pills and told you to take one every half hour, how long would the pills last? _____
7. A house is built so that each side has a southern exposure. If a bear were to wander by the house, most likely the color of the bear would be? _____
8. How far can a dog run into the forest? _____
9. I have in my hand two U.S. coins which total 55 cents in value. One is not a nickel. What are the two coins? _____
10. A farmer has 17 sheep. All but nine died. How many does he have left? _____
11. Two men play chess. They played five games and each man won the same number of games. There were no ties. How can this be? _____
12. Take two apples from three apples and what do you get? _____
13. Divide 30 by one-half and add 10. What is the answer? _____
14. An archaeologist claimed she found gold coins dated 46 B.C. Do you think she did and why? _____
15. An airplane crashed exactly on the U.S.-Mexican border. Where would they bury the survivors? _____
16. How many animals of each species did Moses take aboard the ark with him? _____
17. Is it legal in California for a man to marry his widow's sister? _____
18. How much dirt may be removed from a hole that is 6 ft. deep, 2 ft. wide, and 10 ft. long? _____
19. If your bedroom were pitch dark and you needed a matching pair of socks, how many socks would you need to take out of the bureau drawer if there are 25 white and 25 blue? _____
20. You have four nines (9,9,9,9). Arrange them to total 100. You may use any of the arithmetical processes (addition, subtraction, multiplication, or division). Each nine must be used once. _____
21. If it takes 10 men 10 days to dig a hole, how long will it take five men to dig half a hole? _____

22. Explain the following true boast: "In my bedroom, the nearest lamp that I usually keep turned on is 12 feet away from my bed. Alone in the room, without using any special devices, I can turn out the light on that lamp and get into bed before the room is dark." _____

23. A doctor refuses to operate on a patient who has been injured in an auto accident in which the patient's father was killed. The doctor refuses to operate because the patient is the doctor's son. How can this be? _____

24. There are 12 one-cent stamps in a dozen, but how many two-cent stamps are there in a dozen? _____

25. What four words appear on every denomination of U.S. coin and currency? _____

26. Which is correct: 7 and 8 are 13, or 7 and 8 is 13? _____

27. If 3 cats kill 3 rats in 3 minutes, how long will it take for 100 cats to kill 100 rats? _____

DISCUSSION:

1. Were you surprised at how many questions you could not answer?
2. Were you surprised at how many questions you answered correctly/incorrectly?
3. What did this test tell you about the assumptions you make?

The Uncritical Inference Test

William V. Haney

PURPOSE:

To demonstrate the assumptions/inferences we make upon hearing or reading words.

PROCEDURE:

This test is designed to determine your ability to think *accurately* and *carefully*. Since it is very probable that you have never taken *this type* of test before, failure to read the instructions **extremely carefully** may lower your score.

1. You will read a brief story. Assume that all of the information presented in the story is definitely *accurate* and *true*. Read the story carefully. You may refer back to the story whenever you wish.

2. You will then read statements about the story. Answer them in numerical order. **Do not go back** to fill in answers or to change answers. This will only distort your test score.

3. After you read carefully each statement, determine whether the statement is:
   a. "T"—meaning: on the basis of the *information presented in the story the statement is* **definitely true**.
   b. "F"—meaning: On the basis of the *information presented in the story the statement is* **definitely false**.
   c. "?"—meaning: The statement may be true (or false) but on the basis of the *information presented in the story you* cannot be *definitely certain*. (If any part of the statement is doubtful, mark the statement "?".)

4. Indicate your answer by circling either "T" or "F" or "?" opposite the statement.

Excerpted with permission from "The Uncritical Inference Test" by William V. Haney as it appears in William V. Haney, COMMUNICATION AND ORGANIZATIONAL BEHAVIOR, 3rd edition (Homewood, IL: Richard D. Irwin, Inc., 1973).

Sample Test

STORY A

The only car parked in front of 619 Oak Street is a black one. The words "James M. Curley, M.D." are spelled in small gold letters across the left front door of that car.

Statements about the story

1.	The color of the car in front of 619 Oak Street is black.	T	F	?
2.	There is no lettering on the left front door of the car parked in front of 619 Oak Street.	T	F	?
3.	Someone is ill at 619 Oak Street.	T	F	?
4.	The black car parked in front of 619 Oak Street belongs to James M. Curley.	T	F	?

Remember: Answer **only** on the basis of the information presented in the story. Refrain from answering as you think it **might** have happened. Answer each statement in numerical order. Do not go back to fill in or to change answers.

STORY B

A business man had just turned off the lights in the store when a man appeared and demanded money. The owner opened a cash register. The contents of the cash register were scooped up and the man sped away. A member of the police force was notified promptly.

Statements about Story B

1.	A man appeared after the owner had turned off his store lights.	T	F	?
2.	The robber was a *man*.	T	F	?
3.	The man who appeared did not demand money.	T	F	?
4.	The man who opened the cash register was the owner.	T	F	?
5.	Someone opened a cash register.	T	F	?
6.	After the man, who demanded the money, scooped up the contents of the cash register, he ran away.	T	F	?
7.	While the cash register contained money, the story does *not* state *how much*.	T	F	?
8.	The robber opened the cash register.	T	F	?
9.	After the store lights were turned off a man appeared.	T	F	?
10.	The robber did not take the money with him.	T	F	?
11.	The owner opened a cash register.	T	F	?
12.	The age of the store-owner was not revealed in the story.	T	F	?
13.	The story concerns a series of events in which only three persons are referred to: the owner of the store, a man who demanded money and a member of the police force.	T	F	?
14.	The following events were included in the story: someone demanded money, a cash register was opened, its contents were scooped up, and a man dashed out of the store.	T	F	?

Excerpted with permission from "The Uncritical Inference Test" by William V. Haney as it appears in William V. Haney, COMMUNICATION AND ORGANIZATIONAL BEHAVIOR, 3rd edition (Homewood, IL: Richard D. Irwin, Inc., 1973).

DISCUSSION:

1. Were you surprised at the number of assumptions and inferences you made?
2. Did certain types of words cause you to believe you understood their meaning?
3. What are the implications to your everyday language?

 # Polarization

PURPOSE:

To demonstrate that language forces us to speak and think in a polarized manner.

PROCEDURE:

Fill in the opposites for the words below. Then try to find an in-between word for the opposites and write the words in the middle column.

WORD	IN-BETWEEN	OPPOSITE
tall		
heavy		
strong		
happy		
legal		
leader		
success		
wealthy		
woman		
beautiful		
black		
easy		
teacher		

DISCUSSION:

1. Which is harder to find, an opposite word or an in-between word?
2. Which words are more descriptive—the polar opposites or the in-between words?
3. Is our language structured to make us think in polar opposites?

Owning My Communication

PURPOSE:

To demonstrate that substituting the word "I" for the word "You" (changing the frame of reference) can improve communication.

PROCEDURE:

Read the sentences below which contain the word "You." Note the critical tone that the sentence assumes because of the use of the word "you."

Rewrite the sentences, substituting the word "I" and changing the phrase where necessary and see if that neutralizes the tone of the sentence.

"YOU" Messages	"I" Messages
1. You always give me another job to do before I finish the one I have.	*ex: I need a break between projects.*
2. You never pick up your clothes	*ex: I am frustrated with the mess from these clothes.*
3. You don't make an effort to get along with my friends.	
4. You never show up on time.	
5. Your tests are unreasonable.	
6. You wasted your money on that.	
7. You expect too much from me.	
8. Why can't you communicate?	
9. Why are you so angry?	
10. You hurt my feelings.	

DISCUSSION:

1. What makes changing the frame-of-reference difficult?
2. Why do we tend to use "you"?
3. Consider some recent situations where you could have changed the frame-of-reference. How would the outcome have changed?

Street Talk Test

PURPOSE:

To examine the way words mean different things to different people

PROCEDURE:

Circle the letter for the correct answer of each street term

1. "STALL IT OUT" means:
   a. Stealing a car
   b. Taking a battery out of a car
   c. Stop doing what you're doing
   d. Taking a horse out of the stall

2. "SHAKE THE SPOT" is a phrase used to denote:
   a. Bailing a client out of custody
   b. A boating term used in boat racing
   c. A term used to say you're ready to leave

3. What is meant by the statement "MAKING BANK"?
   a. A construction term used in building
   b. The process of obtaining money
   c. Bank of America's code for instant credit account

4. The term "WHAT'S UP" means:
   a. What's going on
   b. Let's fight
   c. To look up

5. When someone is "TRIPPIN'" they are:
   a. Rapping
   b. Traveling
   c. Falling over themselves
   d. Acting a fool

6. The term "HOMEBOY" means
   a. Lazy person
   b. Immature person
   c. Fellow gang member
   d. A gang member who stays home

7. To "SQUAB" means:
   a. To fight
   b. To set territory aside
   c. How pigeons mate

8. "HOLDING IT DOWN" means
   a. Stop using PCP
   b. Throwing your hand sign downwards
   c. Gang members protecting their territory
   d. Holding a "sherm head" down

9. "CHIPPERS" means:
   a. Police on bikes
   b. Killing somebody with your feet
   c. money

10. I have a "DEUCE-DEUCE" and a "TRAY EIGHT" means:
    a. Number in dice game
    b. .22 cal. and .38 cal. guns
    c. Two gang members talking about the street they live on

11. What is a "SHERM HEAD"?
    a. History major in school
    b. An Uncle Tom
    c. A cool dude
    d. Chronic user of PCP

12. "THAT'S THE BOMB" means:
    a. Trouble
    b. The best thing
    c. Something smelly

13. A "WATER" dealer is:
    a. A Sparkletts man
    b. Radiator mechanic

By permission, Senior Investigator, Ken Bell, Los Angeles District Attorney's Office.

14. To "BUMP SOMEONE'S HEAD" means:
    a. Street robbery
    b. To lie to someone
    c. Gang initiation
    d. Martial arts kick

15. What is a "MUDDUCK"?
    a. Rival gang member
    b. Water fowl
    c. Ugly girl
    d. Ragged car

16. "I don't have any 'CHEDDER'" means:
    a. I don't have any cookies
    b. I don't have any money
    c. I don't have any weapons
    d. I don't have any burglary tools

17. If someone is ON THE "PIPE," it means:
    a. They are an avid pipe smoker
    b. They are free basing (cocaine)
    c. Slang for homosexual activity

18. If someone told you he has a "GLASS-HOUSE," it means
    a. A person into serious gardening
    b. A new modern house
    c. A 1977–78 "Chevy"
    d. A house that's been shot up before

19. Let's do a "GHOST" means:
    a. A magic trick
    b. To leave your present location
    c. Shoot and run
    d. Beat up a "white" person

20. If someone told you "JAMES HAS A BUCKET," it means:
    a. An ugly girlfriend
    b. A new style hat
    c. An old ragged car
    d. James is a janitor

21. "ROLL ON ME" means:
    a. Held me up
    b. Go and see someone
    c. They are an unreliable gang member

22. If someone is "TALKING HEAD" to you, it means
    a. Sign language for deaf and dumb
    b. Silent gang symbols with hands
    c. That they want to fight you

23. What is a "BASE HEAD"?
    a. A person hooked on cocaine
    b. The best tuba player in the band
    c. The leader of the gang

24. A "PRIMO" is:
    a. The best shooter in the gang
    b. A marijuana joint laced with cocaine
    c. The primary target in a gang retaliation

25. "GETTIN' AT"
    a. A rival gang member marked for certain death
    b. Trying to establish contact
    c. Arriving at a destination

DISCUSSION:

1. Were you surprised at the number of questions you had to guess at?
2. What causes words like "Mark" and "Ghost" to change meaning?
3. Why don't words assume a meaning and keep it?
4. Have you used words in a manner different from what the dictionary said? Which ones? Why?

The Ins and Outs of Slang

Cathy Lawhon*

Slang separates the fly-fishermen from the rock turkeys, and the ducks from the live ones.

Don't bother scrambling for a dictionary. You've just discovered the function of slang: If you don't get it, you're not supposed to.

"Slang has a twofold purpose," said Angela Della Volpe, linguistics professor at California State University, Fullerton. "First, it provides identity for a group; it shows you belong. And the other purpose, which is a kind of reversal of the first, is that it's used to exclude those who are not part of the group.

"In Vietnam, the military had its own slang, words that reflected the environment, and it was an 'in' thing that was necessary to keep people who were not privy to the experience out of the interaction," Della Volpe said.

That's how a bombing raid became a "protective reaction strike."

Teenagers use slang to define their cliques, and to close out all non-conforming peers and, of course, parents. The insatiable adolescent appetite for new slang is stimulated by the enormous need for peer identification within an "in" group.

"With kids, slang words stay around only as long as they serve a need," said Dr. Raymond Gibbs, associate professor of psychology at the University of California, Santa Cruz who specializes in psycholinguistics. "And that need is to communicate the things they want to talk about in the way they want to communicate them.

"The main function of slang is not just to transmit information, but show that you have a certain flair," Gibbs said. "It shows you're a member of a social group and that you know how to go about talking about things."

Slang terms are usually coined around everyday ideas or activities within the group. And they are imbued heavily with attitude.

"That's one of the beauties of slang," Gibbs said. "You not only communicate certain information, but your attitude about it as well. It's a way of showing you're hip. If you can use it correctly and appropriately and innovatively, it shows you have a creative sense and puts you at a higher status in some groups. And with children, especially, that is very important."

Slang changes very quickly in teen circles because it becomes passe as soon as parents, teachers or even peers outside the "in" group begin to understand the meaning.

To a lesser degree, members of professions, sporting teams or activities, even members of the opposite sex, use slang to exclude those who don't belong.

"Any kind of jargon or colloquialism is used in that way," Gibbs said. "Reporters, psychologists, we all have our own lingo. I'm not saying that we

---

* Reprinted from the *Orange County Register*

as academic psychologists have a conspiracy going so no one can understand us, but we all do, in fact, use slang as a private code."

Businessmen exclude businesswomen from their conversations by using sports metaphors in their speech, Della Volpe said.

Colleagues within a job or profession develop their own lingo, which lets them communicate while baffling those on the outside. Participants in sports close out the neophytes with their use of jargon.

And while English purists bemoan the proliferation of slang, Della Volpe said it's the life-support system for language.

"People talk in metaphoric terms," she said. "They use the frame of reference they are most familiar with. Since computers are so widespread, for example, we hear a lot of computer jargon."

Consider the noun-turned-verb "interface." It was once a point or means of interaction between two electronic systems. It has become a synonym for personal interaction. Or, 10 years ago, one might have said he didn't feel "up to par" (golf slang) without a morning cup of coffee. These days, he's not "on line."

"That's what keeps language alive," Della Volpe said. "Language has to reflect and evolve parallel with the society. If it doesn't, we can't communicate."

Gibbs said he believes in "linguistic anarchy."

"There are people out there who think slang is definitely a terrible thing. They say the language is deteriorating. Well, the thing to note is that the ancient Greeks said the same thing. I believe there is no one correct way of speaking. Language is there to be created and exploited," Gibbs said.

How slang is created is tough to track.

Slang enters the English language in one of two ways, Della Volpe said. An old word takes on a new meaning (relics of the 1960s remember when "fuzz" meant police as well as something on a peach) or a new word is coined by blending words and meaning. Slang words are created by anyone with enough creativity and imagination to come up with a clever turn of phrase.

To the uninitiated, slang sounds like gibberish. But a little linguistic field-work can reveal the wealth of meaning behind the most colorful slang.

The following are some examples of what's being spoken out there on the Orange County slang front, gathered by a volunteer corps of high school students, sports enthusiasts and workers in a variety of jobs.

Agro: *adj.* Excited, aggressive, aggravated. "Don't get all agro."

Bogus: *adj.* Fake or unnatural. "Those are bogus eyelashes." Also, a bummer. "That exam was bogus."

Bug-out: *n.* A strange or unusual person. "She's a bug-out."

Chill out: *v.* Relax, calm down. "Hey, chill out, dude."

Fresh: *adj.* Cool, worthy of note. "That outfit is fresh."

Full: *adj.* Very; in the fullest sense. "She's a full bug-out."

Lack of oxygen: A phrase used in response to someone who is spacey or absent-minded. "It must be lack of oxygen."

Panic: *n.* A person who is nuts or crazy. "You're a panic."

Put music to it: A phrase used in comeback to anyone who is overly whiny or always complaining. "Aw, come on. Put music to it."

Sketch: *n.* Anyone who's not quite all there. Usually used with full as in, "That teacher's a full sketch."

Jack Lynde, vice president of Orange County Musician's Association Local No. 7 reports from the music business:

Not too tightly wrapped: *adj.* Dumb; not much going on upstairs. Usually used in reference to a backstage groupie. "She's not too tightly wrapped."

Short: *n.* A car. "He lit out of his short on the avenue."

Vine: *n.* Suit of clothes. "That's a fine vine."

The fly-fishing slang report comes from Steven Feldman, a Laguna Niguel attorney:

Hardware man: *n.* A fisherman (not a fly-fisherman) who uses spoons (or lures) to catch fish. "He's a hardware man."

Purist: *n.* A fly-fisherman who won't use wet flies (flies designed to go in or under the water.) "Give the dry flies to the purist."

Rock turkeys: *n.* A bait fisherman, particularly one who stands on rocks at the side of a stream with a fishing rod in one hand and a beer in the other. "Look out for the rock turkeys over there."

Ernie Holliday, manager of Adler Shoes in Montclair, reports on slang in the shoe business:

Dog: *n.* A bad shoe that doesn't sell. "That pump was a dog."

Department 13: *n.* The restroom. "I'll be in department 13."

Drag: *n.* Shoes a salesman left out on the floor from a previous customer. "Pick up your drag."

Duck: *n.* A flat, spread-out foot, or a person with such a foot. "He's got a duck."

Elephant: *n.* A very wide foot, or a person with such a foot. "Who is going to take the elephant?"

Live one: *n.* The salesman's dream. A person who, with a little wining and dining, will buy multiple pairs of shoes. "She's a live one."

Shoe dog: *n.* A career shoe salesman who travels from shoe store to shoe store taking jobs and causing trouble. "The guy is a shoe dog."

Stiffs: *n.* The extras—shoe trees, shoe polish, etc.—that are sold with shoes. "Don't forget to push the stiffs."

Grant Brittain, photo editor of *Transworld Skateboarding Magazine*, supplies slang from skateboarding (or skating):

Betty: *n.* A tongue-in-cheek expression for girl. "There is an awesome betty."

Bio: *adj.* Particularly impressive. Similar to rad only without the element of danger that rad implies. "That was bio, dude."

Flow: *v.* To give or bequeath. "Flow me some bucks."

Grind: *n.* A cool maneuver that consists of scraping the truck (axle) along the ridge of a banked wall. "Hey, gnarly grind."

Sketchy: *adj.* Term used to describe a skater who always looks as though he's about to fall, but doesn't. "He pulled off a sketchy aerial."

Slam: *v.* To fall accidentally and hard. "That was a bad slam."

The surf report comes from Jim Pinkerton at *Surfing* magazine:

Amped: *adj.* Psyched up to surf. Ready to go. "I'm amped."

Bail: *v.* To exit a wave by jumping away or diving off the board. Terminology borrowed from the aviation term "bail out." "I gotta bail, man."

Grind: *v.* To eat a lot of food very quickly. "Let's go grind."

Schralp: *v.* To surf violently on a wave. Synonym for shred, rip and lacerate. "I just schralped that wave."

Stick: *n.* Surfboard. "Got your stick?"

Stoked: *adj.* The adjective that refuses to die. Happy.

Essentially More B.S.

PURPOSE:

To demonstrate the power of words and how people can use words to not only make themselves appear more intelligent, but to confuse an issure. This type of deliberately misleading language is something that any communicator who desires to be viewed as honest would certainly avoid.

PROCEDURE:

This technical writing kit is based on the Simplified Integrated Modular Prose (SIMP) writing system. Using this kit, anyone who can count up to 10 can write as many as 40,000 discrete, well-balanced, grammatically correct sentences packed with EMBS terms and pedagogic gobbledygook.

To put SIMP to work, arrange the modules in A-B-C-D order. Make up four numbers, 7162 for example, and read Phrase 7 off Table A, Phrase 1 off Table B, etc. The result is a SIMP sentence. After you have mastered the basic technique you can realize the full potential of SIMP by arranging the modules in D-B-C-A order. In these advanced configurations some additional commas may be required.

SIMPLIFIED INTEGRATED MODULAR PROSE (SIMP)

SIMP Table A

1. A systematized basis upon which to evaluate competencies and outcomes
2. Initiation and maintenance of a comprehensive, flexible syllabus
3. A curricular formation of meaningful conceptual patterns
4. A ramification of commensurate behavioral objectives
5. A rational entailing subtopic analyses of psychomotor, cognitive and affective domains
6. A noncimitant insight into undergirded knowledge transfer
7. The thrust of instructional objectives which preclude assumed
8. Any reasonably consistent doctrinal guide for curricular innovation
9. The identification of functional modes that equate with educational outcomes
10. A clarifying technique reformulated by the component group

SIMP Table B

1. According to EMBS procedures
2. Technically speaking
3. Based on integral exponential considerations
4. As a resultant implication
5. In respect to specific goals
6. In this regard
7. Relative to the needs assessment program
8. On the other hand
9. Definitively stated
10. In essence then

SIMP Table C

1. Must be based upon developmental conditions and standards with
2. Is further compounded by noncreative concept formulation for
3. Adds vertical organization in complex orientation interplay with
4. Presents extremely interesting subinterval controls to
5. Recognizes and enhances the maximization of individual potential for
6. Effects a significant implementation to functional performance criteria and
7. Neccssitates correlative expertise in specialized areas of
8. Adds dimensional increments to the relevance of theory acquisition for
9. Predicates a viable analysis of multiphasic maturation studies to
10. Postulates that the degree of requisite content mastery is directly proportional to

SIMP Table D

1. The philosophy of affective taxonomy formulated by Krathwohl and others
2. Any interpretive assimilation of the correlative mode
3. The minimum essentials of valid behavioral objectives
4. The scope and focus of all pertinent socioeconomic factors
5. The componential perceptions affecting an integrative approach
6. The transitory utilization of polarized value judgments
7. Any conformation of preestablished divergent assumptions
8. The impetus of value indicators restructured through diverse areas of the continuum
9. Humanistic techniques of career orientation modeled after the Harmin-Simon approach
10. ll nonsupportive and immediate response situations derived from key result Aareas

DISCUSSION:

1. Do you know anyone who uses language that is similar to this? If so, who?
2. What causes people to use EMBS?
3. Does this type of language have any effect on society? If so, in what ways?

Examples of E.M.B.S.

The communication and exchange of ideas on administrative policy matters is encouraged and maintained to optimize the use, mix and cost and administrative inputs in program results. (Treasury Board of Canada Memo)

Now, if you have a strategy you say to yourself, "Well, all right, I'm going to get this out, but I'm going to do it in such a way that I do it in a manner that is compatible, or at least not incompatible with my general thrust.' So what you try to build is the implementation of your strategy by these incremental little things. (Secretary of State George Shultz, quoted in the *Washington Post*)

My position on Vietnam is very simple. And I feel this way. I haven't spoken on it because I haven't felt there was any major contribution that I had to make at the time. I think that our concepts as a nation and that our actions have not kept pace with the changing conditions, and therefore our actions are not completely relevant today to the realities of the magnitude and the complexity of the problems that we face in this conflict. (Nelson Rockefeller, governor of New York, when asked in a press conference for his position on the Vietnam War. When a reporter followed up with a question asking what he meant, Rockefeller answered, "Just what I said.")

Some action of a definite responsive nature probably needs to be taken if it's absolutely clear, but it isn't, at least in the Public sphere, clear that the evidence is overwhelming or without any ambiguity.

Thomas Foley, House Speaker (D-Washington), on the TV program *Face the Nation*, commenting on reports that the Iraqi government had planned to assassinate George Bush.

Facts do not cease to exist because they are ignored. —*A. Huxley*

R E A C T I O N S

Name _____

Date _____

Your professor may require this exercise to be handed in.

Answer the question assigned by your instructor. Remember, openness and honesty are the first steps to being a more effective communicator.

1. Select one of the language barriers to communication that you have experienced in your own communication. Describe the barrier and indicate how it interfered with your communication. What skill will you use in the future to overcome the barrier?

2. In what ways does our reaction to words (semantic reactions) affect our communication?

3. What suggestions would you make to improve communication with respect to semantic reactions?

4. From the very beginning of the day, how long did it take you to slip and use a label or stereotype someone? What was it? What should you have done?

5. If words have power, how is it that "words don't mean; people mean"?

6. Give a recent example of how you reacted to a word because of its connotative impact rather than denotative.

7. Give a recent example of sexism in your language. How might you rid your language behaviors of this barrier?

6 Understanding Self

DEFINITIONS

✳ Self-Image

Definition: How we describe, picture, view ourselves. It is objective, describable, measurable and checkable.

Example: "I am a black female, 24 years old, weighing 123 pounds, 5 feet 6 inches tall." Self-image changes slowly because we develop physically gradually and over extended periods of time.

✳ Self-Esteem

Definition: The value, worth or importance that we put on what our self-image is. It is very subjective.

Example: "I like being black and female. I wish I were a bit older. I would like to lose 10 pounds. I like my height."

✳ Self-Concept

Definition: Our total or world view of ourselves. The complete picture including both our self-image and self-esteem.

Example: "I'm an attractive human being who is intelligent, relates well to others and is generally successful in things I try." Our self-concept changes as our self-image or self-esteem is modified.

✳ Role

Definition: A part we are expected to play in our society.

Examples: Student, mother, brother, worker, athlete, consumer, woman/man, husband, girlfriend, citizen. We are expected to play hundreds of roles in our lives—the more complex our lives, the more roles we are expected to play.

✳ Role Expectations

The parameters or boundaries of the roles we are playing.

✴ Performance Role

Definition: A role where we are paid (or receive some sort of remuneration) for meeting the role expectations as prescribed by the person or agency that "pays" us.

Example: As a student we meet the specifications set by our teacher. If we do so, we receive knowledge, grade, credit, etc. As a worker we do what our boss tells us (often even dressing as directed)—in return, we get a paycheck.

✴ Personality Role

Definition: A role where we have the right to determine the parameters of the role we are playing.

Example: Friend, brother, sex partner, woman, etc. A son or daughter living at home with mom and dad paying the bills is in a performance role since the person is being "paid" her physical upkeep and therefore meets parents' expectations in doing chores around the house or being in at a certain time. However, when son or daughter moves out and begins paying his/her own bills, then son/daughter becomes a personality role.

✴ Self-Disclosure

The process of communicating to others verbally and nonverbally our thoughts, feelings, attitudes, beliefs and values. It is taking our masks off and revealing to another person our "real" self.

THE IMPORTANCE OF UNDERSTANDING SELF

- Who am I?
- How do I feel about myself?
- Do I like (or dislike) parts of my personality or physical appearance?
- Am I comfortable with myself?
- How can I improve my communication both with myself and with others?

These questions are asked by everyone at some time in life. Many of us are confused over the issues of who we really are and the roles we are expected to play to gain societal or peer acceptance. We are frustrated by the demands of people around us who want us to behave according to their expectations of us and our own expectations of who we are and what we want to be.

Is it possible to know and like who we are, to get in touch with the "real me" bur-

ied underneath all the roles we are expected to play in order to be a functioning part of our culture? If it is possible, do we really want to know ourselves? To know and to let others truly know us demands taking risks and being vulnerable. Is it "safer" to live our lives meeting others' expectations and keeping the "real" us hidden from view?

And what does all of this have to do with communication? This, after all, is a book about communication—not psychology.

Here are some things to think about—from people much wiser than the authors of this book.

Honore De Balsac, the great French philosopher-historian, wrote, "Nothing is a greater impediment to being on good terms with others than being ill at ease with yourself."

With regard to meeting the expectations of others, Rabbi Mendel of Kotzk wrote:

> *If I am because I am I,*
> *And you are you because you are you,*
> *Then I am, and you are*
> *But if I am I because you are you,*
> *And you are you because I am I,*
> *Then I am not, and you are not.*

Eleanor Roosevelt, one of the greatest women in American history who survived a lifetime of people attempting to "put her down," wrote, "No one can make you feel inferior without your consent."

Some things to think about? We hope this chapter will give you some answers to the questions we have asked above—and the encouragement to find out and let others know who you really are.

BARRIERS TO UNDERSTANDING SELF

There are real barriers put in place by others and ourselves to our getting to know, accept and like ourselves. Some of them are:

Our confusion between the types of roles we play—those personality roles where we have the right to determine the way the role is played and those performance roles where others have the right to define some of the parameters.

Our fear of risking letting others know what we are truly thinking and feeling because if we do "they" might not like us anymore.

Our unwillingness to change. Even if where we are hurts we sometimes view change as worse than the pain and loneliness we are currently feeling.

Our practice of comparing ourselves with others—not recognizing that when we do that, we automatically make ourselves into losers.

Our problems with accepting ourselves as we are—zits and all—learning that there are some things about ourselves that we cannot change. And that we might just as well learn to accept those things (and maybe like and use them!).

Our false modesty that does not allow us to rejoice in our own uniqueness and to define, refine and emphasize our strong qualities and attributes.

Our failure to prescribe and follow plans which help us to change those things about ourselves that we can change and want to change.

MISS PEACH   By Mell Lazarus

Leading a Good Life Not a Contest for Popularity

Leo F. Buscaglia*

I was recently a guest on a national television talk show that encouraged audience participation. A woman in the audience impatiently awaited her opportunity to comment. When it was her turn to speak, she stood and ventilated her not-so-favorable feelings toward me.

"I don't believe you're for real," she said. "People aren't the way you say they are. Anyone who talks about love and goodness all the time is stupid or phony."

Some in the audience were vocal in their opposition to her statement, some were in agreement. It did not matter. I told her that I long ago gave up the notion that I could (or should want to) please everyone. I've learned to be comfortable with the idea that not everyone will like me or believe in what I do.

There are those who spend years agonizing over the fact that another person may not like us or is offended by something we said or did. Some of us even become what we think others want us to be in order not to offend. We tailor our personalities, our conversation, our behavior to suit others. There are those who make such a studied effort to do this that they begin to lose sight of who they are.

Acting the way you believe others would like you to behave does not win friends. We become indifferent to someone who wants to please all the people all the time. (I would prefer to have someone dislike me rather than be indifferent to me.) Sometimes we have to put ourselves on the line at the risk of alienating others. In the end it is better than the possibility of being alienated from ourselves.

Don't confuse others' disapproval of us with dislike. People are often more accepting and forgiving than we give them credit for. Those who like us and love us for who we are will give us the latitude to have different opinions and even be a real pain once in awhile. No friendship can be based on the assumption that "as long as you agree with me you are my friend." That is enslavement, not friendship.

We all like to make good impressions and have people like us, but why do we take rejection, no matter how mild, so seriously? Perhaps it is based on the false idea that someone else has the power to deprive us of love. Actually, that is something only we can do to ourselves. If artists and musicians and writers worried about being accepted or loved by everyone, they would cease to create.

It is enough that they are appreciated and that they feel the love and acceptance of some people. Whether we care to admit it, most of us respect

---

* By permission, Leo F. Buscaglia

individuals who say, "This is what I feel and I'd like to share it with you. If you like it I'm pleased, but even if you don't, I must continue to express these feelings."

I am not suggesting that we take a "who cares" attitude or be oblivious to how others feel about us. Such individuals are on one end of the scale and those who try to please everybody are at the other extreme. In between these two groups of individuals there is a healthy medium. We have a right and responsibility to be ourselves without worrying whether we are winning friends or influencing people.

The Twelve Year Put-Down

One of the great challenges faced by teachers of college freshmen and sophomores is the large number of these students who feel that they are inadequate human beings. It is not difficult to understand why so many of our students feel this way, when you stop to realize that they have been taught to feel exactly so for twelve long years.

The tragedy of American education is that even our best students usually receive an essentially remedial education. In most U.S. classrooms, at whatever level of schooling, the student is perceived to be in a state of ignorance which must be remedied. By exposing young people in our society to a mandatory twelve years of being thus perceived, we assure the creation of an inferior citizenry. For whatever else our young people learn in this system, they tend to learn to perceive themselves as inferior.

Put yourself in the college freshman's shoes: "For twelve years you have gone to school to be told what you do wrong! Your grades were determined by your errors. A low grade resulted whenever your errors were abundant. A high grade resulted from a notable lack of error. After twelve years in a system which has assumed your ignorance and emphasized your errors, you now probably feel quite inferior. By essentially assuming your incompetence for twelve years, the education system has gone a long way toward assuring your incompetence, because you have formed your self-image from those images of your self which have been most persistently communicated to you by the system in which you operate. Twelve years in a system of negative reinforcement have tended to make you a master of the art of feeling inferior."

By permission, Noel McInnis; © Environment for Learning, 1970, Aspen, CO, 81611

I open myself up to you,
    so you may see inside:
    the past scars
    and present pains.

I place myself before you
    with nothing left to hide:
    no secrets
    or hidden remains.

I present myself to you,
    a package deal:
    the good and strong—
    the weak.

I ask you to accept me,
    for being real:
    your understanding nod
    is all I seek.

By permission, Denelle Hobbs

If . . .

If a child lives with criticism, he learns to condemn.
If a child lives with hostility, he learns to fight.
If a child lives with fears, he learns to be apprehensive.
If a child lives with pity, he learns to feel sorry for himself.
If a child lives with jealousy, he learns to feel guilty.
If a child lives with encouragement, he learns to be confident.
If a child lives with tolerance, he learns to be patient.
If a child lives with praise, he learns to be appreciative.
If a child lives with acceptance, he learns to love.
If a child lives with approval, he learns to like himself.
If a child lives with recognition, he learns to have a goal.
If a child lives with fairness, he learns what justice is.
If a child lives with honesty, he learns what truth is.
If a child lives with security, he learns to have faith in himself and in those about him.
If a child lives with friendliness, he learns that the world is a good place in which to
    live.

The Watchman-Examiner
By permission, Harper & Row, Publishers, *The Treasure Chest, The Watchman-Examiner.*

Exercising Compliments

PURPOSE:

To learn how to give compliments or do something nice for other people and to record their reactions.

PROCEDURE:

For this assignment, you are to give at least 10 compliments or actions to 10 different people. Below, list the person you addressed, what you said or did and the reaction of the person receiving the compliment.

Person:
Compliment:
Reaction:

Person:
Compliment:
Reaction:

Person:
Compliment:
Reaction:

Person:
Compliment:
Reaction:

Person:
Compliment:
Reaction:

Person:
Compliment:
Reaction:

Person:
Compliment:
Reaction:

Person:
Compliment:
Reaction:

Person:
Compliment:
Reaction:

Person:
Compliment:
Reaction:

Showing Appreciation
Saying Thank You

PURPOSE:

To see how people respond to compliments.

PROCEDURE:

1. Divide into groups of five or six people.
2. Select a recorder—a person who will write down everything that is said to a particular individual.
3. Starting anywhere in the circle, one person will be focused upon. Once selected, the group will then start giving compliments to the "focused" person. The best way to do this is to simply go around the circle a few times.
4. After the person has received at least 10 compliments the recorder will hand them the written account of what just transpired. Then another person is selected to be the focus individual. This process will continue until everyone has been focused upon.

DISCUSSION:

1. How did you feel when you were the focus person?
2. Did you find it difficult to give compliments to other people?
3. Is giving compliments to other people a motivational skill?
4. In what aspects of your life can you employ what you did in this group?

The Way We See Me

PURPOSE:

To compare the way you see yourself with the way others see you.

PROCEDURE:

1. Give copies of the questionnaire on the next pages to some of your relatives or friends.
2. Answer "The Way We See Me Questionnaire" as the items apply to you.
3. Take time to compare your questionnaire with each person who answered one.

DISCUSSION:

1. What similarities did you notice among all questionnaire responses? Why?
2. What differences did you notice among all questionnaire responses? Why?
3. What did you learn about yourself from this activity?
4. What effect do our various perceptions of one another have on interpersonal communication?

The Way We See Me Questionnaire (Self)

As part of a class assignment, I am distributing this questionnaire to some of my relatives and friends. It is designed to give me your impressions of my personality. I am attempting to compare the way other people see me with the way I see myself. While it may be difficult for you to express your impressions exactly, I would appreciate as frank a rating as you can give me.

This questionnaire should not take long to complete. First, try to construct an overall view of your impressions about my personality before answering the specific questions. Consider each item briefly and indicate the first choice that occurs to you. If you come to an item which you feel unable to answer with certainty, place a question mark, instead of a check, in one of the spaces to indicate a guess. However, please do answer every question. If you have comments that will help explain any of your answers, please use the space provided or write in the margins. Explanatory comments will be appreciated.

Please begin by considering my main strengths and weaknesses. Describe each as carefully as you can in the spaces below:

Main Strengths:

Main Weaknesses:

How well do the following words apply to me? Please checkmark the word/phrase that applies.

	Not at all	Slightly	Moderately	Rather well	Extremely well
Self-confident					
Tactful					
Irritable					
Quiet					
Emotionally variable					
Serious					
Energetic					
Well-adjusted					
Cooperative					
Prejudiced					
Unpredictable					

	Not at all	Slightly	Moderately	Rather well	Extremely well
Selfish					
Leader					
Considerate of others					
Good natured					
Tense					
Accepts criticism					
Aggressive					
Easy to get to know					
Imaginative					
Sense of humor					
Friendly					
Dogmatic					
Responsible					
Ambitious					
Physically attractive					
Sexually attractive					
Mature					
Trusting of others					
Open					

How accurately do these answers reflect your impressions of me?

How well do you feel you know me?

Additional Comments:

Respondent:

☐ Self

☐ Relative

☐ Friend

The Way We See Me Questionnaire (Relative or Friend)

As part of a class assignment, I am distributing this questionnaire to some of my relatives and friends. It is designed to give me your impressions of my personality. I am attempting to compare the way other people see me with the way I see myself. While it may be difficult for you to express your impressions exactly, I would appreciate as frank a rating as you can give me.

This questionnaire should not take long to complete. First, try to construct an overall view of your impressions about my personality before answering the specific questions. Consider each item briefly and indicate the first choice that occurs to you. If you come to an item which you feel unable to answer with certainty, place a question mark, instead of a check, in one of the spaces to indicate a guess. However, please do answer every question. If you have comments that will help explain any of your answers, please use the space provided or write in the margins. Explanatory comments will be appreciated.

Please begin by considering my main strengths and weaknesses. Describe each as carefully as you can in the spaces below:

Main Strengths:

Main Weaknesses:

How well do the following words apply to me? Please checkmark the word/phrase that applies.

	Not at all	Slightly	Moderately	Rather well	Extremely well
Self-confident					
Tactful					
Irritable					
Quiet					
Emotionally variable					
Serious					
Energetic					
Well-adjusted					
Cooperative					
Prejudiced					
Unpredictable					

	Not at all	Slightly	Moderately	Rather well	Extremely well
Selfish					
Leader					
Considerate of others					
Good natured					
Tense					
Accepts criticism					
Aggressive					
Easy to get to know					
Imaginative					
Sense of humor					
Friendly					
Dogmatic					
Responsible					
Ambitious					
Physically attractive					
Sexually attractive					
Mature					
Trusting of others					
Open					

How accurately do these answers reflect your impressions of me?

How well do you feel you know me?

Additional Comments:

Respondent:
☐ Self

☐ Relative

☐ Friend

The Way We See Me Questionnaire (Relative or Friend)

As part of a class assignment, I am distributing this questionnaire to some of my relatives and friends. It is designed to give me your impressions of my personality. I am attempting to compare the way other people see me with the way I see myself. While it may be difficult for you to express your impressions exactly, I would appreciate as frank a rating as you can give me.

This questionnaire should not take long to complete. First, try to construct an overall view of your impressions about my personality before answering the specific questions. Consider each item briefly and indicate the first choice that occurs to you. If you come to an item which you feel unable to answer with certainty, place a question mark, instead of a check, in one of the spaces to indicate a guess. However, please do answer every question. If you have comments that will help explain any of your answers, please use the space provided or write in the margins. Explanatory comments will be appreciated.

Please begin by considering my main strengths and weaknesses. Describe each as carefully as you can in the spaces below:

Main Strengths:

Main Weaknesses:

How well do the following words apply to me? Please checkmark the word/phrase that applies.

	Not at all	Slightly	Moderately	Rather well	Extremely well
Self-confident					
Tactful					
Irritable					
Quiet					
Emotionally variable					
Serious					
Energetic					
Well-adjusted					
Cooperative					
Prejudiced					
Unpredictable					

	Not at all	Slightly	Moderately	Rather well	Extremely well
Selfish					
Leader					
Considerate of others					
Good natured					
Tense					
Accepts criticism					
Aggressive					
Easy to get to know					
Imaginative					
Sense of humor					
Friendly					
Dogmatic					
Responsible					
Ambitious					
Physically attractive					
Sexually attractive					
Mature					
Trusting of others					
Open					

How accurately do these answers reflect your impressions of me?

How well do you feel you know me?

Additional Comments:

Respondent:
☐ Self
☐ Relative
☐ Friend

 # Turning Points in My Life

PURPOSE:

To identify events in your life which have affected you and your intra/interpersonal communication.

PROCEDURE:

1. In the space below, list at least 10 events in your life which could be said to have been turning points—i.e., travel experiences, school experiences, births, deaths, embarrassments, milestones, etc.
    a.
    b.
    c.
    d.
    e.
    f.
    g.
    h.
    i.
    j.

2. Briefly state how each of these affected you and your intra/interpersonal communication.
3. Once you have completed these, form small groups and discuss what each has written. Also, discuss the following questions.

DISCUSSION:

1. Specifically, how have these events related to your own intra/interpersonal communication?
2. How might these events relate to the self-fulfilling prophecy which states that people tend to become what they are told they are or think they are?
3. Are there any similar events which have affected people in your group? Discuss.
4. Do people of other cultures react differently than you do to your turning points? How/why?

"Who Are You?"

"Who are you?" said the caterpillar. Alice replied rather shyly, "I-I hardly know, sir, just at present—at least I know who I was when I got up this morning, but I must have changed several times since then."

Lewis Carroll

HARLEM RAIN

Sometimes it comes on my favorite day
the rain, that is, on Saturday
    Rain makes me think . . .
    Don't like the rain
Momma, umbrellas can't shelter the rain
no, not as long as I got a brain
    Newsman says scattered showers
    Don't see no scatterin'
    just rain
Rain drains plugged, they don't want no rain
Ha! funny, I feel the same
    Momma's best pot
    ain't smellin' of stew,
    just catchin' rain . . .
Tonight it'll stop when I'm sound asleep
at dawn returning . . . afraid to peep
    Got a friend named Josh
    lives uptown . . .
    Never talks about the rain
    must never seen it
Momma is this how they felt in slavery,
body in prison, mind roaming free
    Newsman say rain gon' stop
    sure hope so
    cause my mind is tired . . .
Preacher preached "Storm Clouds Don't Come To Stay!"
And all I see is rain today . . .
    Clouded windows
    Clouded dreams . . .
    That ol' sun must be in mournin' . . .
When I get grown I'm gon' catch a train
somewhere . . . somewhere . . . where it ain't no rain
    Peering out my window
    thru glass that's fogged
    from heat inside
    I write . . . my name

Raymond Porter

Comfort Survey

PURPOSE:

To identify the feelings that each person is comfortable with and can express.

PROCEDURE:

First, complete the survey below. Circle the number which expresses how well you deal with each feeling listed.

Rating Scale	
1	Can express completely in any situation
2	Can express 75% of the time
3	Can express 50% of the time—with difficulty
4	Express only 25% of the time—with reservation
5	Do not express except on a very rare occasion

caring	1	2	3	4	5	displeasure	1	2	3	4	5
sharing	1	2	3	4	5	tension	1	2	3	4	5
love	1	2	3	4	5	hurt	1	2	3	4	5
liking	1	2	3	4	5	disappointment	1	2	3	4	5
concern	1	2	3	4	5	disgust	1	2	3	4	5
sadness	1	2	3	4	5	joy	1	2	3	4	5
depression	1	2	3	4	5	excitement	1	2	3	4	5
fear	1	2	3	4	5	pride	1	2	3	4	5
anger	1	2	3	4	5	patriotism	1	2	3	4	5

Complete the sentences below:

a. I am disgusted when _____

b. I get angry when _____

c. The thing that frightens me most is _____

d. Love is a feeling _____

e. To like someone is _____

f. I am disappointed with _____

g. I take pride in _____

h. I feel tense _____

i. I am concerned about _____

j. The last time I felt real joy was _____

k. I am excited about _____

l. The thing that hurts me most is _____

m. The thing which depresses me most frequently _____

n. I very much care about _____

o. I enjoy sharing _____

p. I feel _____

q. Patriotism _____

r. I am displeased with _____

Form dyads and discuss your answers from the above.

DISCUSSION:

1. What part do feelings play in verbal communication? In nonverbal communication?
2. Is there a feeling that you absolutely cannot deal with? If so, what?
3. How important are feelings to you?
4. How can you work on dealing more effectively with your feelings?
5. Which feeling do you think you deal with most successfully?
6. How do feelings affect your perception?

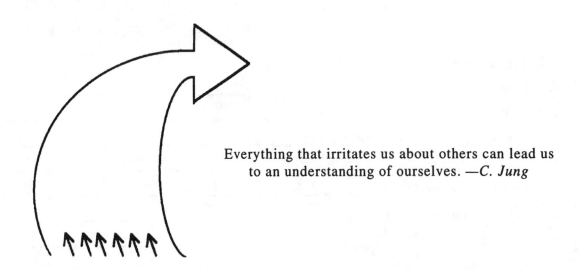

Everything that irritates us about others can lead us to an understanding of ourselves. —*C. Jung*

Rate Your Self-Confidence

PURPOSE:

To determine the nature of self-confidence and how to increase it.

PROCEDURE:

Next to each situation, rate how strong your self-confidence is, based on the rating scale.

Rating Scale
1 Feel completely self-confident and capable
2 Feel capable, but have some feelings of self-consciousness
3 Feel very self-conscious, but do an adequate job
4 Feel inferior to the point that it hampers my ambition, willingness to try, for fear of failure
5 Complete fear of failure—no self-confidence—will not try at all—don't get in these kinds of situations

_____ 1. In front of a group—acting as the leader

_____ 2. In sports (tennis, basketball, etc.)

_____ 3. In scholastic competition

_____ 4. In my looks

_____ 5. My ability to communicate

_____ 6. My ability to do my job

_____ 7. Taking on added responsibilities

_____ 8. Organizing a big program

_____ 9. As a husband/wife/boy friend/girl friend

_____ 10. Acting as the stabilizing factor

_____ 11. As a parent or a future parent

_____ 12. Artistic/creative abilities

_____ 13. Carry on a conversation

_____ 14. Going on an interview

_____ 15. Volunteering for demonstration

_____ 16. Entering a new situation—new group of people

_____ 17. Speaking out in a group of strangers

_____ 18. Ability to begin a task and carry it through

_____ 19. Risk-taking

_____ 20. Trusting others

DISCUSSION:
1. Will your self-confidence affect your future success? If so, how?
2. Will it affect your interpersonal relationships? How?

I care not what others think of what I do, but I care very much about what I think of what I do: that is character! —*T. Roosevelt*

 **Interpersonal Confidence Walk**

PURPOSE:

To examine the ways in which you gain interpersonal confidence or trust.

PROCEDURE:

1. Your instructor will assign you a partner.
2. Have your partner blindfold you. She will take you around the room, building or campus.
3. When the blindfolded partner has developed a high degree of confidence or trust, switch places and continue your walk.

RULES FOR TRUST WALK:

1. Walk—**Don't run.**
2. Remain in body contact with your partner from the instant the blindfold goes on.
3. Talk to your partner. Share **thoughts** and **feelings**.
4. Remove blindfold and return to the classroom if any of the following happens:
   a. Your partner says she cannot continue.
   b. Your partner violates your trust in **any way**.
   c. Your partner becomes frightened, dizzy or disoriented.
5. Follow the prescribed route.
6. After you have reversed roles, and both persons have been on the trust walk, thank each other and talk about your experience.

DISCUSSION:

1. How long did it take you to develop confidence in your partner?
2. How was this confidence developed? Be specific.
3. Describe the communication between you and your partner during your walk.

If you aspire to the highest place,
it is no disgrace to stop at the second or even the third.
—*M. Cicero*

 **Role Analysis**

PURPOSE:

To examine more closely the roles you play and how these roles affect aspects of communication.

PROCEDURE:

Answer the following questions individually and then we will discuss the responses as a class.

1.   Try to list five of the roles which you commonly play, making each role separate and distinct from the others—i.e., student, mother, wife, etc.
2.   How are each of the following altered by each of the above roles?
     a. Language
     b. Appearance
     c. Attitude
     d. Values
     e. Quantity and quality of communication
3.   What major role expectations do you have for each of the following roles?

     a. Teacher   k. Clergyman
     b. Student   l. Parishioner
     c. Wife   m. Doctor
     d. Husband   n. Patient
     e. Boy friend   o. Policeman
     f. Girl friend   p. Citizen
     g. Mother   q. Employer
     h. Father   r. Employee
     i. Son   s. Clerk
     j. Daughter   t. Customer

4.   Analyze the following situations according to how different people might deal with them.
     a. What questions might each person ask?
     b. What factors would determine their reaction to each situation?

How would a . . .	**deal with . . .**
mother	buying a car
father	selecting a college
fashion model	seeing a ball game
preacher	going on vacation
boy friend	selling a boat
girl friend	stealing an orange
cab driver	punishing a small child
salesperson	getting a speeding ticket
police officer	going to the dentist
rich student	paying a fine
poor student	using leisure time

DISCUSSION:

1.   How do roles affect interpersonal communication?
2.   Discuss role playing as a means of solving problems which occur in interpersonal communication situations.

four portraits of women

hang
   before
the world's equal rights
amendment
    wearing
horn-rimmed
mental frames.

figure one is
    innocent
freezer paper,
as simple as
    a box
folder on the tomatoe
conveyor belt
of campbell's soup.

number two is painted
hot coal,
aborting many
corset
   loves,
only to prove
devotion in america's
welfare.

the next frame
   clicks
buttons in stock
x changes,
lights fires on stimulating
nights
with
   the gas log
of her
fireplace—
being shrewdly convinced
that one, two
and four
must certainly have
castrated
minds.

and what of portrait
four?
   well, it's blank
textured
rice paper
because I haven't been
levered by pushers
or red sylvania light bulbs;
all women feel right
at home sitting on my
intelligence seat,
especially when i can
paint
self-portraits to new
amendments
   with notes
for timing one final rhyme
just for
   them:
"you say i'm a monkey
so i'll stand on my head
and wait for you to laugh
your three selves to
death."

four portraits of women
hang
   before
the world's equal rights
amendment
    wearing
horn-rimmed
mental frames that all
could use
   a mortifying
intestinal
mud pack.

S-Grace

The Childless Couple

KFI Editorial[*]

There is nothing sadder than the childless couple. It breaks the heart to see them stretched out relaxing around swimming pools in Florida, sitting all suntanned and miserable on the decks of their boat—trotting off to Europe like lonesome fools. It's an empty life. There's nothing but money to spend, more time to enjoy and a whole lot less to worry about. . . .

The poor childless couple gets so selfish and wrapped up in their own concerns that you have to feel sorry for them. They don't fight over the child's discipline, they don't blame each other for the child's most nauseous characteristics, and they miss half the fun of doing without things for the child's sake. They go along in their own dull way, doing what they want, buying what they want and liking each other. It's a pretty pathetic picture.

Everyone should have children. No one should be allowed to escape the wonderful experience attached to each stage in the development of the young. The happy memories of the baby days, the alert nights, coughing spells, debts, diaper rash, "dipso" baby sitters, saturated mattresses, spilled food, tantrums, emergencies and never ending crises.

Then comes the real fulfillment as the child grows like a little acorn into a real nut. The wonder of watching your overweight ballerina make a fool of herself in a leotard. The warm smile of the small lad with the sun glittering on 500 bucks worth of braces ruined on peanut brittle. The rollicking, merry, carefree voices of hordes of hysterical kiddies, gently massaging potato chips into the rug at the birthday party.

How dismal is the peaceful home without the constant childish problems that make for a well-rounded life and an early breakdown; the tender thoughtful discussions when the report card reveals the progeny to be one step below a moron; the end of the day reunions with all the joyful happenings related like well-placed blows to the temple.

Children are worth it all. Every moment of anxiety, every sacrifice, every complete collapse pays off as a fine sturdy adolescence is reached. The feeling of reward the first time you took the baby hunting; he didn't mean to shoot you; the boy was excited; remember how he cried? How sorry he was? How much better you felt after the blood transfusion? These are the times with a growing son that a man treasures. . . . These memories that are captured forever in the heart and the limp. . . .

Think back to the night of romantic adventure when your budding daughter eloped with the village idiot. What childless couple ever shared in the stark realism of that drama? Aren't you a better man for having lived richly, fully, and acquiring that tic in your left eye? Could a woman without children touch

---

* By permission, KFI Radio, Los Angeles, CA.

the strength and heroism of your wife as she tried to fling herself out of the bedroom window? The climax when you two became really close in the realization that, after all, your baby girl was a woman with the mind of a pygmy?

The childless couple live in a vacuum. They fill their lonely days with golf, vacation trips, dinner dates, civic affairs, tranquility, leisure and money. There is a terrifying emptiness without children, and the childless couple is too comfortable to know it. You just have to look at them to see what the years have done: he looks boyish, unlined and rested; she's slim, well-groomed and youthful. It isn't natural. If they had had kids, they'd look like the rest of us—tired and gray, wrinkled and sagging. In other words, Normal. . . .

JOHARI WINDOW

The Johari Window provides a way to look at the self. There are things you know about yourself and things you don't know. There are things other people know about yourself and things they don't know. These four aspects represent the various areas of the self.

AREA 1 (I know, others know) represents your public self. The information is common knowledge and you feel free about sharing that information with others.

AREA 2, blind area (others know, I don't know) includes information others have about you, but that you do not have. This, for example, is the way you look to other people.

AREA 3, the hidden area (I know, others don't know) represents the things that you know about yourself, but have been unwilling to share with others. This area includes your secrets and things you are ashamed of.

AREA 4, the unknown area (I don't know, others don't know) represents those things about yourself which you don't understand. This is the area of needs, expectations and desires that you have which you cannot understand.

The four areas are interdependent, that is, a change in the size of one area affects the size of the other areas. By self-disclosing, an individual increases the free area and decreases the size of the hidden area. As a result of the hidden area being decreased, the unknown area is likewise decreased. Such disclosing on the part of an individual makes feedback easier by others and, therefore, the blind area and unknown area are also reduced in size.

Self-disclosure can then be seen as a means to aiding an individual in learning more about the self.

The Johari Window

Free Self	Blind Self
Hidden Self	Unknown Self

The Johari Window Exercise

PURPOSE:

To examine the degree of overall "openness" of your communication.

To provide insight into the hidden areas of your personality.

To demonstrate self-disclosure as a situational variable.

PROCEDURE:

Draw your Johari Window for each of the following environments: speech class, close family, friendship group, spouse, boy friend/girl friend.

DISCUSSION:

How do the windows for each of the environments differ?

MASLOW'S HIERARCHY OF NEEDS

Maslow has classified the basic needs of man into five broad categories:

1. PHYSIOLOGICAL NEEDS—these are necessary for survival. They include the need for food, drink, shelter, sex, avoidance of injury, pain, discomfort, disease, or fatigue, and the need for sensory stimulation. If physiological needs are not satisfied, they are stronger in their motivation than any higher needs.
2. SAFETY NEEDS—these focus on the creation of order and predictableness in one's environment. They include preference for orderliness and routine over disorder, preference for the familiar over the unfamiliar.
3. LOVE NEEDS—are of two types: love and affection between husband and wife, parents and children and close friends; and the need for belonging—identifying the larger groups (church, club, work, organization, etc.). When these needs are not met, feelings of rejection and isolation result with subsequent feelings of mistrust and suspicion toward others.
4. ESTEEM NEEDS—refer to the desire for reputation, prestige, recognition, attention, achievement and confidence. Some sociologists believe that esteem needs are powerful motivators in America.
5. SELF-ACTUALIZATION—the fulfillment of one's capabilities and potentialities. Self-actualization needs take on strong motivating power only when other more basic needs have been fulfilled.

According to Maslow, higher needs act as motivating forces only when those preceding them on the hierarchy have been satisfied.

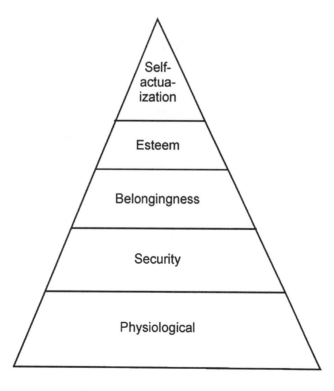

Maslow's Needs Hierarchy

Maslow Activity

PURPOSE:

To help you understand and explore Maslow's theory of human motivation and how it relates to communication.

PROCEDURE:

1. Read the following story and determine the order in which you would make your requests.
2. Form a small group and reach a group consensus on the order of the request.
3. After the groups have reached consensus, compare the groups' ranking with Maslow's hierarchy.

Situation

You are the sole survivor of your wrecked ship. You have been rescued by a wealthy and eccentric recluse who lives on an uncharted island somewhere in the South Pacific with a small group of his followers. Because the island is uncharted, there is no hope of rescue. Your host, who discovered the island years earlier with his small band of followers, has indicated that you are welcome and all your needs and wants will be satisfied—all you have to do is ask. Below are five requests which you may make. Place them in the order in which you would make them.

Individual	Group	
_____	_____	companionship of others
_____	_____	the ability to determine your goals and strive to achieve them
_____	_____	food, drink, shelter, sex
_____	_____	recognition and attention from others
_____	_____	a set of guidelines describing how life on the island is structured

DISCUSSION:

1. How does your ranking and that of your group compare with Maslow's hierarchy?
2. Do you agree or disagree with Maslow's theory? Why?
3. Why do you think Maslow felt most Americans were at level 4?
4. Is there anything about our society which may keep a person from meeting their esteem needs?
5. How does a self-actualized person behave?
6. What role does communication play in meeting needs at each level?
7. What kind of communicator is a self-actualized person?
8. Using communication, how can you help a person move from level 4 to level 5?

R E A C T I O N S

Name _____

Date _____

Your professor may require this exercise to be handed in.

1. Is it possible to know and like who we are?

2. What does knowing who we are have to do with our communication skills?

3. Are the risks of revealing our "real selves" to others worth it? Why or why not?

4. What harm does role playing do to the communication process? When is it appropriate to play roles?

5. Is it true that we have to know and love ourselves before we can know and love others? Why or why not?

6. Are there any cautions to be observed when we are trying to be open and honest in our communication? If so, what are they?

Values

DEFINITIONS

Valuing is one of our most precious personal rights. Yet it seems increasingly clear that all too few humans understand what they value. This chapter describes the process of "valuing" and helps participants to not only clarify their values, but ascertain the relationship of these values to the attitudes and behaviors that they exhibit. Do you always understand why you are making a decision? On what principle it stands? Is your behavior consistent or inconsistent with what you say? Are you consistent in how you apply standards, expectations or judgments from one person to the next?

In order to understand the relationship of values to behavior, attitudes and perception, we first need to look at some basic definitions inherent to the discussion of values.

✴ Values

Long-enduring ideas of what is desirable, which influence choices from available possibilities for action.

✴ Beliefs

Our perceptions about reality which drive our attitudes.

✴ Attitudes

Our views about things which usually give direction to our behaviors.

✴ Behaviors

The acting out of our desires, fears, decisions; the process of making our body take some action in one direction or another—following up on our intentions—with action; to proceed with, discharge, enact, play one's part, conduct oneself

✴ Attributes

Definition:

Those characteristics that define something—that by which it can be described and put into perspective against other things.

Example: Height, gender, personality, intelligence

✳ Consequences

Definition:

The possible outcomes of any given action(s).

Example: Break the law—pay the price

✳ Choosing

Definition:

The act of placing in a higher priority one thing over another—the act of selection, picking, using discretion to select among alternatives.

Example: Selecting a life partner

✳ Preferences

Definition:

Those things which we place a higher priority on than on others; if we had our way and were free to choose—we would go with these things.

Example: All children will be safe and cared for

✳ Decision Making

The process of:

1. Clarifying the problem or choice
2. Gathering pertinent data
3. Identifying possible alternatives
4. Verifying the consequences of alternatives
5. Choosing one alternative over the other

✳ Judging

The process of evaluating someone, an action or outcome, on the basis of self-established criteria—the discrimination between options; the imposing of values on someone else; the process of estimating, awarding, reviewing, critiquing and reporting the conclusion thereof.

——————— ✩ ✩ ✩ ———————

THE IMPORTANCE OF VALUES

Values are not just important in their own right. They serve as a base for decisions, actions and judgments and are crucial to making decisions. In those instances when an individual (or group) either knows or is able to explain her values related to the problem, she can use those values directly, deliberately and openly in making the decision. In those instances in which the individual is unaware of her values, those values act at a subconscious level. That is, a plausible solution is that making the decision may be highly frustrating because there are competing values acting on the individual but she is unaware of the source of conflict and thereby unable to respond to the real issue.

It is the purpose of this chapter to present information and exercises that will enable you, by the end of the chapter, to answer the following questions:

1. What is a value?
2. How do values relate to my everyday life?
3. How do values affect the decision making process?
4. How are values formulated?
5. How do values affect my interpersonal communication?
6. What are factors that alter the existence of values in my life?
7. How does "information" affect the valuing/decision making process?

BARRIERS TO UNDERSTANDING VALUES

In our information and highly technological society today, we are constantly being bombarded by conflicting opinions, views, beliefs and desires of other people, groups, family, friends and general public opinion. This information, and the influence with which it is displayed to us, presents many potential barriers to actually developing clear values for ourselves.

Confusion often exists between what we were taught to believe as youngsters and **what we believe as adults.**

Think for a moment about what opinions and values you borrowed from your parents; about those aspects of your current lifestyle that are similar or very different from those of your family members. Think back on those cliches or traditions that you participated in and/or heard as a child that have affected you today.

All of us receive some of our values initially from our families and sometimes those values are based in our religion, nationality, race, socioeconomic status and political upbringing. As we grow older, we sometimes re-examine the values that we "absorbed"—usually because a behavior facing us comes into conflict with our belief system.

LACK OF ACCURATE INFORMATION

Ignorance for some is bliss . . . and it can allow us to not see the total picture. When we don't have as much relevant information as possible—when we have only seen one side versus all sides, and when certain key and relevant facts, perspectives, are not known to us—we choose from what is known and the choice may, in the larger context, be inappropriate.

PERSONAL BIASES OF OTHERS WHICH HAVE NO BEARING IN THE RATIONAL WORLD

If we care about or admire someone, we tend to give their thoughts and feelings more credence and priority. Sometimes, because we do not want to offend people we care about, are close to, or are related to, we do not take the risk of offending them by "owning" values different than theirs.

PEER—FAMILY—WORK PRESSURE

All of us are subject to pressures from all of those around us. All of the avenues within which we function—family, work, social—have organizational cultures which reflect values. This culture, both directly and subtly, forces us to confront its values. The threats of noncompliance, rejection and ostracism are usually present. And some of us are not comfortable with "being in the minority" in our thought—of not conforming and being part of whatever "normative" culture we are a part of.

CONFLICTING VALUES

At one time or another, we are all faced with alternatives to the decision process that are based on values that seem to conflict. For example, a person who has a priority on stability and security—who values his house and wants to stay there—may be faced with a job promotion that requires him to move somewhere else. Upward mobility and success may also be a high priority. But when placed against the security and stability of a house, which one will prevail?

LACK OF EMPOWERMENT

People with self-confidence usually do not have any problem being able to articulate their values. They may change their values—but they feel empowered—they feel able to be in charge of the changes. A lack of this feeling—knowing that you are and have a right to be in control—can be a barrier in that you may not be able to exercise the control to identify for yourself and be comfortable with your choice.

CONSISTENCY

As choices emerge, in a variety of circumstances, especially if they include passing judgment on ourselves vs. others, we sometimes have the tendency to be inconsistent in what values guide our decisions. But, if something is truly a value for us, should or shouldn't it apply to all circumstances?

CHANGING CIRCUMSTANCES

As circumstances and events change, so does pertinence of our decisions. We all must re-evaluate from time to time our choices based on emerging circumstances. And these can pose a challenge to our value system. If we value something because it has certain attributes—and the attributes change—what happens to how we feel about the value?

The greatest discovery of my generation is that a human being can alter his life by altering his attitude.
—*W. James*

My World Now: Life in a Nursing Home, from the Inside

Anna Mae Halgrim Seaver[*]

This is my world now. It's all I have left. You see, I'm old. And I'm not as healthy as I used to be. I'm not necessarily happy with it but I accept it. Occasionally, a member of my family will stop in to see me. He or she will bring me some flowers or a little present, maybe a set of slippers—I've got 8 pair. We'll visit for awhile and then they will return to the outside world and I'll be alone again.

Oh, there are other people here in the nursing home. Residents, we're called. The majority are about my age. I'm 84. Many are in wheelchairs. The lucky ones are passing through—a broken hip, a diseased heart, something has brought them here for rehabilitation. When they're well they'll be going home.

Most of us are aware of our plight—some are not. Varying stages of Alzheimer's have robbed several of their mental capacities. We listen to endlessly repeated stories and questions. We meet them anew daily, hourly or more often. We smile and nod gracefully each time we hear a retelling. They seldom listen to my stories, so I've stopped trying.

The help here is basically pretty good, although there's a large turnover. Just when I get comfortable with someone he or she moves on to another job. I understand that. This is not the best job to have.

I don't much like some of the physical things that happen to us. I don't care much for a diaper. I seem to have lost the control acquired so diligently as a child. The difference is that I'm aware and embarrassed but I can't do anything about it. I've had 3 children and I know it isn't pleasant to clean another's diaper. My husband used to wear a gas mask when he changed the kids. I wish I had one now.

Why do you think the staff insists on talking baby talk when speaking to me? I understand English. I have a degree in music and am a certified teacher. Now I hear a lot of words that end in "y." Is this how my kids felt? My hearing aid works fine. There is little need for anyone to position their face directly in front of mine and raise their voice with those "y" words. Sometimes it takes longer for a meaning to sink in; sometimes my mind wanders when I am bored. But there's no need to shout.

I tried once or twice to make my feelings known. I even shouted once. That gained me a reputation of being "crotchety." Imagine me, crotchety. My children never heard me raise my voice. I surprised myself. After I've asked for help more than a dozen times and received nothing more than a dozen condescending smiles and a "Yes, deary, I'm working on it," something begins to break. That time I wanted to be taken to a bathroom.

I'd love to go out for a meal, to travel again. I'd love to go to my own church, sing with my own choir. I'd love to visit my friends. Most of them are gone now or else they are in different "homes" of their children's choosing. I'd love to play a good game of bridge but no one here seems to concentrate very well.

My children put me here for my own good. They said they would be able to visit me frequently. But they have their own lives to lead. That sounds normal. I don't want to be a burden. They know that. But I would like to see them more. One of them is here in town. He visits as much as he can.

Something else I've learned to accept is loss of privacy. Quite often I'll close my door when my roommate—imagine having a roommate at my age—is in the TV room. I do appreciate some time to myself and believe that I have earned at least that courtesy. As I sit thinking or writing, one of the aides invariably opens the door unannounced and walks in as if I'm not there. Sometimes she even opens my drawers and begins rummaging around. Am I invisible? Have I lost my right to respect and dignity? What would happen if the roles were reversed? I am still a human being. I would like to be treated as one.

The meals are not what I would choose for myself. We get variety but we don't get a choice. I am one of the fortunate ones who can still handle utensils. I remember eating off such cheap utensils in the Great Depression. I worked hard so I would not have to ever use them again. But here I am.

Did you ever sit in a wheelchair over an extended period of time? It's not comfortable. The seat squeezes you into the middle and applies constant pressure on your hips. The armrests are too narrow and my arms slip off. I am luckier than some. Others are strapped into their chairs and abandoned in front of the TV. Captive prisoners of daytime television; soap operas, talk shows and commercials.

One of the residents died today. He was a loner who, at one time, started a business and developed a multimillion-dollar company. His children moved him here when he could no longer control his bowels. He didn't talk to most of us. He often snapped at the aides as though they were his employees. But he just gave up; willed his own demise. The staff has made up his room and another man has moved in.

A typical day. Awakened by the woman in the next bed wheezing—a former chain smoker with asthma. Call an aide to wash me and place me in my wheelchair to wait for breakfast. Only 67 minutes until breakfast. I'll wait. Breakfast in the dining area. Most of the residents are in wheelchairs. Others use canes or walkers. Some sit and wonder what they are waiting for. First meal of the day. Only 3 hours and 26 minutes until lunch. Maybe I'll sit around and wait for it. What is today? One day blends into the next until day and date mean nothing.

Let's watch a little TV. Oprah and Phil and Geraldo and who cares if some transvestite is having trouble picking a color-coordinated wardrobe from his husband's girlfriend's mother's collection. Lunch. Can't wait. Dried something with puréed peas and coconut pudding. No wonder I'm losing weight.

Back to my semiprivate room for a little semiprivacy or a nap. I do need my beauty rest, company may come today. What is today, again? The afternoon drags into early evening. This used to be my favorite time of the day. Things would wind down. I would kick off my shoes. Put my feet up on the coffee table. Pop open a bottle of Chablis and enjoy the fruits of my day's labor with my husband. He's gone. So is my health. *This* is my world.

Note: Seaver, who lived in Wauwatosa, Wis., died in March. Her son found these notes in her room after her death.

70,800,000 JOB MARKETS IN THE UNITED STATES (THAT'S THE TOTAL NUMBER OF NON-FARM PAYROLLS), including 19,400,000 Manufacturers' Job Markets. • You narrow this down by deciding just what area, city • or county you want to work in. This leaves you with however many thousands or millions of job markets there are in that area or city. • You narrow this down by identifying your Strongest Skills, on their highest level that you can legitimately claim, and then thru research deciding what field you want to work in, above all. This leaves you with all the hundreds of businesses/ community organizations/agencies/schools/hospitals/ projects/associations/foundations/institutions/firms or government agencies there are in that area and in the field you have chosen. • You narrow this down by getting acquainted with the economy in the area through personal interviews with various contacts; and supplementing this with study of journals in your field, in order that you can pinpoint the places that interest you the most. This leaves a manageable num- ber of markets for you to do some study on. You now narrow this down by ask- ing yourself, can I be happy in this place, and, do they have the kind of prob- lems which my strongest skills can help solve for them? This leaves you with the companies or organizations which you will now carefully plan how to approach . . .

---

* By permission, Richard Bolles, © 1989 *What Color Is Your Parachute*; Ten Speed Press, Berkeley, CA.

Values Model

PURPOSE:

To examine the basis for the things that we believe.

PROCEDURE:

Form groups of 5–6 and answer the discussion questions below. Have one member record your group responses.

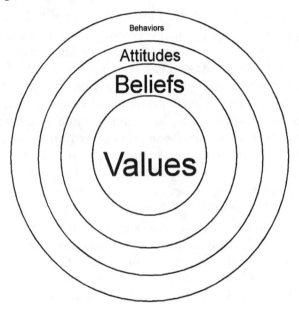

DISCUSSION:

1. Define
   a. Value
   b. Belief
   c. Attitude
   d. Behavior
2. Where do values come from?
3. Is it possible to have a **belief** about something that is not supported by a **value**? How? Example?
4. Consider your feelings about taking an elective class in Music Appreciation. Trace those feelings from the attitude you have to the **belief** and ultimately the **value**. Can you do the same thing with your attitude about next Saturday's plans? Or your position on abortion?
5. Can we change our **values**? How? What effect would changing a **value** have on the rest of your life?

One cannot have wisdom without living life. —D. McCall

VALUES IN A CHANGING SOCIETY

INTRODUCTION

The values present in a society in any given period are time and culturally bound. This chart illustrates the contrast between the values an individual holds as she progresses through her environments from decade to decade.

Time Factor	Environmental Setting	Resulting Values
Present Age: 70 Years *Value Processing period—1920s	Close Family-WWI "Model T" Flappers	Security-Economic Materialism Team Effort
Present Age: 60 Years *Value Processing period—1930s	Depression	Work Ethic
Present Age: 50 Years *Value Processing period—1940s	WWII Family Decay Mobility	Traditionalism Puritanism
Present Age: 40 Years *Value Processing period—1950s	Affluence Permissiveness T.V.-Jets-Technology Change-"Rock" Music	Change Acceptance Experience Individualism
Present Age: 30 Years *Value Processing period—1960s	Civil Rights Individual Freedoms War	Self-expression Equality Sensualism
Present Age: 20 Years *Value Processing period—1970s	Distrust/Tension Turmoil-Emotional/Social "Me" generation Computers	Emotional Security Experimentation Participation
Present Age: 10 Years *Value processing period—1980s	Affluence Crime/Drugs Peace	Materialism? Conservatism? Emotional Security?
Age: Born in the '90s		

A STUDY OF AMERICAN YOUTH

Some contrasting highlights of student attitudes and values appear below:

1960s	Early 1970s	1990s
Campus rebellion in full flower.	Campus rebellion dead.	Student awareness/ change within the rules.
New life-styles and radical politics appear linked: commune living, pot smoking and long hair, student protest marches.	Almost total divorce between radical politics and new life-styles.	Acceptance/tolerance of divergent lifestyles.
Campus search for self-fulfillment *in place* of conventional career.	Campus search for self-fulfillment *within* a conventional career.	Movement towards financial security, interest in career secondary to its potential for material gain.
Growing criticism of our "sick society."	Lessening of such criticism.	Constructive criticism, active, informed opinions.
Women's movement has little impact on youth values and attitudes.	Wide and deep penetration of women's lib ideas.	Concept of equality accepted by significant numbers of students.
Violence on campus condoned, romanticized.	Violence-free campus, violence rejected.	Violence continues to be rejected.
Value of Education severely questioned.	Value of Education strongly endorsed.	Value of Education seen as requirement for success.
Widening gap in values, morals and outlook between young people and their parents, especially college youth.	Younger generation and older mainstream America moving closer in values, morals and outlook.	Students aware of and interested in what parents and middle America believe.
Sharp split in social and moral values found within youth generation and between college students and the noncollege majority. Gap *within* generation proves to be larger and more severe than gap *between* generations.	Gap within generation narrows: noncollege youth virtually caught up with college students in new social and moral norms.	Gap between generations very narrow, gap between economic groups (college students vs. disenfranchised) becoming quite large.

---

* Adapted from *The New Morality* by Daniel Yankelovich

1960s	Early 1970s	1990s
Challenge to traditional work ethic confined to campus.	Work ethic strengthened on campus; growing weaker among noncollege youth.	Work ethic continues to grow weaker.
New code of sexual morality, centering on greater acceptance of casual premarital sex, abortion, homosexuality and extramarital relations confined to minority of college students.	New sexual morality spreads to mainstream of both colleges and working class youth.	Sexual morality significantly affected by sexually transmitted diseases.
Harsh criticisms of major institutions, political parties, big business, military almost wholly confined to college students.	Criticism of some major institutions tempered on campus, taken up by working class youth.	Criticism reflects more enlightened mature judgments.
Campus is main focus of youthful discontent—noncollege students quiet.	Campuses are quiet. Many signs of latent discontent and dissatisfaction among working class youth.	Campuses reflect growing political/social involvement but within the law.
Much youthful energy and idealism devoted to concern with minorities. Blacks considered most oppressed.	Concern with minorities lower. American Indians considered most oppressed.	Minority awareness very high on campus, even leading to political action.
Political interest of college youth left or liberal.	No clear-cut political center; pressures from both right and left. New left and radicals decline.	Significant swing to conservative values and ideals.
Law and order anathema to campus.	Campus shows greater acceptance of law and order.	Law and order on campus is norm. Disorder is abnormal behavior.

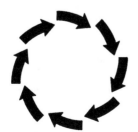

There must be more to life than having everything.
—M. Sendak

Gallup Poll: Four generations say what's gone wrong

Americans believe the nation is in a serious decline, but four key age groups differ on how to get the country back on track

MOST AMERICANS ARE DISCOURAGED, BUT SEE RAYS OF HOPE

American decline: Percent who think the U.S. is in an economic, moral and spiritual or military decline

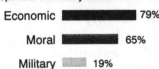

Economic — 79%
Moral — 65%
Military — 19%

Gloom about the future: Are you satisfied with the opportunity for the next generation to live better than its parents?

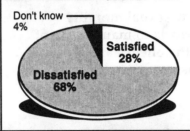

Don't know 4%
Satisfied 28%
Dissatisfied 68%

Hard work pays off: Are you satisfied with Americans' willingness to work hard to better themselves?

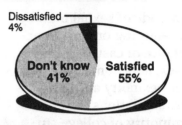

Dissatisfied 4%
Don't know 41%
Satisfied 55%

BABY BUSTERS: IDEALISTIC BUT CAUTIOUS

(18-31 yrs. old)

Don't favor big change: Percent who said it will take fundamental change to improve the economy

18-31 yrs.	40%
32-49 yrs.	59%
50-67 yrs.	63%
68 and over	50%

Want to help the needy: Percent who said government should spend more on the most needy, even if others get less

18-31 yrs.	42%
32-49 yrs.	36%
50-67 yrs.	39%
68 and over	34%

Want to solve social problems: Percent who want defense savings spent on education, poverty and other social needs instead of the deficit

18-31 yrs.	74%
32-49 yrs.	63%
50-67 yrs.	55%
68 and over	48%

MIDDLE AGERS: LITTLE TRUST IN GOVERNMENT

(32-49 yrs. old)

Think taxes favor rich: Percent who believe if they pay more taxes, they can count on the government to make the wealthy pay their share

18-31 yrs.	12%
32-49 yrs.	6%
50-67 yrs.	14%
68 and over	19%

Look to the private sector: Percent who want to give tax incentives to business and industry to encourage job creation

18-31 yrs.	46%
32-49 yrs.	53%
50-67 yrs.	47%
68 and over	41%

Concern for their children: Percent who say the next generation will be able to live better than their parents

18-31 yrs.	30%
32-49 yrs.	23%
50-67 yrs.	30%
68 and over	27%

SILENT GENERATION: DOWNBEAT AND DISILLUSIONED

(50-67 yrs. old)

Worry about losing ground: Percent who said their standard of living is going down

18-31 yrs.	24%
32-49 yrs.	32%
50-67 yrs.	35%
68 and over	30%

Feel the economy is sliding: Percent who think the country has lost ground with the economy and jobs

18-31 yrs.	59%
32-49 yrs.	66%
50-67 yrs.	76%
68 and over	62%

Fear U.S. can't compete: Percent who are satisfied with America's success at competing economically with other countries

18-31 yrs.	41%
32-49 yrs.	32%
50-67 yrs.	23%
68 and over	28%

DEPRESSION ERA: KEEPING THE FAITH

(68 yrs. and over)

Trust Social Security: Percent who say they can count on Social Security and Medicare when they grow old

18-31 yrs.	30%
32-49 yrs.	21%
50-67 yrs.	43%
68 and over	72%

Trust government more: Percent who think they can trust the government to do what is right most of the time

18-31 yrs.	13%
32-49 yrs.	13%
50-67 yrs.	11%
68 and over	23%

Doubts about work ethic: Percent who are satisfied with America's willingness to work hard to better themselves

18-31 yrs.	59%
32-49 yrs.	57%
50-67 yrs.	52%
68 and over	47%

SOURCE: A Gallup Poll of 1387 adults taken Aug. 31-Sept. 2, 1992; margin of error 3 percent for full sample, 6 percent for generation samples

258 B

The Lawrence Kohlberg Moral Development Scale

The Scale
1   Is universal, consistent and unchanging—the world over!
2   Is inflexibly sequentially upwards (a person may be halfway in one stage and "spill over" in the neighboring two).
3   Focuses on *why* (the reason) a decision is made, not *what* the decision is (two people at differing stages on the scale can make the same decision—but for different reasons).
4   Is dependent on conflict (either direct or empathic) for upward growth.
5   Upper levels (5–6) demand high cognitive development high intelligence, well educated).

Scale Level	Description	Behavioral Reasoning
1	Deference to Authority	"I did it because _____ told me to."
2	Sense of satisfaction of own needs	"I did it because I wanted to."
3	Seeking approval through being "good" or "nice"	"I did it because _____ will approve of (like) me for making that choice."
4	Respect for Law & Order	"The rules are. . . . The law is. . . . The book says. . . ."
5	Societal Needs	"What is the greatest good for the greatest number?" "Considering everybody involved, what is the best decision?"
6	Universal Ethical Principle	"I make my moral decisions based on a carefully thought out, personally chosen ethical standard that emphasizes the worth and dignity of life."

It Was Because. . . .

PURPOSE:

To examine your position in moral maturity according to the Kohlberg scale.

PROCEDURE:

1. Write down the last time you did something you **knew** was wrong. The more significant the issue, the more meaningful this lesson will be. Try to choose something that you had to **think** about. **Everybody** exceeds the speed limit. We often do it without any guilt at all, so pick something of **consequence**.
2. The issue may be one of ethics, morals, legality or conduct.
3. You may be 100 percent honest. This assignment will **not** be turned in or shared with anyone else.
4. Identify (as close as you can) the reason(s) that best represents your justification to do the above mentioned wrong (check all that apply).

_____ A. "I was asked to, and I told 'em I would, so I went ahead and did it."

_____ B. "My decision was really best for everyone involved."

_____ C. "I know better than those who say 'It's wrong'."

_____ D. "It was a deal, I had to keep my word."

_____ E. "Hey, I was told to do it. I had to do it."

_____ F. "I was just doing my duty."

_____ G. "Well, I could have gotten into trouble if I hadn't done it."

_____ H. "Everybody else was doing it."

_____ I. "I had a job to do and I did what I was supposed to do."

_____ J. "I didn't want to disappoint anybody."

_____ K. "My rules take precedence over other rules."

5. Your instructor will explain the concepts behind Moral Development and show you what level each item above corresponds to. Remember, this brief exercise is only an indication of your level, only **you** can accurately place yourself on the scale.

DISCUSSION:

1. Does Kohlberg's scale fairly reflect Moral Development?
2. Do you agree with your "position" on the scale based on the exercise? Why?
3. What value to you as a communicator is this knowledge of your position?
4. What can you do to advance on Kohlberg's scale?

Complete the Thought

PURPOSE:

To engage in free association and inductive reasoning in determining values you have.

PROCEDURE:

1. Complete the following thoughts in the various sections.
2. Pair off and discuss your responses, letting someone else read yours first.
3. Discuss with your partner the "I" thoughts you like most and why.
4. Resume in a large group to share responses and answer discussion questions.

IN GENERAL

1. When it rains, I . . .

2. Crowded, bustling places make me feel . . .

3. In my spare time, I . . .

4. Abortion is . . .

5. Sex before marriage . . .

6. As a societal institution, marriage . . .

7. I think homosexuals . . .

8. I think that marijuana . . .

9. Minority groups in this country . . .

10. To me, money . . .

PERSONAL THOUGHTS

1. I cry when . . .

2. I feel most comfortable in a small group when . . .

3. People bother me when . . .

4. I feel self-conscious . . .

5. I am warm and sincere . . .

6. I get ticked off . . .

7. Religion is something . . .

8. The out of doors makes me feel . . .

9. The mountains make me aware . . .

10. Ocean waves remind me of . . .

11. The beach is a place that . . .

12. If I had 6 months to live, I would . . .

13. My mother . . .

14. My father . . .

15. The quiet activity I enjoy most is . . .

16. The sport that interests me the most is . . .

17. The most influential person in my life has been . . .

18. More than anyone else, I respect . . .

19. The single most motivational *factor* or event in my life was . . .

20. If I could change one thing about myself, I would . . .

21. The thing I like most about myself is . . .

22. I feel very inferior when . . .

23. The situation I feel most secure in is . . .

24. Of all the many faces of myself, I like the role of . . .

25. Game-playing is something that . . .

26. Most of all, I want to . . .

27. What I like least about myself is . . .

28. The physical characteristic about me that I like most is . . .

29. Intellectually, I . . .

30. I make myself laugh when I . . .

DISCUSSION:
1. What, if anything, did you learn about yourself?
2. What values did you become aware of or reaffirm?
3. Are you a very social person, or private?
4. Did you find this hard to do? Why/why not?

Self-Appraisal

PURPOSE:

To look at the ways you relate to others and the values behind your behavior. The form was originally developed by Edgar Schein, Bernard Bass and James Vaughan. On the basis of this form you may analyze the way in which your values affect the manner in which you relate to others.

PROCEDURE:

For each of the statements below, circle the number that best describes your place on the scale. Next draw a diamond around the number which best expresses where you would like to be.

1. Ability to listen to others in an understanding way.

    Not at all able 1 2 3 4 5 6 7 8 9 10 Completely able

2. Willingness to discuss feelings with others.

    Not at all willing 1 2 3 4 5 6 7 8 9 10 Completely willing

3. Awareness of feelings of others.

    Not at all aware 1 2 3 4 5 6 7 8 9 10 Completely aware

4. Understanding why I do what I do.

    No understanding 1 2 3 4 5 6 7 8 9 10 Complete understanding

5. Tolerance of conflict and antagonism.

    Not at all tolerant 1 2 3 4 5 6 7 8 9 10 Completely tolerant

6. Acceptance of expressions of affection and warmth among others.

    Uncomfortable 1 2 3 4 5 6 7 8 9 10 Readily

7. Acceptance of comments about my behavior from others.

    Rejecting 1 2 3 4 5 6 7 8 9 10 Welcoming

8. Willingness to trust others.

    Completely suspicious 1 2 3 4 5 6 7 8 9 10 Completely trusting

9. Ability to influence others.

   Completely unable 1 2 3 4 5 6 7 8 9 10 Completely able

10. Relations with peers.

    Wholly competitive 1 2 3 4 5 6 7 8 9 10 Completely able

DISCUSSION:

1. Identify which area you plan to concentrate on first to improve your communication.
2. How must your change improve your communication?

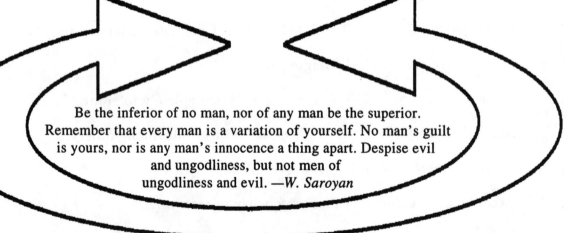

Be the inferior of no man, nor of any man be the superior. Remember that every man is a variation of yourself. No man's guilt is yours, nor is any man's innocence a thing apart. Despise evil and ungodliness, but not men of ungodliness and evil. —*W. Saroyan*

Lost in a Lifeboat

PURPOSE:

To employ decision making techniques using values to guide your choices.

PROCEDURE:

You are aboard a luxury liner that is in the middle of the Pacific Ocean. As dusk approaches, you hear the alert signal to abandon ship. Passengers pour onto the lifeboats, but many do not clear the ship before a bomb explodes and kills hundreds, completely destroying everything on the ship. The remainder of the ship sinks. You are in a lifeboat with 15 people; your boat is equipped to transport eight. You only have enough water for 10 people for three days, but you decide to try to carry all 15. To plan ahead, you feel the group should rank the persons from 1–15, with one being the most necessary person to stay and 15 being the first to go.

Your task: With the description given below and information provided in the story, rank the persons as instructed, first by yourself and then in a small group.

Your Decision	Group Decision		
_____	_____	1.	Minister, age 25, single, male.
_____	_____	2.	Electrical Engineer, 40s, female.
_____	_____	3.	Olympic Swimmer, 40s, male.
_____	_____	4.	Doctor, female, married, with 3 children at home, age 35.
_____	_____	5.	Artist, male, 60, widowed.
_____	_____	6.	Navy Captain, retired, age 70, male, divorced.
_____	_____	7.	Nurse, married, with no children, female, age 30.
_____	_____	8.	Pregnant lady, unmarried, age 27.
_____	_____	9.	Teenage boy, 14, epileptic.
_____	_____	10.	A rabbi, male, age 40.
_____	_____	11.	A campus militant, age 21, female.
_____	_____	12.	Scientist, male, married with 2 kids, 36 years old.

Your Decision	Group Decision		
_____	_____	13.	Youngster, male, 7 years old, only child.
_____	_____	14.	45-year-old housewife, married, 2 children, can't swim.
_____	_____	15.	31-year-old ex-con, armed robbery, male, unmarried, 2 children.

DISCUSSION:

1. On what values were your decisons based? Your group's decision?
2. Did your values remain the same throughout, or did they change under peer pressure?
3. What further implications does this activity have for you in the real world?

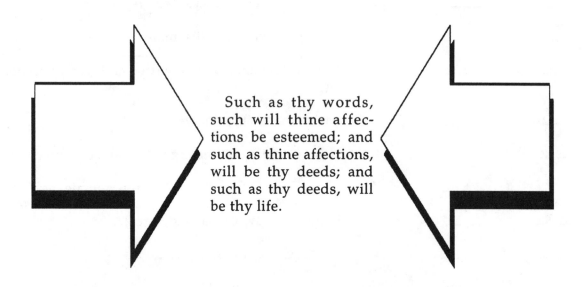

Such as thy words, such will thine affections be esteemed; and such as thine affections, will be thy deeds; and such as thy deeds, will be thy life.

REACTIONS

Name _____

Date _____

Your professor may require this exercise to be handed in.

1. List three reasons why an understanding of values can help you be a more effective communicator.

   a.

   b.

   c.

2. If values are learned, why are they so difficult to change?

3. Identify the most significant event in your experience that caused you to evaluate a value. What was the outcome of that evaluation? How did it affect your beliefs? Your decisions? Your life?

4. What effect will an understanding of values have the next time you face an ethical decision? Do we always try to do what is "Right"? Why?

8 Conflict

DEFINITIONS

✳ Conflict

Definition: The perception of two or more objectives, choices or courses of action which motivates people to resolve the situation. The idea here is based on one generally agreed principle of communication and psychology. That is that humans prefer a state of balance—a consistency within ourselves, our beliefs, our attitudes and our view of the world. Just as we seek to maintain or restore this balance, we seek to avoid or eliminate imbalance.

Example: If I have two good friends who like me and also like each other, I can be said to be in a state of balance in this situation. However, if these two friends suddenly begin to dislike each other, I begin to experience imbalance.

✳ Productive conflict management

Those communication behaviors which lead to positive feelings and results for all parties involved in the conflict.

✳ Destructive conflict management

Those communication behaviors which cause negative feelings and results on the part of any parties involved in the conflict.

✳ Competition

Actions on the part of two or more people to each acquire some scarce resource to the exclusion of the other.

TYPES OF CONFLICT: Following are the seven types of conflict.

✳ Content Conflict

Definition: Conflicts which arise over perceived differences in facts or information.

Example: If you and I are in a conflict over who won the Super Bowl in a given year, we are experiencing a "content" conflict.

✳ Decisional Conflict

Definition: Conflicts which revolve around decisions that an individual or individuals must face. Sometimes these decisions involve simply ourselves and can therefore be classified as intrapersonal. In this case the conflicts often arise from alternatives which appear equally attractive or unattractive.

Example 1: A decision over which car to buy can confront an individual with equally attractive alternatives.

Example 2: A decision over whether to quit your job and risk unemployment or stay in your job and continue to be dissatisfied would be an example of equally unattractive alternatives.

✳ Material Conflict

Definition: Conflicts are exclusively interpersonal and involve competition for a limited resource, such as money, a job, property, food or any other limited resource. The more of a limited resource which one person gets, the less there is for someone else.

Example: People often find themselves competing for things which are actually not in limited supply. Conflicts over love or esteem are examples of this misinterpretation.

✳ Role Conflict

Definition: This involves disagreements in role expectations between two people or conflicting role expectations in the case of intrapersonal role conflict.

Example: Conflicts between couples over their expectations of one another's behavior are prime examples of role conflicts. Sometimes the intervention of a third party, such as a marriage counselor, is necessary to encourage people to identify their expectations of one another and freely share those expectations with the other person.

✳ Judgmental Conflict

Definition: Judgmental conflicts revolve around conflict value statements as to the worth of something.

Example: Conflicts about whether or not a particular movie, book or political candidate is good or bad.

✳ Expectancy Conflict

It is a natural part of living to make expectations about people and situations but if these expectations are unrealistic, the "reality" can never measure up and we doom ourselves to increasing amounts of dissatisfaction with life.

✳ Ego Conflict

In this type of conflict, the competition is over which person is the better person. Once our ego defense mechanisms come into play, good communication goes out the window and people begin attacking each other.

TYPES OF BEHAVIOR

✳ Assertive Behavior

Communicating in a direct, calm, honest, nonmanipulative manner, with a respect for the rights of self and others.

✳ **Aggressive Behavior**

Communicating in a direct, emotional, threatening, manipulative manner, with a disregard for the rights of others.

✳ **Nonassertive (Passive) Behavior**

Behavior which is characterized by an inability or unwillingness to communicate one's true feelings or ideas to others.

THE IMPORTANCE OF MANAGING CONFLICT

A classroom discussion about conflict will reveal some interesting ideas. One prevalent notion is that seeking conflict is a sign of mental illness. Conflict is considered a dirty word, or at least a bad thing to bring to a relationship. Why would any right minded individual deliberately bring it about? You think about Aunt May and Uncle Bill who never argued. They LOOKED happy and they stayed married.

A second popular concept is that good relationships are free from conflict. Somehow we learned from others that it is not okay to be involved in conflicts. People get hurt when conflicts arise. If you ignore it, you are the better person and it will go away. You know this is true because you remember Beau and Bulah. They fought all the time. It was painful to be around them. Eventually it was too painful for them too and they divorced.

CONFLICT DOESN'T GO AWAY

Unfortunately, conflict doesn't go away if we turn our backs on it. For example, you and your boyfriend were used to spending a lot of time being together in the evenings. Then he got a new job and had to work five nights a week. Another example is that your girlfriend was elected to a major student body office and is working closely with a very popular guy who is on one of her committees. Perhaps you need to move back home with the family in order to save up some money to get "back on your feet" again. In each of these situations changes occurred between the way

it was and the way that it is now. If the conflict that results from the change is ignored, resentment will probably lead to serious problems in the relationship.

UNRESOLVED CONFLICT CAN LEAD TO PROBLEMS

You have probably experienced the emotional reaction to conflict. You feel nervous, upset, anxious and up-tight. Perhaps you can't concentrate on what's happening at school or at work. You may even become physically ill from being "stressed out." Often our conflict is a creation that doesn't exist—expectations or assumptions we place on a situtation—or a by-product of a previous conflict, such as yelling at the spouse when we are angry at the job.

The way most of us "ignore" conflict is to pretend that "everything will work out." The fact of the matter is that things don't work *themselves* out. We have to make them work out. If you fell and broke your arm would you allow healing to take its own path? Probably not. Even though your arm can mend itself, you would probably seek assistance for it to heal without deformity. Yet given "broken relationships," we willingly allow healing to take its own path. Just as a broken arm needs guidance with a watchful eye, broken relationships need care.

The purpose of this chapter is to show that conflict is inevitalbe in our daily lives. A second purpose is to help you see that ignoring conflict leads to problems and that confronting the conflict in assertive ways leads to positive results.

CONFLICT IS INEVITABLE

There are several reasons why conflict is inevitable. We are confronted at home, at work and at play with a limited amount of resources such as money, time, space and availability of people. We have clashes with others over differences of values or interests. Poorly defined responsibilities among members of a group lead to conflict. The different roles that each of us assumes in groups lead to conflict. The aggressive nature of some of those with whom we interact can lead to conflict. Finally, whenever we introduce change, we can have conflict.

CONFLICT CAN BE BENEFICIAL

The skills that are necessary for creative thinking (the process of bringing something new into existence) are derived from the ability to manage controversy. These skills involve discovery of diverse information and viewpoints, handling controversy among persons with diverging ideas and perspectives with assertivness and maintaining open-mindedness by viewing a problem from various vantage points.

Knowing that it is not good to ignore conflict, and being aware that conflict is inevitable should lead us to be on the look-out for potential conflict and use it for the improvement of our relationships and our lives.

By understanding the nature of conflict, developing a positive outlook about it, learning to recognize the types of conflicts in which we can find ourselves, we can begin to deal with our conflicts in a far more constructive and productive manner. However, it is also necessary to learn to recognize and control the barriers to productive conflict management.

THROUGH MANAGING CONFLICT, WE CAN LEARN TO PRACTICE ASSERTIVENESS SKILLS

Assertiveness is really nothing more than asking for what we want. A lot of people miss the point that we are not likely to get what we want if we do not ask for it. If we are in a grocery store and cannot find Cheerios, we do not hesitate to ask a clerk where we might find the product. We forget that simple lesson, however, when it comes to making requests of our friends or family or when we want to let them know that we do not want to do something that they would like us to do. And so, rather than asking for what we want or telling them how we feel, we beat around the bush, hoping that they will guess what it is we want. It would seem silly to play 20 Questions with the clerk at the grocery store to have him guess that we wanted Cheerios. Isn't it equally silly to do the same thing with our friends and family?

One of the most valuable tools that we can use to manage conflicts is assertiveness. If we are willing to let the other person know what we want, how we feel, and what we are willing to give up to get what we want, we can save ourselves a lot of time and difficulty in working out conflicts with others.

Each time that we manage a conflict with another person by using assertiveness, we go another step forward in practicing the use of assertiveness in our daily lives. By regularly speaking out for what we want, our relationships will be more direct and honest. And we will likely begin getting the things that we want—because we ask for them.

Later in this chapter, we will learn how assertiveness can be used as a tool to help us manage conflict.

The great thing in this world is not so much where we stand,
as in what direction we are moving.—*Oliver Wendell Holmes*

BARRIERS TO CONFLICT MANAGEMENT

Below are some of the barriers to managing conflict in a productive way. It is important to recognize and overcome these barriers in order to manage conflicts productively.

AVOIDANCE

As was mentioned at the outset, people tend to have a negative attitude about conflict and therefore tend to avoid dealing with conflicts once they are perceived, hoping that the conflict will simply go away.

NONASSERTIVENESS (PASSIVENESS)

Not being willing to speak your own mind and allow others the same opportunity increases frustration and distorts communication.

MISANALYSIS

Buying into someone else's conflict or failing to analyze what is actually in conflict causes inappropriate behavior and may cause us to apply the wrong management strategy. Not being able to correctly determine who owns the problem is also an example of misanalysis.

ESCALATION (AGRESSIVENESS)

Becoming defensive and thereby escalating the situation to an ego conflict produces disastrous effects.

DIRTY FIGHTING

Using strategies associated with nonassertive or aggressive behavior promotes poor communication and leads to escalation.

COMPETING

Failing to recognize that interpersonal conflict management requires cooperation and good will between the parties generally brings about competition among the individuals involved in a conflict. Rather than cooperatively seeking a "win-win" solution, people go after a "win-lose" answer and ultimately everyone loses.

By understanding the true nature of conflict, developing a positive outlook about it, learning to recognize the types of conflicts in which we find ourselves, avoiding destructive types of conflicts and the barriers to effective conflict management, we can begin to deal with our conflicts in a far more constructive and productive manner. The remainder of this chapter will provide you with opportunities to explore your thoughts and feelings about conflict in more depth. You will have a chance to learn and practice constructive communication and conflict management techniques as well as to avoid destructive types of conflict.

Attitudes about Conflict

PURPOSE:

To allow you to explore feelings associated with conflicts.

PROCEDURE:

1. Complete each statement as openly and honestly as possible, reflecting your feelings about conflict.
   a. When I win a conflict situation, I feel _____ .
   b. When I win an argument, I feel _____ .
   c. When I lose an argument, I feel _____ .
   d. When I'm in a conflict that is not resolved, I feel _____ .
   e. I get defensive when _____ .
2. Form a group and discuss your responses.

DISCUSSION:

1. How did your answers compare to others in your group?
2. What general conclusions can you make about people's feelings regarding conflict?

MANAGING GROUP CONFLICTS ASSERTIVELY AND EFFECTIVELY

If sufficient information and needed materials are available, conflicts can be resolved to meet the needs of all involved. If people *want* to work together assertively and respectfully, they *can* work together to solve mutual problems. If people respect each other's right to participate in decisions that affect then, respect each other's integrity, respect each other's capabilities and share common goals, they can manage conflicts.

In order to successfully manage conflict, individuals involved must commit to:

- Being prepared, be "present" and participate.
- Valuing the unity of the team.
- Listening to the contributions and reactions of fellow team members and refraining from interrupting.
- Committing to achieving the team purpose.

- Keeping actions purposeful.
- Making sure the recorder's key words express the intent.
- Not letting egos get too involved in the problem-solving process.
- Taking responsibility for changing unconstructive habits or negative attitudes that are limiting.
- Presenting a position as clearly as possible and avoiding blindly arguing for individual ideas.
- Avoiding changing ideas just to agree and avoid conflict. Supporting only ideas which can be lived with.
- Acknowledging and accepting differences of opinion that improve the team's chances of reaching the best solution.
- Looking for the next most acceptable alternative that all team members can live with when the team reaches a stalemate.

Interpersonal conflicts (conflicts between people) result from differences in

- goals
- perceptions
- preferences
- beliefs
- experiences

What do we do about differences when they arise? There are several options, but conflict solution guidelines are basic:

- Agree on the basics.
  - ✓ the at-hand task and the process to be used
  - ✓ secure shared commitment with whole group together in difficult times
- Search for interests in common.
- Experiment (the way to move beyond stalemate without admitting defeat).
- Doubt your own infallibility. Be willing to admit mistakes and change direction.

Everyone needs to play a part in helping a group resolve conflicts. Each person can help do so by

- helping the group develop a sense of direction and a commitment to that direction
- agreeing that it is a shared responsibility and is only determined by who can do best in this situation and assume responsibility

Researchers show that leadership plays a critical role in *group effectiveness* and *member satisfaction*. As a leader, it is important to be sensitive to

- group dynamics
- task orientation
- clear structure
- understanding leadership responsibilities

It is critical for a leader to have his head on straight. As leader you must

- Accept responsibility for your own behavior. Learn from failure. Do not repeat past errors.

- Receive constructive criticism with an open mind and be glad for the opportunity to improve.
- Don't expect special treatment.
- Meet emergencies with poise.
- See the world in shades of gray rather than simple black and white. Realize that no person or situation is wholly bad or good.
- Don't be impatient with reasonable delays. Realize that the world runs according to its own pace. Expect to make reasonable compromises.
- Win without gloating. Endure defeat and disappointment with equanimity. Try to learn from every loss.
- Harbour no jealousy. Be sincerely pleased for others when they enjoy success or good fortune.
- Be considerate of the opinions of others, and be a careful listener. Don't become defensive, closed-minded or unduly argumentative when discussing your opinions.
- Plan for the future rather than trusting to the inspiration of the moment.

Use judgment. Judgment is a higher order of skill than mere reasoning, for it involves

- weighing the problem at hand
- scanning all knowledge and experience—much of it stored in the unconscious mind—in order to discover which set of principles might render the best solution
- applying logic and reason to the problem in terms of those principles
- monitoring the result attained, and if it seems unacceptable, going back into the unconscious to bring forth and apply yet another set of principles

Judgment is a function of education and experience, as well as reasoning, logic, and intuition. Reasoning is using logic to examine all the elements of a puzzle, and working out the correct answer. Judgment is the infinitely more refined capability of considering an ambiguous situation, and using both logic and intuition to make a really good guess.

Identifying Conflicts Activity

PURPOSE:

To help you in identifying the types of conflict which we encounter in our daily lives.

PROCEDURE:

Following is a list of the seven types of conflict discussed at the beginning of this chapter. For each example, write which type you think it is in the space provided.

CONFLICT TYPES:

CONTENT—disagreement over "facts"
DECISIONAL—decision about different courses of action to take
MATERIAL—competition for material goods such as money, job, etc.
ROLE—disagreement over role expectations and/or behavior
JUDGMENTAL—disagreement over the value or worth of something
EXPECTANCY—difference between our expectations of something and the perceived reality
EGO—disagreement over the worth of yourself or someone else

EXAMPLES:

1. You are disagreeing with your boyfriend/girlfriend over which movie to see. _____

2. You are arguing with your brother or sister over who gets use of the family car on Friday night. _____

3. Your boss and you disagree about how you should act around the other employees in your area of responsibility. _____

4. You have had plans for a vacation in Hawaii for several months. You have arrived and now feel upset at how it is turning out. _____

5. You and your father or mother are having an argument over what time you need to be home from a date. _____

6. You are having a disagreement with a friend over who won the Oscar for Best Picture in 1988. _____

7. You are having an argument with a co-worker about the new sick leave policy which has been enacted. _____

8. You have decided to show another player on the team that you are better than him/her. _____

9. You are having a disagreement with your instructor about your study habits. _____

10. You and another employee are competing for the same promotion. _____

DISCUSSION:

1. Compare your answers with others in the group.
2. As you identified these conflict types, what personal examples did you think of?

CRAZYMAKERS

What's your conflict style? To give you a better idea of some unproductive ways you may be handling your conflicts, we will describe some typical conflict behaviors that can weaken relationships. In our survey we will follow the fascinating work of Dr. George Bach, a leading authority on conflict and communication.

Bach explains that there are two types of aggression: clean fighting and dirty fighting. Either because they cannot or will not express their feelings openly and constructively, dirty fighters sometimes resort to "crazymaking" techniques to vent their resentments. Instead of openly and caringly expressing their emotions, crazymakers (often unconsciously) use a variety of indirect tricks to get at their opponent. Because these "sneak attacks" don't usually get to the root of the problem, and because of their power to create a great deal of hurt, crazymakers can destroy communication. Let's take a look at them.

THE AVOIDER

The avoider refuses to fight. When a conflict arises, he will leave, fall asleep, pretend to be busy at work or keep from facing the problem in some other way. This behavior makes it very difficult for the partner to express his feelings of anger, hurt, et cetera because the avoider won't fight back. Arguing with an avoider is like trying to box with a person who won't even put up his gloves.

THE PSEUDOACCOMMODATOR

Not only does the pseudoaccommodator refuse to face up to a conflict, she pretends that there is nothing at all wrong. This really drives the partner, who definitely feels there is a problem, crazy and causes that person to feel both guilt and resentment toward the accommodator.

THE GUILT MAKER

Instead of saying straight out that he doesn't want or approve of something, the guilt maker tries to change the partner's behavior by making that person feel responsible for causing pain. The guilt maker's favorite line is, "It's o.k., don't worry about me...." accompanied by a big sigh.

THE SUBJECT CHANGER

Really a type of avoider, the subject changer escapes facing up to aggression by shifting the conversation whenever it approaches an area of conflict. Because of these tactics, the subject changer and the partner never have the chance to explore their problem and do something about it.

THE CRITICIZER

Rather than come out and express feelings about the object of her dissatisfaction, the criticizer attacks other parts of the partner's life. Thus, she never has to share what is really on her mind and can avoid dealing with painful parts of relationships.

THE MIND READER

Instead of allowing a partner to honestly express feelings, the mind reader goes into character analysis, explaining what the other person really means or what's wrong with the other person. By behaving this way the mind reader refuses to handle her own feelings and leaves no room for her partner to express himself.

THE TRAPPER

The trapper plays an especially dirty trick by setting up a desired behavior for his partner, and then when it is met, attacking the very thing he requested. An example of this technique is for the trapper to say, "Let's be totally honest with each other," and then when the partner shares his feelings, he finds himself attacked for having feelings that the trapper doesn't want to accept.

THE CRISIS TICKLER

This person almost brings what is bothering her to the surface, but she never quite comes out and expresses herself. Instead of admitting her concern about the finances she innocently asks, "Gee, how much did that cost?" dropping a rather obvious hint but never really dealing with the crisis.

THE GUNNYSACKER

This person does not respond immediately when he is angry. Instead he puts his resentment into his gunnysack, which after awhile begins to bulge with large and small gripes. Then, when the sack is about to burst, the gunnysacker pours out all his pent-up aggressions on the overwhelmed and unsuspecting victim.

THE TRIVIAL TYRANNIZER

Instead of honestly sharing his resentments, the trivial tyrannizer does things he knows will upset his partner: leaving dirty dishes in the sink, clipping his fingernails in bed, belching out loud, turning up the television too loud and so on.

THE JOKER

Because she is afraid to face conflicts squarely, the joker kids around when her partner wants to be serious, thus blocking the expression of important feelings.

THE BELTLINER

Everyone has a psychological "beltline," and below it are subjects too sensitive to be approached without damaging the relationship. Beltlines may have personality traits a person is trying to overcome. In an attempt to "get even" or hurt his partner the beltliner will use his intimate knowledge to hit below the belt, where he knows it will hurt.

THE BLAMER

The blamer is more interested in finding fault than in solving a conflict. Needless to say, she usually does not blame herself. Blaming behavior almost never solves a conflict and is an almost surefire way to make the receiver defensive.

THE CONTRACT TYRANNIZER

This person will not allow his relationship to change from the way it once was. Whatever the agreements the partner had as to roles and responsibilities at one time, they will remain unchanged. "It is your job to . . . feed the baby, wash the dishes, discipline kids, etc."

THE KITCHEN SINK *Fighter*

This person is so named because in an argument she brings up things that are totally off the subject ("everything but the kitchen sink"): the way her partner behaved last New Year's Eve, the unbalanced checkbook, bad breath—anything.

THE WITHHOLDER

Instead of expressing her anger honestly and directly, the withholder punishes her partner by keeping back something—courtesy, affection, good cooking, humor, sex. As you can imagine, this is likely to build up even greater resentments in the relationship.

THE BENEDICT ARNOLD

This character gets back at his partner by sabotage, by failing to defend her from attackers, and even by encouraging ridicule or disregard from outside the relationship.

```
PEACE

Fight for me,
        Cry for me,
Some even die for me.
        Command me,
            Demand for me,
Some cannot stand me.
        Teach of me,
            Preach for me,
Extend a hand, reach for me.
        Mask me,
            Grasp for me,
Ever try . . . to just ask for me?


by Raymond Porter
```

Nonproductive Conflict Styles

PURPOSE:

To help you explore the nonproductive ways we manage conflict.

PROCEDURE:

1. Read the following descriptions of nonproductive styles and try to identify those of which you may be guilty.
2. Form groups and answer the discussion questions below. Indirect conflicts often result in games because the individuals involved do not openly and directly acknowledge the real conflict. These games are called "crazymakers" or "dirty fights" by George Bach and they lead to a worsening of the conflict rather than to a satisfactory solution. There are three basic "crazymakers" styles:

A. *The Avoider.* This person denies the conflict by refusing to face up to it directly and assertively.
    Typical Behaviors:
    —pretending there is nothing wrong
    —refusing to fight (falling asleep, leaving, pretending to be busy)
    —changing the subject whenever conversation approaches the
      area of conflict
    —hinting at the conflict or talking in generalities but never quite
      coming out and expressing self

—changing the subject whenever conversation approaches the area of conflict

—hinting at the conflict or talking in generalities but never quite coming out and expressing self

—kidding around when other person wants to be serious thus blocking expression of important feelings

—attacking other parts of other person's life rather than dealing with real problem

B. *The Manipulator.* This person wants to "win." She attempts, in an indirect way, to get the other person to behave as she wants them to rather than dealing in a direct way.

Typical Behaviors:

—trying to change other person's behavior by making them feel guilty or responsible ("It's OK, don't worry about me . . .")

—going into character analysis by explaining what's wrong with the other person or what the other person really means rather than allowing them to express themself directly

—refusing to allow the relationship to change from what it once was

C. *The Avenger.* This aggressive behavior often results from nonassertive behavior. Because of an unwillingness to deal with the conflict openly and directly, this person attempts to get back at the other person in a number of indirect ways. An especially dirty fighter, he creates fights because he experiences second order conflicts for which he wants to "pay back" or get even.

Typical Behaviors:

—storing up resentment and dumping it all on the other person all at once

—doing things to upset them

—finding fault by blaming other person for things

—bringing up things in an argument that are totally off the subject (other behavior, bad breath, etc.)

—attempting to punish partner by withholding

—encouraging others to ridicule or disregard partner

DISCUSSION:

1. Which of the preceding styles have you been guilty of?
2. What were your feelings when employing any of these styles?
3. What were the results when you used these styles?

You cannot shake hands with a clenched fist. —*I. Gandhi*

ASSERTION TRAINING

We have discussed two basic reasons for conflict. The first reason is that individuals fail to properly analyze the type of conflict that exists. They, therefore, get caught up in an ego struggle when the conflict is about something in which ego should really not have a role—such as material conflict or decisional conflict. By properly defining the type of conflict, it may be considerably easier to resolve it.

The second reason for conflict may be a failure to act assertively. If we see conflict as a win-lose struggle, we will typically approach it from one of two perspectives. One is *aggressively*—communicating in a direct, emotional, threatening, manipulative manner—with a disregard for the rights of others. This approach is based on the notion that if you do not win you lose. When the aggressor wins, the other person loses. The conflict may appear to be resolved, but one person is angry at having lost, and even the winner may feel uneasy about possible future retaliation.

The second way in which one may fail to act assertively we call *nonassertive*. Nonassertive behavior is characterized by an inability or unwillingness to communicate one's true feelings or ideas to others. This person disregards his or her own rights. This person would also like to win but may have a greater fear of losing and, therefore, is unwilling to compete. Another reason that many people choose to be nonassertive is so they will not appear aggressive. What nonassertive people often do is to play manipulative games in hopes of winning, or they hope that the other will "read their mind" and know what they want. When such people lose in a conflict situation, they are likely to feel angry that they were not understood or cared for by the other.

Assertive behavior is defined as communicating in a direct, calm, honest, nonmanipulative manner, with respect for the rights of self and the other. An assertive person is likely to see their world from a position of win-win. They take the position that each person can probably be satisfied if they openly communicate about what they need, why they need it, and what they will give up to get it. Through open and honest communication, they seek to understand the other and to be understood.

Many people have difficulty behaving in an assertive fashion because our society has not encouraged people to speak up for what they want while recognizing that others also have the right to do so. We will now examine ways to ask for what we want. Speaking up for what we want, respecting ourselves and others, and talking about what bothers us will help us to manage conflicts.

YOUR RIGHTS (AND MINE)

To begin with, Assertion Training is based on the assumption that **all** human beings have certain rights. It may be interesting to note that these "rights" have been based on the United Nation's "Bill of Human Rights" and have been modified over time to the list below:

1. I have the right to assert myself as a worthy individual.
2. I have the right to express myself.
3. I have the right to be listened to.
4. I have the right to change my mind.
5. I have the right to express my feelings without always justifying them.
6. I have the right to not always need the goodness of others to survive.
7. I have the right to say, "I don't know."
8. I have the right to say, "I don't understand."
9. I have the right to avoid what I don't want.
10. I have the right to decide whether I want to be responsible for the problems of someone else.
11. I have the right to make mistakes and to accept responsibility for my actions.

12. I have the right, as an assertive person, to decide when and if I want to act assertively, aggressively or nonassertively.

One note of caution before proceeding to our next main area: Assertion Training can lead to too much "I-am-number-one." Many recent books and seminars written and presented under the guise of teaching people how to be assertive are really just teaching people how to get their way—all the time—no matter what. Always remember as you communicate with someone else that just as you have "rights," the other person has those **same** "rights."

Three Behaviors

Now that you understand that you have certain rights as you communicate with others, let's identify the three behaviors generally associated with Assertion Training, one of which will become our preferred focus, with the other two behaviors being the boundaries of that preferred behavior.

NONASSERTIVE BEHAVIOR

First, nonassertion is the act of withdrawing from a situation. The emotions, such as fear, anxiety, guilt, depression, fatigue and hurt, are kept within the person.

The nonverbal communication associated with nonassertion is aversion to eye contact, teary eyes, shifting of balance, slumped posture, wringing of hands, biting lips, adjusting clothing, or nervous jitters. As the nonassertive person verbalizes, there are rambling statements, many qualifiers (maybe's, if's), speech fillers (uh's, you-knows), and negatives (don't know's, I don't care's and whatever's).

In general, the nonassertive person denies his own feelings and permits others to act and make decisions. The result is intrapersonal conflict, depression, helplessness, stress, addiction, loneliness and poor self-image.

AGGRESSIVE BEHAVIOR

Next, let's identify aggression. Aggression is the act of emotionally over-reacting to a situation. The emotions of fear, anxiety, etc. that we mentioned are used by this person as a build-up to inappropriate anger, rage, self-righteousness and superiority. (Physiologically, the body temperature is above normal.)

The nonverbal behaviors of aggressiveness are glaring, narrowed eyes, a rigid, forward-leaning posture, clenched fists or pointing fingers and a raised haughty voice. While speaking, there are clipped or interrupted statements, threats (you-betters, watch-outs), name calling, defensiveness, sarcasm, put-downs, judgments (should's, bad's), sexism and racism. In the extreme, aggression is characterized by verbal or physical violence.

ASSERTIVE BEHAVIOR

Finally, we identify assertion. Assertion is the act of declaring "This is what I am, what I think and feel, and what I want" and doing so as soon as it occurs.

The nonverbal communications associated with assertiveness are eye-contact that isn't uncomfortable for the listener; standing relaxed; hands loose at the sides; steady, firm, clear tone of voice. Assertive statements are concise. Assertive individuals characteristically use words like "I" ("I think/I feel/I want"); cooperative words ("let's resolve this/compromise"); and show openness/willingness ("What do you think/Is this workable").

Aggression - - - Assertion - - - Nonassertion

Some conclusions about assertiveness: Assertive responses are characterized by the use of "I," instead of "you." Assertive responses are usually effective in getting people to change or to reinforce behaviors. Assertive responses run a low risk of hurting a relationship. Assertive responses do not attack the other person's self-esteem or put others on the defensive. Assertion prevents "gunny sacking"—i.e., saving up a lot of bad feelings until you explode.

ASSERTIVE TECHNIQUES

In terms of possible techniques or verbal strategies, there are various approaches which can be used. The model that is perhaps most widely used in this field comes from M. Smith's *When I Say No, I Feel Guilty*, in which the author presents seven basic techniques. For each technique, we will give a brief explanation and then present a sample situation and dialogue to illustrate their use.

1. BROKEN RECORD

Repeat your goal/request over and over without getting distracted and until you wear the other person down.

Situation: You have just received your credit card bill and find charges for purchases you never made—you (Y) contact customer service (S).

Y: You have my transaction on your screen? You see the $39.95 charge for shoes from Shu-World? I never shop at that store and I would like my account credited for that amount, please.
S: Well, we have the receipt and your signature is on it.
Y: You may have something that looks like my signature, but I never shop at that store and I would like my account credited for that amount, please.
S: It is highly unlikely that anyone would forge your signature for $39.95.
Y: I realize that you think it is highly unlikely, but I never shop at that store and I would like my account credited for that amount, please.

Skills for Dealing with Criticism

2. FOGGING

Calmly and politely agreeing with your critic that there *may be* **some truth in what they are saying** or telling them that **you can understand why they** *might* **feel that way.** This buys time and puts you in control of the situation.

Situation: At the office, your boss (B) starts complaining that you (Y) are taking too many breaks and using the copier for personal use.

B: Not only do you take too many breaks but now you are using the company copier for your own personal use.
Y: Perhaps I should be more concerned about my break times and use of the copier.

3. NEGATIVE ASSERTION

Openly and honestly admitting your mistakes instead of hiding or lying about them. We all make mistakes.

Situation: At a friend's (F) party, you (Y) knock over a glass, which breaks.

F: That ruins my set which has a lot of sentimental value.
Y: I feel very badly that I broke the glass and I wish I would not have.

4. NEGATIVE INQUIRY

Asking for more criticism of yourself in order to get rid of criticism that is manipulative. It makes people tell you the truth about why they are angry.

Situation: You (Y) have decided to go away to college and now your closest friend (F) is criticizing your decision.

F: Why did you choose that diploma factory to go to? You won't learn anything there.

Y: I like the school. I don't know why you're so against me going there.

F: I can't believe you don't want to go to a good school.

Y: This is a good school and I still don't understand what you have against me going there.

F: But the students are all rejects from other colleges.

Y: I like this school. I know some of the students who go there and they like it. Are you sure there isn't some other reason you don't want me going to this school?

Conversation Skills

5. FREE INFORMATION

This is a listening skill. You learn to ask lots of questions about others and their concerns, opinions, etc., rather than talking about yourself too much.

Situation: You (Y) have just started a new job and during lunch break meet another person (P), who mentions that they have just gotten back from vacation.

Y: That sounds great. What did you do during your time off?

6. SELF-DISCLOSURE

Admitting openly and honestly your strengths, weaknesses and opinions without apologizing for them.

Situation: Your boss (B) asks you (Y) to do something that you do not know enough about.

B: When you've finished that report, take this software, make the spreadsheet and a graph of it.

Y: I know how to make the spreadsheet, but I'm not sure about the graph.

7. WORKABLE COMPROMISE

This is for two assertive people. For example, when you are both using broken record, you must compromise. This compromise does not have to be **fair**—it only has to **work**. Never use it if you feel that your self-respect will be jeopardized.

Situation: Your boss (B) needs a report by 10 a.m. the next day and asks you (Y) to stay late to finish it.

B: I need you to stay late and finish this report tonight. It must be done for an important meeting I have tomorrow at 10 a.m.

Y: I know this report is important to you, but I have a very important meeting after work.

B: But I **want** this report finished tonight.

Y: O.K. I will stay an extra hour today and if I don't finish, I will come in early tomorrow so that you have it for your 10 o'clock meeting.

How Assertive Are You?

PURPOSE:

To help you assess your level of assertiveness.

PROCEDURE:

1. Place an "X" on the following scale indicating generally how assertive you believe yourself to be.

| nonassertive | 60 | 120 | 180 | 240 | 300 | completely assertive |

2. For each of the statements below, circle the number that best describes you. If an item describes a situation unfamiliar to you, try to imagine what your response would be. Of course, you will not achieve an accurate self-evaluation unless you answer all questions honestly.

Rating Scale	
1	Never
2	Rarely
3	Sometimes
4	Usually
5	Always

1.	I do my own thinking.	1	2	3	4	5
2.	I can be myself around wealthy, educated or prestigious people.	1	2	3	4	5
3.	I am poised and confident among strangers.	1	2	3	4	5
4.	I freely express my emotions.	1	2	3	4	5
5.	I am friendly and considerate toward others.	1	2	3	4	5
6.	I accept compliments and gifts without embarrassment or a sense of obligation.	1	2	3	4	5
7.	I freely express my admiration of others' ideas and achievements.	1	2	3	4	5
8.	I readily admit my mistakes.	1	2	3	4	5
9.	I accept responsibility for my life.	1	2	3	4	5

10.	I make my own decisions and accept the consequences.	1 2 3 4 5
11.	I take the initiative in personal contacts.	1 2 3 4 5
12.	When I have done something well, I tell others.	1 2 3 4 5
13.	I am confident when going for job interviews.	1 2 3 4 5
14.	When I need help, I ask others to help me.	1 2 3 4 5
15.	When at fault, I apologize.	1 2 3 4 5
16.	When I like someone very much, I tell them so.	1 2 3 4 5
17.	When confused, I ask for clarification.	1 2 3 4 5
18.	When someone is annoying me, I ask that person to stop.	1 2 3 4 5
19.	When someone cuts in front of me in line, I protest.	1 2 3 4 5
20.	When treated unfairly, I object.	1 2 3 4 5
21.	If I were underpaid, I would ask for a salary increase.	1 2 3 4 5
22.	When I am lonely or depressed, I take action to improve my mental outlook.	1 2 3 4 5
23.	When working at a job or task I dislike intensely, I look for ways to improve my situation.	1 2 3 4 5
24.	I complain to the management when I have been overcharged or have received poor service.	1 2 3 4 5
25.	When something in my house or apartment malfunctions, I see that the landlady repairs it.	1 2 3 4 5
26.	When I am disturbed by someone smoking, I say so.	1 2 3 4 5
27.	When a friend betrays my confidence, I tell that person how I feel.	1 2 3 4 5
28.	I ask my doctor all of the questions for which I want answers.	1 2 3 4 5
29.	I ask for directions when I need help finding my way.	1 2 3 4 5
30.	When there are problems, I maintain a relationship rather than cutting it off.	1 2 3 4 5

31.	I communicate my belief that everyone at home should help with the upkeep rather than doing it all myself.	1	2	3	4	5
32.	I make sexual advances toward my husband or sex partner.	1	2	3	4	5
33.	When served food at a restaurant that is not prepared the way I ordered it, I express myself.	1	2	3	4	5
34.	Even though a clerk goes to a great deal of trouble to show merchandise to me, I am able to say "No."	1	2	3	4	5
35.	When I discover that I have purchased defective merchandise, I return it to the store.	1	2	3	4	5
36.	When people talk in a theater, lecture or concert, I am able to ask them to be quiet.	1	2	3	4	5
37.	I maintain good eye contact in conversations.	1	2	3	4	5
38.	I would sit in the front of a large group if the only remaining seats were located there.	1	2	3	4	5
39.	I would speak to my neighbors if their dog was keeping me awake with its barking at night.	1	2	3	4	5
40.	When interrupted, I comment on the interruption and then finish what I am saying.	1	2	3	4	5
41.	When a friend or spouse makes plans for me without my knowledge or consent, I object.	1	2	3	4	5
42.	When I miss someone, I express the fact that I want to spend more time with that person.	1	2	3	4	5
43.	When a person asks me to lend something and I really do not want to, I refuse.	1	2	3	4	5
44.	When a friend invites me to join her and I really don't want to, I turn down the request.	1	2	3	4	5
45.	When friends phone and talk too long on the phone, I can terminate the conversation effectively.	1	2	3	4	5
46.	When someone criticizes me, I listen to the criticism without being defensive.	1	2	3	4	5
47.	When people are discussing a subject and I disagree with their points of view, I express my difference of opinion.	1	2	3	4	5

48.	When someone makes demands on me that I don't wish to fulfill, I resist the demands.	1 2 3 4 5
49.	I speak up readily in group situations.	1 2 3 4 5
50.	I tell my children or family members the things I like about them.	1 2 3 4 5
51.	When my family or friends make endless demands on my time and energy, I establish firm notions about the amount of time I am willing to give.	1 2 3 4 5
52.	When my husband phones to tell me he is bringing home an unexpected guest for dinner and I've had a hard day at work, I level with him about it and request that he make alternative plans.	1 2 3 4 5
53.	When one friend is not meeting all of my needs, I establish meaningful ties with other people.	1 2 3 4 5
54.	When my own parents, in-laws or friends freely give advice, I express appreciation for their concern without feeling obligated to follow their advice or suggestions.	1 2 3 4 5
55.	When someone completes a task or job for me with which I am dissatisfied, I ask that it be done correctly.	1 2 3 4 5
56.	When I object to political practices, I take action rather than blaming politicians.	1 2 3 4 5
57.	When I am jealous, I explore the reasons for my feelings, and look for ways to increase my self-confidence and self-esteem.	1 2 3 4 5
58.	When a person tells me she envies me, I accept her comments without feeling guilty or apologizing.	1 2 3 4 5
59.	When I am feeling insecure, I assess my personal strengths and take action designed to make me feel more secure.	1 2 3 4 5
60.	I accept my husband's, wife's or boy/girl friend's interests in other people without feeling I must compete with them.	1 2 3 4 5

Total Score _____

DISCUSSION:

1. How does your initial general rating compare to your actual score? If there is a significant difference, how can you account for it?
2. How important is it to you to be a more assertive person? Why?
3. In what ways can you go about being more assertive?

Five Sample Situations

PURPOSE:

To be able to identify responses as either assertive, nonassertive or aggressive.

PROCEDURE:

Read through each of the following situations and determine which of the three responses is assertive, which is nonassertive and which is aggressive.

1. Cousin Jessie with whom you prefer not to spend much time is on the phone. She says that she is planning to spend the next three weeks with you.

   Responses:
   a. "We'd love to have you come and stay as long as you like."
   b. "We'd be glad to have you come for the weekend, but we cannot invite you for longer. A short visit will be very nice for all of us, and we'll want to see each other again."
   c. "The weather back here has been terrible,"—not true—"so you'd better plan on going elsewhere."

2. You have bought a toaster at Sears that doesn't work properly.

   Responses:
   a. "I bought this toaster and it doesn't work and I would like my money back."
   b. "What right do you have selling me junk like this. . . ."
   c. You put it in the closet and buy another one.

3. One of your workers has been coming in late consistently for the last three or four days.

   Responses:
   a. "I have noticed that for the last few days you have been a little late and I am concerned about it."
   b. "The next time you're late you're fired."
   c. You mumble to yourself and hope he'll be on time tomorrow.

4. You are in a meeting and someone starts smoking, which offends you.

   Responses:
   a. "Hey, man, that smoke is terrible."
   b. You suffer the smoke in silence.
   c. "I would appreciate it if you wouldn't smoke here. I am bothered by it."

5. You are at a lecture with 400 other people. The speaker is not speaking loud enough for all to hear.

   Responses:
   a. You continue straining to hear and end up daydreaming.
   b. You yell out, "Speak up; we can't hear you if you talk to yourself."
   c. You raise your hand and get her attention—"Would you mind speaking a little louder, please."

DISCUSSION:

1. Was it easy or difficult to distinguish among the three behaviors?
2. Which of the situations were easier to distinguish and why?

Assertion Training: Practicing Behaviors

PURPOSE:

To be able to construct assertive, nonassertive and aggressive comments in different situations.

PROCEDURE:

1. Form small groups.
2. As a group, take each of the 10 situations and write a nonassertive, aggressive and assertive response for each.
3. As a class, discuss the various responses to each situation.

1. You are in charge of a meeting and Jean walks in somewhat intoxicated.
2. You are talking with some other people and they start talking about Jose. Someone calls him a "wetback," which offends you, because Jose is your friend.
3. You are taking an English class. Your handwriting is the "pits." As a result, your teacher keeps giving you a lower grade, which you feel is unfair.
4. You and a group of friends have decided to go out to dinner. Everyone else wants to go somewhere that you do not like.
5. You want to go out for the weekend with a group of friends. Your parents object. You still want to go.
6. Someone moves into the apartment next to you and you would like to meet them.
7. You are standing in the check-out line at Super Market. Someone keeps pushing their cart into your back.
8. You and a friend are shopping. You see him stealing something, which you feel is wrong.
9. You are wearing a new outfit and someone compliments you on it.
10. Your friend has said she will meet you for lunch at 12:30. She arrives at 1:15—with no apologies—and you are irritated!

DISCUSSION:

1. Did you find it easier to come up with nonassertive and aggressive comments than with assertive ones? Why?
2. Did you find it harder to come up with assertive comments to some situations as opposed to others? If so, which ones? Why?

Managing Conflict through Assertiveness

PURPOSE:

To apply assertiveness principles to the management of conflicts

PROCEDURE:

1. Working on your own, complete the steps below.
2. After you have completed the steps, role-play the situation with a partner.

Step 1.   Define the conflict that you are having with another person and the other person's shared responsibility in that conflict.

Step 2.   Make an appointment with the other person. (Be sure to allow yourselves enough time to work through steps 3 through 6.)

Step 3.   Describe the problem and your needs to the other person. (Describe the behavior, your interpretations. your feelings, and the consequences to you)

Step 4.   Seek to understand your partner. (Ask your partner to paraphrase what you said. Ask your partner to share what he or she wants from you. Be sure to paraphrase or do perception checking on what you hear.)

Step 5.   Use the *Workable Compromise* that is described in this chapter. (Remember, the key to workable compromise is that each party feels that it will work for them.)

Step 6.   Put the solution into effect and plan a follow-up appointment to evaluate the extent to which your solution is working for each of you.

DISCUSSION:

1. Which step(s) did you find the most difficult?
2. What changes in your own behavior will you need to focus on?

Copyright 1997, Dr. Katz. Distributed by Los Angeles Times.

REACTIONS

1. Write your personal definition of conflict.

2. Describe your own comfort level in conflict situations.

3. Would you classify yourself as basically nonassertive, assertive or aggressive?

4. In what kinds of situations do you find it most difficult to be assertive?

5. Describe a situation where it might be better to react aggressively.

6. Describe a situation where it might be better to be nonassertive.

7. Which simple concept from this chapter do you plan to apply first in your next conflict? How?

9 Decision Making

DEFINITIONS

Most people have no difficulty choosing between A and B if A is a lot better than B. We frequently come face to face, however, with the need to choose between two or more alternatives that are attractive for different reasons. Perhaps one choice gives us what we want at a high cost while another choice gives us only part of what we want at a more affordable cost. Decisions are not made in a vacuum. Most decisions that we make have consequences that may be difficult to determine at the time we need to decide.

Choices are difficult. But they also present options for us as well as opportunities. In order to move forward we neeed to make the best decision possible in a timely manner.

In this chapter, we will look at 1) why making timely, competent decisions is important; 2) what prevents us from making such decisions; and 3) how we can become more effective decision makers.

Decision making presents us with opportunities to utilize our intrapersonal communication abilities described in this text while demanding that we exercise interpersonal skills when our decisions involve others.

✳ Decision Making

A process that individuals use to select among alternatives to determine the best choice given the circumstances available at that time. Conceptualizing decision making as a process means that each of us can learn how to use decision making strategies for our benefit as we would learn to use any other tool.

✳ Indecision

An interruption in the decision making process. Many people see indecision as an end result, a stopping point. However, by seeing indecision as merely a step in the process, one can learn how to move to the next step in the process and on to the desired conclusion.

✳ Rational/Analytic Reasoning

A logical, systematic (step by step), linear (follows a path), approach to evaluating the available choices in order to determine which one is the most capable of bringing about the desired results. Use of a rational/analytic approach as a basis for our decision making can assist us in making sound decisions.

✱ Intuition

The use of one's subjective, subconscious feelings in the decision making process. If you have ever had a "hunch" or a "feeling" about what you should do in a given situation, that has probably been your intuition at work. Many people ridicule intuition; others rely on it entirely. Intuition can be a valuable tool in the decision making process.

✱ Values

Those things to which a person attaches worth. The outcomes that an individual hopes will result from a correct decision are reflective of his/her values. Our values are usually developed over such a long period of time without our being aware of the changes occurring in us that we may be unaware of their influence in our decision making. Effective decision makers are very clear about their values and apply them in the decision making process.

✱ Irreversibility

The belief, often erroneous, that once we make a decision we cannot change our minds or alter our course. Have you ever said to yourself, "If I buy that and I don't like it, then I'm stuck with it"? Most decisions are not that irrevocable. It may take time or cost some money; we may even have to endure other's attempts to make fun of us for the choice that we made. But we can usually take back a decision that we made. The belief that decisions are irreversible prevents us from making timely decisions.

✱ Disaster Fantasies

A focus on the bad things that will happen if a decision is made. As we dwell on these, we generally expand them out of proportion to reality. In making any decision, it is important to accurately estimate what negative outcomes may occur. But we should look at the possible harms, costs and problems in the same objective way that we estimate the possible profits and pleasure that will occur if the decision turns out the way we want it.

———————— ✩ ✩ ✩ ————————

He who never made a mistake
never made anything.

THE IMPORTANCE OF EFFECTIVE DECISION MAKING

One of the major differences between humankind and animals is that animals are controlled by instinct and humans control by making decisions. The ability to make decisions, although not unique to humans, gives us the ability to control our destiny and to change our directions so that yesterday's mistakes do not have to be repeated. On a personal level, it is through our ability to make decisions that we choose our friends, careers, spouses and every other aspect of our lives including how successful we will be.

When you recognize the importance of effective decision making to your future, can you allow yourself to go through life letting decisions "happen"? Let's take a case in point. What if you know that you have a chance for a part-time apprenticeship in your future occupation. If you take the apprenticeship, however, you will have to take a leave of absence from college for the next semester. Rather than make a decision, you "worry and fret" about what to do until the apprenticeship is given to someone else.

How many times have you allowed decisions *about you* to be made by *someone else* because you failed to decide. You can see then that effective decision making really gives you control over your life. In the above situation, perhaps it would have been better for you to have stayed in school and not taken the apprenticeship. But by not deciding yourself, you gave up control over your own life and you lost the chance for some wonderful learning opportunities.

As we go through life, many opportunities will present themselves to us. Some will be financial, professional, social, political, personal, recreational or healthful in nature. The decisions that we make about each of those opportunities will help us to make the next one. Decisions should meet three criteria. They should be 1) timely, 2) competent and 3) capable of teaching us lessons about future decisions that we will make.

Notice, we did not include in our list that the decision should be "perfect." That is because we cannot always guarantee that we will make the perfect choice. On the other hand, if our choices meet the three criteria listed, we will be successful more times than the odds predict.

TIMELINESS

It may seem self-evident to say that a decision needs to be timely because if we delay too long, we may lose the opportunity. On the other hand, we live in a time when we have so much information available to us—via media and technology—that it seems there is always more time needed to sift through it all to find the answer. Whenever we make a decision, we leap from what we know to what we don't know. Having more information can help us to know more about our chances but it will never completely tell us about the future. At some point, we must risk. Successful decision makers use all of the data that is available within the time frame they are dealing with. Then they decide.

COMPETENCY

A competent decision is one about which the decision maker has a good feeling. She believes she carefully determined the outcomes that were desired and evaluated the ability of each alternative to bring about those outcomes. Believing in your ability to make good decisions is important. If you believe that you made a good decision, you will probably work harder to make that decision successful. If you think that you made a poor decision or if someone else made the decision for you, you will not put the energy into making it a success. Each time you use a process for decision making that works for you, you gain confidence in your ability to make decisions and you will, in turn, make even more competent decisions in the future.

CAPABLE OF TEACHING US LESSONS

Even though our decisions are timely and competent, we may still fail to achieve our desired outcomes through no fault of our own. This is where the third criterion of decision making is operative. If we can look back on the process that we used in making the decision and see where we may have improved our system, we will gain insight that will help us in our next decision. When people allow decisions to be made by procrastination or by flipping a coin, they never have a chance to insure that their next decision will be any better than the last one they made. Effective decision makers use a process to make their important decisions.

After the decision is made, they ask "how can I do it better the next time?"

To make the kind of decisions that are beneficial to us, we need to understand our values and how they were communicated to us; we need to be effective at processing information at the intrapersonal level; and in many cases, we need to be effective in our ability to communicate with others.

Effective decision making is an important tool that people today can use to insure that their lives will be as rich and full as they desire. Like any tool, we only become successful when we learn the proper way to use it and practice every chance we get.

BARRIERS TO DECISION MAKING

In this section, we present some of the main reasons why people often fail to make effective decisions.

FEAR OF RISK

Every time we make a decision, we venture into unknown territory. We have not been there before. We do not know for sure if our choice will produce the results we want. If our decision requires a financial commitment, we may lose our money. If our decision requires that we give someone our word or puts us in a place where we can be personally criticized, we can lose our self-respect. Such losses can be hard to take; none of us likes to lose. When we fear the loss that risk brings, it sometimes feels better to not decide because that way we cannot be blamed. The fact is, if the thing turns out badly, we lose whether we actively or passively decided.

Someone you know is willing to sell you a car that is worth $1,000 for only $500. You think, "Hey, I can sell the car by advertising it in the newspaper." You have the $500 needed to purchase the car, plus the money necessary to advertise in the newspaper, but cannot decide whether or not to buy it. There is an obvious risk involved. You

could spend $300 advertising the car and then sell it for $600; but if that happens, you would lose $200. On the other hand, if you could only spend $50 for advertising and resell it for $1,000, you could make a fast $450.

Some risks are not worth taking. Others are almost sure things. Some people only focus on the potential for loss so that they are unable to objectively weigh the evidence necessary to make an effective decision.

UNSUCCESSFUL PAST DECISIONS

Another reason that people are reluctant to make decisions is because of unsuccessful decisions that they have made in the past. If our past decision making is marred by failure and we have no idea how our decision making led to the failure, we will be very wary of making other decisions that could lead us to failure again. People learn from every experience in life whether they are aware of what they learn or not. When we make a decision and it turns out badly, we may be criticized, demeaned or we may lose something of material value. The next time we are faced with a decision, we remember the consequences of previous decisions and seek to avoid the consequences by avoiding the decision.

BELIEF THAT OUR DECISIONS ARE IRREVERSIBLE

Most things in life that we do can be undone. For example, if you decide to major in law and decide after a year in law school that you would rather be a marine biologist. You cannot get the year back that you spent in law school. On the other hand, you can leave law school and go to a college that specializes in marine biology. The year in law school could actually help you to increase your commitment to being a marine biologist.

Unfortunately, many people do not realize that they can continue to make progress when a decision they made did not produce the results that they wanted. When people believe that their decisions are irreversible, the fear of failure increases. Imagine how you would feel if you knew you had to get everything correct the first time you tried it. People who believe in the irreversibility of their decisions apply the same limited thinking to their decisions.

DISASTER FANTASIES

Disaster fantasies keep many people from making effective decisions. Effective decision makers recognize that they may lose something (e.g., money or prestige) if they make the wrong decision. These losses are carefully calculated and weighed against the possible gains from making a good decision. The effective decision maker knows that she can handle the loss.

The ineffective decision maker has no idea how much can be lost. Rather than carefully calculate the potential loss, the ineffective decision maker lets his imagination run wild. Every past real and imaginary frightful experience is free to jump into the mind of one who allows his imagination no limits. Take a minute before you leave home today and imagine all of the terrible things that can happen to you outside of your home. If you applied the same disaster fantasies to all of your decisions, you would freeze into immobility.

LACK OF KNOWLEDGE OF THE DECISION MAKING PROCESS

Many people simply do not realize that there are decision making models that can be learned. There are a lot of things that we don't naturally know how to do. If you know how to type, use a computer or drive a car, you know that you did not do any of those things without learning first how to do them. It is easy to recognize the things that obviously require learning before we can do them. On the other hand, there are many things that we assume that we should know how to do even though we have never been taught. Many people have never been taught how to use a systematic method for effective decision making.

By becoming aware of the barriers to effective decision making, we are able to be alert to our own tendencies to hamper our decision making process. Such recognition is the first step in moving ahead to competent, timely and appropriate decisions.

Wise men admit their mistakes,
foolish men defend them.

Historically, people have competed against each other for resources, customers and reputations. Individuals and institutions strive to be the first and the best in areas of specialization. The focus has been on individual or institutional reputation and position rather than quality for the community or larger society. Times have changed, and so have the processes we can all use to make good decisions.

Thriving in the future depends on foresight about

✓ where our possibilities will intersect with future needs
✓ unanticipated demands
✓ future competition
✓ costs of doing business

A person who makes good decisions is able to keep her/his pulse on all of these variables and translate them into information which can be used to facilitate the decision process by individuals, groups and organizations.

Assertive and effective decision makers are transformational. They convince subordinates to transfer their own self-interest into the interest of the group through concern for a broader goal. They also ascribe their power to personal characteristics (like charisma), personal skill, hard work and personal contacts rather than to their organizational stature (position and formal authority) and are interactive. They try to make interactions positive for everyone involved.

Assertive and effective decision makers also encourage participation, share power and information, enhance self-worth, and get others excited about their work. They believe that allowing people to contribute and to feel powerful and important is a win-win situation—good for the employees and good for the individual groups. Effective decision makers don't covet formal authority; they have learned to live without it.

Instead, they concentrate on energizing others.

Processes to Follow

Regardless of the environment in which decision making takes place, there are certain steps which are integral to the decision-making process. In many cases, we use these steps instinctively. However, in managing a complex organization, we are sometimes confronted with extremely difficult situations which may influence the decision making process. In such a case it is helpful to return to the steps of decision making to help clarify the picture. The following may be used as an outline:

Step 1 Identify and define the problem and recognize related issues.

Define the problem broadly, try not to restrict options and continue to refocus on the central problem or issue so that bonfire solutions and treatment of only the symptoms are avoided. Don't lose sight of the perspective or environment in which the problem exists so that a sense of proportion is established,

Step 2 Analyze the difficulties in the existing situation.

In unique circumstances, creative decisions require going beyond policies or rules for a decision. Solutions may require modification of the existing organizational structure.

Ask: What is involved? Why? Where? When? To what extent?

Then: Collect data.

Step 3 Establish criteria for problem resolution.

Ask yourself what are the criteria for adequacy or "boundary conditions?" What is good enough?

Step 4 Develop an action plan which contains your strategy.

A systematic plan specifies alternatives, predicts consequences, and aids in your deliberating and selection of the alternatives for action.

Identify factors which mediate the choice of a preferred alternative. These include the values of the administrator, the cultural context in which the decision is made and implemented, the perceptions of those involved in the process, the potency of the situation, the force and pressure on the decision maker and the importance of the goal.

Step 5 Initiate the plan of action.

Steps of action include:

Programming: The mechanics and specific details for implementing the plan; specific programs for allocating authority and physical and human resources.

What impacts a good decision?

✓ Clear Expectations: Without clear conditions of individual responsibility, authenticity and accountability, little can be accomplished. (Legitimacy is an essential condition of the quality of the decision.)

✓ Uncertainty: Expertise must be certain, rewards meaningful and empowerment and inspiration likely.

✓ What is going on outside.
✓ The ability to become an enabler.
✓ The ability to see the bigger picture.
✓ Our ability to develop policy to enable meaningful coalitions/partnerships to be found.

Use Your Judgment

Utilize your best judgment at all times. Ask yourself:

✓ Is it fair and reasonable?
✓ Is it honest?
✓ Does it make good sense in the context of our established objectives?

If you can answer "yes" to all of these, then proceed. Remember, you are accountable against these criteria for your actions.

Follow the "Triple A" Formula for Success

ATTITUDE   To achieve, you must have the right attitude and apply yourself to the situation

APTITUDE   You must have the knowledge—if you don't, get it!

ACTION   Execution makes the plan work—get started and keep going!

THE CHANGE PROCESS: MANAGING CHANGE

Flexibility is the key to survival in a changing world. Only those individuals who are flexible enough to react to a constantly changing environment thrive personally and on the job. Major decisions in industry come at the rate of two per day. This will impact how, what and with whom we do what we do. The leading characteristic of corporate and individual success is the ability to respond with agility in an environment determined by constant, unrelenting change. Why?

✓ Things keep happening faster and faster.

✓ Markets and competition are changing rapidly.
✓ All the steps and styles are no longer necessary—we have instant models and products.

Each person must be able to accommodate whatever is necessary at the moment. With the growing technological capability and economy throwing new ideas, new competitors, new technologies and new customer demands at us faster than we can anticipate, rapid response must become a core competency. We must be able to reconfigure both human resources and information technology structures—we must be able to move from one job function/personal situation to the next as needs and demands change. We must be capable of functioning in a new way, in a flattened organization versus a cumbersome, deep hierarchy which guards against making mistakes and improvements. In a world where technology products, processes and competitors were changing slowly, that system worked. Now, we are experiencing a new paradigm where things are changing too fast for hierarchical organizations to respond.

Now, each of us must be willing to be part of an empowered unit where

✓ decisions are processed at the point of maximum knowledge and
✓ the activity actually occurs and people are best versed in dealing with that activity.

To become fully empowered, we must be responsible, act assertively, use self-direction to encourage pride of ownership for results, and be willing to make an ally of change. We must be willing to change course quickly, efficiently and economically in an unpredictable environment, see unexpected opportunities and respond rapidly and decisively to unforeseen events. In es-

sence, effective change masters must be able to manage cacophony, diversity and sometimes downright incivility. This response requires:

✓ subtlety
✓ courage
✓ self-discipline (to submerge one's ego)
✓ an ability to invent relationships between events/people where there were none.

As Lothair I (795–855 A.D.) said, "The times change, and we change with them.")

While resistance is inherent in the changing process, resistance isn't bad: rather, it gives us a healthy chance to effect long-term change. Human beings resist change for sane and logical reasons. In order to be successful at creating and continuing change, you must celebrate resistance!

As you work toward change, an "unfreezing" of what needs to be changed must occur. This can be done in at least three ways:

- Via strain
  ✓ Do individuals feel stress about change or about problems linked to change?

Sources of Resistance	Possible Antidotes
Lack of ownership	Involvement
Lack of benefit to changes	Payoff
Increased work load	Lighten load
Lack of top support	Top brass support
Loneliness (from being a pioneer)	Collegiality
Insecurity	Security
Norm incongruence	Shared values/norms
Boredom	Participation
Chaos	Control
Superiority	Empathy
Differential (levels) of knowledge	Equal information
Lack of recognition	Involvement
Sudden, wholesale change	Gradual, understandable timetable
Fear of failure	Affirmation of successes
Extremes of organizational structure (high centralization—no opportunity, no change)	Moderate centralization, formalization or stratification
Unique problems	Unique solutions

- Via potency
  - ✓ Does the "changee" believe he/she can change?
  - ✓ Does the individual changee perceive the possibility of success? (Perception is important.)
  - ✓ Potency deals with beliefs, not facts.
- Via value
  - ✓ Is there something valuable to head toward?
  - ✓ Is point "B" something that moves you forward?
  - ✓ If you lack a clear vision of your objective, you most definitely will not leave the point where you are.

Change strategies are as plentiful as the people who use them. There are three basic strategies:

- Rational (empirical) Strategy which
  - ✓ Assumes people change to new information via natural process
  - ✓ Is shown by research to be the least effective
- Coercive (power) Strategy which
  - ✓ Is the fastest, most effective
  - ✓ Depends on power
  - ✓ Is short-term because it increases resistance and sows the seeds of ultimate dissatisfaction, and
- Normative (re-education) Strategy which
  - ✓ Links a change to people's needs and drives
  - ✓ Tries to identify payoffs for changes
  - ✓ Includes positive reinforcement of individuals involved
  - ✓ Has the most long-range impact
  - ✓ Takes the most time

In any change process, all individuals must recognize the importance of ownership and participation. People will resist what they consider alien. The best predictor of ownership is participation (both defining the change and implementing it) and involving others in defining the "what" and the "how."

It is important to go slowly and employ the "Theory of Small Wins."

- Don't attempt too great a change "early-on."
- Nothing succeeds like success. (Successive approximation of success.)
- Break down long-term objectives into a series of near-term successes.

It is equally important to put the *urgency for making the change* into perspective. So many times, changes are "sold" as heavy, overreaching, impossible challenges. When we link change with gravity, we increase resistance. When we link it with excitement and joy, people want to join. People love parties and will jump on the bandwagon. When people are having a good time, they are more open to possibilities.

Change takes guts. It requires a basis for action. Change is more often a process than a result. Greatness in planning change lies not in reaching a goal, but in how you journey toward it. What makes a success is not the ability to avoid failure, but rather the capacity to get up and try once more.

Folk Wisdom of Change	Antidote
1. The grass is always greener on the other side of the fence.	We will change when there is sufficient reason to do so.
2. Guess what? Not everyone is like me.	We must not only look at our motives (benefits to us of the change), but we must look at the benefits to other stakeholders.
3. Stress is fertile ground for success.	Curiosity and anxiety are necessary preconditions to learning. In physical systems, strain is necessary for the development of musculature. Nearly every innovation is a product of stress—a response to inadequacy.
4. You can't make it if you believe you are faking it. If you say you can, or you say you cannot, you are right.	If you have no faith in your current skills and knowledge, how can you think about learning more? (Belief in self is the foundation of change.)
5. If they haven't bought it, they aren't going to keep it.	Participation is critical to ownership
6. Push me, and I'll push you back.	People resist pressure. People have an infinite capacity to get even.
7. If you want a change, have a party.	When people are having a good time, they are open to possibilities.
8. One hundred proof change, like 100 proof whiskey, is hard to stomach.	Change comes in stages. If we learn to celebrate the early stages, the later stages will eventually emerge.
9. Change is loss.	Change always means loss. Changers need to recognize the natural grief and resistance that come from loss. (People need to be allowed to work through their sense of loss.)
10. You learn to walk only by taking baby steps.	Theory of small wins. Baby steps are less scary.
11. To err is not only human but divine.	If I have no failures, they ought to fire me on the spot because it means that I'm not trying enough. I'm not trying to reach beyond my ready grasp.
12. Risk is not Russian Roulette.	The real question is how much of a chance? Bounded risk is the sign of a thriving and surviving change agent.

McDonnell Douglas Ethical Decision Making Check List

Kirk Hanson[*]

Analysis

What are the facts?
>   Have I defined the problem correctly?
>   What decision am I asked to make?
>   Who will be affected by the decision?
>   What events or actions have led to the situation?
>   Do others define the problem the same way I do?

Who is responsible to act?
>   What are my formal and informal obligations in this case?
>   What role do I play that gives me these responsibilities?
>   What general responsibilities do I have which apply?
>   To whom are these responsibilities owed?
>   Will my decision be understood by others?
>   Am I willing for my decision to become a general rule in the company?

Are all parties treated fairly in my proposed decision?
>   Are all persons treated the same or can I justify any differential treatment I propose?
>   Can I justify the distribution of the benefits and burdens resulting from my solution?
>   Are there any groups I have not considered who will believe that they are not being treated fairly?

Implementation

Who should be consulted and informed?
>   Do some individuals have a right to be consulted before a decision is made?
>   Do some individuals have a right to be notified first?
>   Will some persons be harmed if they are not told first?

What actions will assure that my decision achieves its intended outcome?
>   What implementation steps are critical to achieving my goals?
>   What can interfere with the implementation and what have I done to prevent/hedge against interference?
>   With which groups or individuals must I communicate to assure that the decision is carried out?
>   What steps must be taken to follow up on the implementation and the effects of the decision?

Implement.

---

[*]   By permission, Kirk Hanson and McDonnell Douglas.

Follow up

> Was the decision implemented correctly?
>
> Did the decision maximize benefits, reduce harms, respect rights and treat all parties fairly?

Select the Optimum Solution

What are the potential consequences of my solutions?

> Who will be affected by my alternative decision and how?
>
> Are there any second order or unintended effects?
>
> Does the good I will do outweigh the bad?

Which of the options I have considered does the most to maximize benefits, reduce harm, respect rights and increase fairness?

> Am I satisfied that I have found the best solution possible?
>
> Can I comfortably explain the decision to my family, my subordinates or my boss?
>
> Will the decision look as good in time as it does today?
>
> Will my decision be understood for what it is?
>
> Am I willing for my decision to become a general rule?
>
> Does my role give me special responsibilities toward certain individuals or groups?
>
> Do I have a responsibility to a larger group than is involved here?

What are the consequences of actions (benefit/harm analysis)?

> Who will be affected by my alternate decisions and how?
>
> Are there any second order effects? unintended effects?
>
> Does the good I will do outweigh the bad?

What and whose rights are involved (rights/principles analysis)?

> Whose rights may be affected here?
>
> Are there any civil or basic human rights involved?
>
> Are there any job or employment rights involved?
>
> Is there any other type of contract or implied contract?

What is fair treatment in this case (social justice analysis)?

> What individuals or groups deserve equal or balanced treatment?
>
> Are all persons treated the same or can I justify the differential treatment I propose?
>
> Can I justify the way the benefits and burdens conferred by my solution are distributed?
>
> Are there any groups I have not considered who will believe they are not being treated fairly?

Solution Development

What solutions are available to me?

> To reduce harms?
>
> To maximize benefits?
>
> To respect rights?
>
> To be fair to more parties?

Have I considered all of the creative solutions which might permit me to reduce harms, maximize benefits, respect more rights or be fair to more parties?

> Would brainstorming bring better solutions to mind?
>
> Can I increase the positive effects of the solution?
>
> Can I decrease the negative effects of the solution?

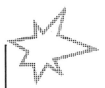

Observation Activity

PURPOSE:

To utilize your observational skills and your increasing knowledge of group dynamics that you may draw valid conclusions regarding a given group's effectiveness.

PROCEDURE:

1. Your assignment is to twice attend a meeting of a group—any group of your choice except family, close friends, job or a group of which you are already a member—observe the proceedings and respond to the questions below.
2. Some groups which have been observed in the past include: city and/or utility board meetings, Alcoholics and/or Parents Anonymous, religious conferences, Parent-Teacher Associations, Weight Watchers, Gay Awareness, therapy and/or sensitivity training groups, etc. It may be necessary to obtain advance permission to attend meetings of your target group. Check with a group representative regarding this.
3. Take the information you have received in class through lectures, films, textbook and participation and apply that information to answering the questions. Explain your answers! Devote at least one paragraph to each question so you may have sufficient space to reflect your thinking.
4. After submitting your written report, get into small groups and be prepared to:
   A. Relate your experiences and observations to other group members;
   B. Discuss whether you felt "competent" decisions were made;
   C. Identify those elements of group interaction that you think either contributed to or interfered with the participants' ability to resolve issues.

DISCUSSION:

1. What gathering did you observe? When/where did you observe?
2. Why do these particular meetings take place? That is, what kinds of decisions are being made? Are they related to therapy? commitment? learning? problem solving? communication? motivation? living skills? crisis/stress management, etc.?
3. How did communication flow? Did it go back and forth evenly, around in a circle, from a facilitator to participants and back to facilitator? Did any member try to dominate? Did the other members allow or block the behavior?
4. How were decisions formulated? Did the participants utilize the seven step Creative Problem Solving Process described in The Elements of the Decision Making Process article? Did they use a process developed by members? Was each individual allowed to use what ever method s/he chose? How did the other members support or critique the efforts of one individual to decide something?
5. In your opinion, were "competent" decisions made? Why or why not?

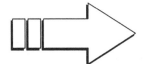

Once to every man and nation comes the moment
to decide, in the strife of Truth with Falsehood,
for the good or evil side.
—*J. R. Lowell*

Decision Making Model

PURPOSE:

To help structure the decision making process so that one systematically considers all of the factors necessary for making a competent, timely and appropriate decision.

PROCEDURE:

1. Along the top of the diagram, place the options you have in the decision you are making.
2. Brainstorm to determine the values you wish to have as outcomes to your decision.
3. Rank the values so that you determine which is the most important value that you wish to occur, the second most important value and so on.
4. Give the values a weighting so that the most important value will be counted more heavily than the least important value.
5. List these weighted values along the left side of the diagram.
6. Rate or rank each option according to each weighted value. (For example, if you are ranking each option for Criterion 1, the first choice would receive a score of 5—1 x 5 = 5—and the last choice would receive a score of 20—4 x 5 = 20. The option with the lowest total score would be the "best" choice based on the criteria (values) which you chose.
7. Sum the scores for each option.
8. If the first and second choices are close, sleep on the decision overnight. If you wake up feeling okay about the number one choice, go with it. If you don't feel okay about the number one choice, go with number two. This allows for the use of intuition.

	Option 1	Option 2	Option 3	Option 4
Values (Criteria)				
Criterion (5 x the score)				
Criterion 2 (4 x the score)				
Criterion 3 (3 x the score)				
Criterion 4 (2 x the score)				
TOTAL SCORE				

DISCUSSION:

1. How did clarifying your values help you to make your decision?
2. For what kind of decisions would you use this process? Why?
3. For what kinds of decisions would you not use this process? Why not?

R E A C T I O N S

Name _____
Date _____
Your professor may require this exercise to be handed in.

1. Think about a very difficult decision you have had to make. What were some of the psychological/emotional barriers or obstacles that made it so difficult? What was the outcome? Are you still satisfied with the quality (remember the concept of competency?) of your decision? Given the same situation today, would you follow a similar or different process?

2. What are at least four interpersonal elements that affect the "process" of decision making when you attempt to make a decision with someone else? Now that you have done the above, add these four—personality, culture, aggressiveness, expectations—and comment further on what effect they may have.

3. How does one's sense of self-confidence affect decision making behavior? Give an example from your own life where you operated from either high or low self-confidence and explain how it affected your actions.

4. What are at least five sources you can go to for information when you seek to make a "competent" decision?

Relational Communication

DEFINITIONS

We share a large part of our lives with other individuals in what we call "relationships." All relationships involve elements of interpersonal communication; however, the study of relational communication focuses specifically on the communication that occurs between two people who are in the process of beginning, continuing or ending a relationship with each other. Although we have many relationships (i.e., with neighbors, our boss, teachers), this chapter will address the intimate communication between family members, close friends or significant love relationships. In order to gain an understanding of the communication process that occurs in these relationships, we will define several terms that will be used in this chapter:

✳ **Relational Communication**

Definition: Communication that affects our willingness, and that of others, to initiate, continue or terminate our relationships.

Examples: Greeting people, handshakes (initiating), expressing our commitment to the relationship (continuing), telling someone we no longer want to be friends (terminating), etc.

✳ **Relational Identity**

Definition: The perception of two individuals in a relationship as something different than who they are as individuals.

Examples: We may see ourselves as a "couple," "twosome," or a "duo." We begin to refer to ourselves as "we" or "us" instead of "you and me."

✳ **Intimacy**

Definition: According to Adler, Rosenfeld and Towne in their book *Interplay*, this can be classified in three areas: intellectual, emotional or physical intimacy. Intimacy is characterized by extended and concentrated communication in any of these areas. It is also not the goal in all relationships.

Examples: We may share our life philosophies with a friend (intellectual), our feelings of love with a parent (emotional), and have a sexual relationship with a girlfriend or boyfriend (physical).

✳ **Self-Disclosure**

Definition: Sharing information about oneself that the other individual is unlikely to find out by other means.

Examples: Sharing secrets, discoveries, confidential information, past history and experiences or information that we do not commonly express.

——————— ✩ ✩ ✩ ———————

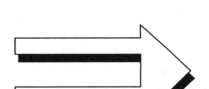

If you judge people, you have not time to love them. —*Mother Teresa*

THE IMPORTANCE OF RELATIONAL COMMUNICATION

Imagine for a moment that you are suddenly alone in the world. You woke up this morning and found that the people you share your home with are gone. You stepped outside and your neighborhood was void of the sounds of people awakening and preparing for a new day—no car engines running or doors closing as other individuals go about their daily routines. You leave for work or school only to find the streets empty. Every store, school or business you see is the same: deserted. As far as you know you are the only person left in the world!

This is not a very pleasant scene but it does allow us to examine how we feel about those who share our lives. Whether it be a parent, a roommate or a spouse, we would sorely miss the company of others if we suddenly found them absent from our lives. The reality is that we are social creatures by nature and our relationships provide the foundation of our daily lives. Under-

standing how and why we establish these relationships and what barriers we face in successfully maintaining them can help us avoid the "disappearance" of important relationships from our lives. And, most importantly, the more we understand about how we communicate in these relationships the greater the opportunity we have to make them work well.

RELATIONSHIPS ARE INEVITABLE

Relationships are, fortunately, unavoidable. From business contacts to friendship to intimate love, relationships pervade our lives. We begin by being born into families where we learn the basics of communicating in relationships. Babies learn, through nonverbal communication with their parents, that certain people are more important to their existence than others. Toddlers discover that developing more relationships makes life more interesting. Brothers, sisters, grandparents and more provide social opportunities and stimulation.

Relationships also fulfill basic human needs. Simply communicating with others is not enough. We need to know that significant people share a future with us. We need companionship, love and a sense of belonging. And we don't fulfill these needs in any one relationship. Instead, we often have several or many relationships that serve us differently. We may socialize with one friend and confide in another. And we fulfill others' needs as well. This is the reciprocal nature of relationships. As long as we are both having our needs met we can be quite satisfied with each other. However, as soon as one person starts to expect more than the other person is willing to give or if one person feels she is giving more than she is receiving, then we have a "needs" imbalance and the relationship may suffer as a consequence.

RELATIONSHIPS DEVELOP IN STAGES

Effective relationships need to be carefully created and constructively maintained. The path a relationship takes does not happen by accident and we can exercise some degree of control by understanding how communication influences the development of relationships. According to researcher Mark Knapp in the book *Interpersonal Communication and Human Relationships*, relationships develop through the following 10 stages:

Initiating—in this stage we want to create the impression that we are an interesting person worth knowing. At the same time we are evaluating the other individual's reaction to us. Initiating is often characterized by communication such as a handshake or "nice to meet you." And if we are really interested in initiating a relationship, we often strategically plan our approach. Being "accidentally" in the same place at the same time, smiling or nodding may gain us the entrance we desire.

Experimenting—at this point we try to find things that we have in common with the other person. We often engage in "small talk." Now, you may be one of those people who find small talk to be superficial and useless but at this early stage of a relationship it serves an important communication function. Besides finding out if we have anything in common, it helps us determine if we want to pursue the next step. For instance, Anthony had wanted to meet Brenda for a long time. When he finally got the courage to introduce himself, he suddenly started telling his life story, including some intimate details. When he asked her out to dinner, she turned him down. Little did he know that she was very uncomfortable with what he had told her. Brenda felt that Anthony was either insecure or moving "too fast!" Small talk would have broken the ice for Anthony and allowed the relationship to develop along a more natural path.

Intensifying—At this point we begin to develop a relationship that will, hopefully, meet our needs. This stage is characterized by informal communication. We start referring to each as "we" rather than "I" or "you." We begin disclosing more about ourselves as the potential for growth becomes obvious. It is here that we find the courage to start expressing our feelings about commitment. Sheri, a college student, stated in class, "I have a friendship that has become very important to me. Yesterday my friend told me that we're going to be friends forever! I can't tell you how nice it is to know I can count on her."

Integrating—In this stage a relational identity is developed. We are recognized by others as a "couple," "partners" or "buddies." We begin interacting with each other based on this new identity called "us." For example, Matthew canceled an appointment so he could go to his girlfriend's company picnic with her. When we integrate, we often take on relational commitments rather than continue to follow our individual schedules.

Bonding—Now we make our commitment known through public rituals. A wedding is an example of such a ritual. Research in psychology indicates that public commitments create in us a stronger desire to make the relationship work. We decide to let the "world" know that we are having a relationship.

Differentiating—We reach a point where the relational identity may be too restricting and we want to re-establish our own identities. Often this is a reaction to conflict in the relationship. For instance, a wife may stop referring to a family automobile as "our car" and start calling it "my car" in an effort to communicate her individuality. This doesn't mean that differentiation cannot have a positive outcome. Recognizing the other person's need for individuality and personal space can strengthen the original commitment to each other.

Circumscribing—Hopefully all relationships will have happy endings. But we all know this is not realistic. At some point what we have with another person begins to deteriorate. The first stage of this disintegration is circumscribing wherein we reduce the quantity or quality of time and energy we put into the relationship. For example, Tony and Sophie became a clear case of a relationship in this stage when they both started spending more time with other friends, avoiding each other's phone calls and responding to each other by saying "you wouldn't be interested" or "it doesn't concern you." The sad part about this is that, while avoiding each other, we often avoid the fact that we are both contributing to the disintegration of what we called "us."

Stagnation—Here we really begin to live life in a rut! The relationship has no novelty or excitement and we react to it in a very routine way. Have you ever had a job that you disliked but you continued to perform? It becomes robotic, repetitive and boring. The same thing happens to a relationship if we allow it to stagnate. We become the stereotypical picture of the old couple living in the same house and never speaking a word to each other.

Avoiding—Stagnation may develop to the point that we cannot handle any contact with each other so we go out of our way to avoid one another. For example, Angela, who dated Mario for 2 months, wanted so badly to avoid him that she dropped out of two classes that they attended together. Avoiding is a clear sign of the death of the relational identity. We no longer talk about "us," rather we communicate in terms "you" or "me."

Terminating—This is, of course, when one or both parties involved end the relationship. It can be brought on by the death of one of the individuals or a decision that staying together is no longer beneficial. This is one of the most difficult stages for it can often be painful to the parties involved. How it occurs often depends on how intimate the relationship was. A casual friendship may end, but a marriage or cutting the ties with a family member may take more negotiation and expressing of feelings.

Most communication researchers agree that all relationships follow a systematic development. However, that doesn't mean that every time we get involved with someone it is destined for termination. What is important is that we discover how to stop the pattern when we've reached a stage where both participants are happy and maintain the relationship at that level.

BARRIERS TO DEVELOPING RELATIONSHIPS

INITIATING RELATIONSHIPS

There are many barriers to maintaining good communication in a relationship. However, the first major barrier is how to begin a relationship, how to initiate contact. We have probably all experienced the desire to meet someone and the uncertainty about how to go about communicating with them. Regardless of the kind of relationship we're interested in establishing (we may want a new friend or a new love), we face the barriers of overcoming our own shyness, having our advances rejected and taking the risk of putting ourselves on the line. But if a relationship is going to exist, someone has to make the first move. Arthur Wassmer, in his book *Making Contact*, recommends the SOFTENS Technique to help make the initial contact more productive. He uses each letter of the word "softens" to represent nonverbal behaviors that we can use when breaking the ice with someone new. Taking these nonverbal signals into consideration can help us overcome the fear we often feel on the initial contact. The technique is as follows:

Smiling—genuinely done, helps establish a positive climate

Open posture—communicates interest

Forward lean—communicates involvement

Touching by shaking hands—establishes physical contact

Eye contact—communicates interest, listening and builds rapport

Nodding—communicates listening and can help you focus on what the other person is saying

Space—can promote closeness depending on culture and the kind of relationship you want to encourage

MAINTAINING A RELATIONSHIP

The second barrier we face is communicating within the relationship in such a manner that we maintain the relationship.

The more intimate the relationship is, the more complex it may become to maintain, whether it is with a family member, a friend or a lover. Intimacy, whether it be physical, emotional or intellectual, can enhance the relationship by allowing two people to bond to each other through this closeness, or it can drive them apart if one or the other is not ready or prepared to maturely deal with the intimacy. Intimacy involves vulnerability and therefore requires trust in each other. If we feel like we are being manipulated or played with, we often find it difficult to be intimate with someone. This can happen when we encounter "control factors." Control factors are any issues in a relationship that cause one or more participants to feel a lack of balance in the relationship. In other words, these factors set things out of control. Several major communication control factors that surface in many relationships are as follows:

Unequal participation—Teresa feels she puts out a lot more effort in the marriage than her husband, Chris. She is feeling very dissatisfied with this imbalance and wants him to contribute his share to the relationship.

Simultaneous Relationships—Rod and Mike have been friends for a long time. Recently, Mike became involved in a club at school and has been spending a lot of time with other people and not much time with Rod. Rod, who has no interest in the club's activities, has made a request for more of Mike's time. Mike feels a tremendous imbalance. He wants to see Rod, but also wants to continue developing his new relationships. He feels like he's doing a juggling act with friends.

Incompatibility—Jennifer and Troy are very attracted to each other. They feel there is a real chemistry between them. However, as they start to spend time together, they find they have little in common. They want to see each other because of the interpersonal attraction, but when together, they have a tendency to argue over opposing viewpoints. They want to resolve this imbalance but don't know how.

Game Playing—Matt feels confused about his relationship with his father. They can be getting along well one day, but the next his dad is putting "some guilt trip on me." He would like to spend more time at home but the emotional "yo-yo" is getting to be more than he can handle.

Control—Jesse is realizing that she is tired of being considered a "little girl" by her parents. Granted, they controlled her life when she was small but she wants to make her own decisions now. She does not want the scales to lean so heavily in her parents' favor.

In each of these situations, the individuals involved feel an imbalance in their relationships. Each one has a choice—they can continue to feel the lack of satisfaction, they can reduce the amount of involvement in the relationship or they can try to resolve the conflict by communicating with their partners about the factor that is causing the problem. This last option is necessary if the relationships are going to be maintained at a positive stage. But this step also requires the willingness to self-disclose feelings in an honest and supportive fashion. If they are willing to take the risk of disclosure then they have the chance to bring balance back to the relationship. But disclosure must be given in appropriate amounts. We can overwhelm another person with our inner feelings and literally chase them away. But if handled sensitively, self-disclosure has two benefits for relationships: it encourages reciprocal disclosure (I will be more motivated to share if you are equally willing) and it can increase the intimacy of the relationship. Lastly, it is important to be aware of the influence self-disclosure has in our lives. It is not only important in maintaining healthy relationships, but it is also one of the first things to diminish as the relationship begins to deteriorate. Relation-

ships that are stagnating are often characterized by a lack of disclosure—the individuals just won't share!

ENDING A RELATIONSHIP

The last barrier we'll address here deals with ending a relationship. For most of us this is one of the most difficult communication situations. Few of us want to play the "bad guy." Yet, if our partner is the one ending the relationship, we may suffer feelings of rejection and a loss of self-esteem. It is very rare to have an outcome where both parties are happy; however, this can happen. For example, Raul was tired of his girlfriend, Janie, playing games and Janie was fed up with Raul continually trying to control her time so they mutually agreed to call it quits and both were happy. Most of us, however, suffer a feeling of loss when we lose relationships whether they be through the death of a family member or the breakup of a love relationship. This is because we are literally in mourning for the relational identity, that element that was composed of ourselves and another. We not only miss the other person but we miss that identity that was "us." As in any mourning situation, acknowledging our grief and allowing it to run its course is one of the best treatments to the pain of an ended relationship.

Knowing why we need relationships in our lives helps us understand the way we communicate within them. We are striving to start and maintain them and, sometimes, find ourselves in one that is ending. Relationships, like life, work in a cycle. And, like life, how much we give them will determine how much we gain from them. The activities in this chapter are designed to help you determine the kind of relationships you want, how to improve the ones you are currently involved in and aid you in acquiring the skills to start new ones. With this information you will, hopefully, never find yourself alone in the world.

Are You Made for Love?

Diane Ackerman[*]

A naturalist and prize-winning poet, contributing editor Diane Ackerman holds a Ph.D. from Cornell University. In addition to her four poetry collections, she's the author of five works of nonfiction, including the best-selling "A Natural History of the Senses." This article—an exploration of the biology of love—is adapted from her new book, "A Natural History of Love," published by Random House.

Among the many handicaps that can befall human beings, few are sadder than the inability to feel love. Because we imagine love to be wholly psychological, we don't even have a word for people who are biologically unable to love. But there are some unlucky souls who, through trauma to part of the brain, cannot feel emotion.

Antonio Damasio, a neurologist at the University of Iowa College of Medicine, reports a curious case in which a man we'll call John had been living a normal life as accountant, husband and father. At 35, John had a benign tumor removed from the front of his brain. The operation was a success. But soon afterward his personality changed dramatically. He divorced his wife, became involved with a prostitute, lost one job after another, became penniless—all without feeling anything, not even bewilderment or concern.

Using magnetic resonance imaging to peer inside the brain, Damasio found that a region of John's frontal cortex was damaged. Most likely, this had occurred during the tumor operation, injuring a small portion of gray matter between the eyebrows that seems to be a factory for emotions.

Damasio hooked John up to a machine similar to a lie detector and presented him with emotionally charged slides, sounds and questions. Some were violent, some pornographic. John had no response. A field of flowers registered no differently than a murder.

If the ability to love is something that can be so destroyed, then it has a physical reality, it is matter. But where does love reside in the body?

Throughout history, people have located love in the heart, probably because of its loud, safe, regular, comforting beat—that maternal two-step that babies follow from before birth. The image of the heart adorns greeting cards, coffee mugs, bumper stickers and paintings of the crucifixion. A real heart, viewed during open-heart surgery, seems a poor symbol for so much emotion. "In my heart of hearts," we say, making a *matrioshka* doll of it; in the innermost cave

---

in the labyrinth of my feelings. The heart is vital to being alive, the unstated logic runs, and so is love.

Love develops in the neurons of the brain, and the way it grows depends on how those neurons were trained when we were children. Evolution hands out a blueprint for the building of the house of one's life. But, as with a house, much depends on the skill and experience of the builders; the laws and codes of society; the qualities of the materials; not to mention the random effect of landslides or floods or plumbing catastrophes; and the caprices of inspectors or supervisors, of hooligans or neighbors. How we love is a matter of biology. How we love is a matter of experience.

- *The cuddle chemical.* Oxytocin, a hormone that encourages labor and the contractions during childbirth, seems to play an important role in love, especially mother love. The sound of a crying baby makes its mother's body secrete more oxytocin, which in turn erects her nipples and helps the milk to flow. As the baby nurses, even more oxytocin is released, making the mother want to nuzzle and hug the baby. It has been called the "cuddle chemical" by zoologists, who have artificially raised the oxytocin level in animals and produced similar behavior.

Later in life, oxytocin seems to play an equally important role in romantic love, as a sexual arousal hormone that prompts cuddling between lovers and sweetens pleasure during lovemaking. Unlike other hormones, oxytocin flows from either physical or emotional cues—a certain look, voice or gesture is enough—and can be tied to one's personal love history, so a lover's voice alone can trigger more oxytocin. So might a richly woven and redolent sexual fantasy.

This outpouring of hormone may help explain why more women than men prefer to continue cuddling after sex. A woman may yearn to feel close and connected, tightly coiled around the mainspring of the man's heart. In evolutionary terms, she hopes the man will be sticking around for a while—long enough to protect her and the child he just fathered.

- *The infatuation chemical.* When two people find one another attractive, their bodies quiver with a gush of PEA (phenylethylamine), a molecule that speeds up the flow of information between nerve cells. An amphetaminelike chemical, PEA whips the brain into a frenzy of excitement, which is why lovers feel euphoric, rejuvenated, optimistic and energized, happy to sit up talking all night or making love for hours on end. Because amphetamine, or "speed," is addictive—even the body's naturally made speed—some people become what Michael Liebowitz and Donald Klein of the New York State Psychiatric Institute refer to as "attraction junkies," needing a romantic relationship to feel excited by life.

Driven by a chemical hunger, they choose unsuitable partners. Soon the relationship crumbles, or they find themselves rejected. In either case, tortured by lovesick despair, they plummet into a savage depression, which they try to cure by falling in love again. Liebowitz and Klein think this rollercoaster is fueled by a craving for PEA. When they gave some attraction junkies MAO inhibitors—antidepressants that can subdue PEA and other neurotransmitters—the researchers were amazed to find how quickly their patients improved. No longer craving PEA, they were able to choose partners more calmly and realistically. All this strongly suggests that when we fall in love, the brain drenches itself in PEA, a chemical that makes us feel pleasure, rampant excitement and well-being. A sweet fix, love.

- *The attachment chemical.* While the chemical sleigh ride of infatuation carries one at a fast clip over uneven terrain, lives become blended, people mate and genes mix, and babies are born. Then infatuation subsides and a new group of chemicals takes over—the morphinelike opiates of the mind, which calm and reassure. Being in love is a state of chaotic equilibrium. Its rewards of intimacy, dependability, warmth, empathy and shared experiences trigger the production of that mental comfort food, the endorphins. It's a less steep feeling than falling in love, but it's also steadier and more addictive.

The longer two people have been married, the more likely it is that they'll stay married. Stability, friendship, familiarity and affection are rewards the body clings to. As much as we love being dizzied by infatuation, such a state is stressful. It also feels magnificent to rest, to be free of anxiety or fretting and to enjoy one's life with a devoted companion.

That's a hard tonic to give up, even if the relationship isn't perfect. Shared events (including shared stresses and crises) are rivets that draw couples closer together. Soon they are fastened by so many that it's difficult to pull free.

- *The chemistry of divorce.* Monogamy and adultery are both hallmarks of being human. After the seductive fireworks of infatuation—which may last only a few weeks, or a few years—the body gets bored with easy ecstasy. Then the attachment chemicals roll in their thick cozy carpets of marital serenity. Might as well relax and enjoy the calm and security, some feel. Separated even for a short while, the partners crave the cradle of each other's embrace. Is it a chemical craving? Possibly so, a hunger for the soothing endorphins that flow when they're together.

Other people grow restless and search for novelty. They can't stand the tedium of constancy. So they begin illicit affairs or divorce proceedings.

One way or another, the genes survive, the species prevails. Even when the chemical cycle falters and breaks, it picks itself up and starts again.

Talking to People in Our Lives

The following five activities are designed to teach you the communication skills of initiating, maintaining and ending a conversation. The activities may be done singly or in a series.

Skill #1: Figuring Out to Whom to Talk

PURPOSE:

To learn to identify nonverbal signals that tell us if a person is willing to have a conversation.

PROCEDURE:

1. For three days observe people you do not know but to whom you are attracted (as a possible friend or love interest).
2. Identify nonverbal signals that communicate to you whether a person is approachable or not (state specifically what the person is doing that makes you feel this way).
3. Describe the communication behavior below.

Not Approachable	Approachable
1.	1.
2.	2.
3.	3.
4.	4.
5.	5.
6.	6.
7.	7.

DISCUSSION:

1. What did the "approachable" people do that made you feel this way? The "unapproachable?"
2. Which person seemed to be the most approachable and why?
3. Which person seemed to be the most unapproachable and why?
4. How approachable do you think other people perceive you and why?
5. How will these observations help you in your future relationships?

Skill #2: The Art of Small Talk

PURPOSE:

To examine the value of small talk as a way to initiate communication in a new relationship.

PROCEDURE:

1. Select someone you do not know very well and initiate a conversation on one of the following topics: the weather, your favorite foods or hobbies, your jobs, a TV program or movie you've recently seen, a current news event or the surrounding environment.
2. Carry on the conversation for at least 15 minutes, changing subjects if necessary to maintain dialogue.

DISCUSSION:

1. How comfortable/uncomfortable were you using small talk?
2. Did small talk help you find areas of common interest?
3. Did small talk lead to any in-depth conversation? Explain.
4. How can small talk help you start a relationship with someone you're interested in?

Skill #3: Sharing Yourself— More In-Depth Conversations

PURPOSE:

To explore the value of sharing personal information as a means of encouraging in-depth conversation.

PROCEDURE:

1. Over the next week monitor the conversation you have with family members, friends and in significant love relationships. Select five occasions when you share personal information about yourself with one or more of these people.
2. If you do not normally share personal information, then select five opportunities to do so.
3. For each occasion describe the following:
   a. My partner was:
   b. The information I shared was:
   c. His/her response was:

DISCUSSION:

1. Did the personal information encourage more conversation? Why or why not?
2. How did the person respond? How did you feel about his/her response?

Skill #4: Encouraging Your Partner to Talk

PURPOSE:

To explore the use of open-ended questions (questions that invite a variety of responses rather than a short, specific answer) as a means to maintain a conversation.

PROCEDURE:

1. For each situation below write two open-ended questions that could keep the conversation going.
2. Divide into dyads.
3. Ask each other the questions you have just written. Take turns role-playing and responding.

Situation 1: You are out on a blind date. You and your partner are sitting in a nice restaurant and are looking at the menus. The restaurant overlooks the ocean and it is sunset.

    1.

    2.

Situation 2: You are visiting a good friend's home for the first time and have just sat down for lunch. The friend's two young children are playing in the next room.

    1.

    2.

Situation 3: It's the first meeting of class. You sit down next to a person whom you have been attracted to for some time but haven't approached before now.

    1.

    2.

Situation 4: You've just met your fiance's/fiancee's parents for the first time. You are alone with them in their living room.

    1.

    2.

DISCUSSION:

1. Was it difficult to come up with your questions and if so, why?
2. Did the open-ended questions encourage conversation between you and your partner? Why or why not?
3. How might open-ended questions enhance communication in your relationships?

Skill #5: It's Hard to Stop Talking

PURPOSE:

To experience the process of ending a conversation.

PROCEDURE:

1. You will practice the following methods of ending a conversation:
    a. Summary—identifies the main points of the discussion: "I really understand how to organize this surprise party, Mom. I'll get started on the supplies right away."
    b. Value—a supportive statement that points out something that you found useful or are appreciative about: "This talk has helped so much! I really appreciate how much you've listened to my problem."
    c. Future Interest—identifies your desire to meet again: "I would really like to talk further with you about this. Could we get together later today?"
2. For each of the following situations write an example of one of the three preceding methods of ending a conversation. Identify which one you are using:

Situation 1: Disagreement with a parent:

Situation 2: After listening to a close friend who talked about his troubled love life all evening:

Situation 3: After an unenjoyable dinner date:

Situation 4: After having a great date with someone you haven't seen in several years.

DISCUSSION:

1. Do you normally find it difficult to end conversations? Explain.
2. Was it difficult to come up with these endings? Why or why not?
3. How can using specific endings help your communication in your relationships?

Are Men and Women Really Different?

Communication between the sexes has long been the brunt of jokes. Several popular sitcoms base episodes on family problems, with the fun being poked at the difference between the way the man and woman see things. It does make us laugh, until we find ourselves living the joke. What has created the stereotype that is so prevalent? The late Dr. Paul Popenoe, founder of the American Institute for Family Relations in Los Angeles, wrote a brief article in which he discussed the differences between men and women.

Beginning with the obvious, the functions of menstruation, pregnancy and lactation, men and women are found to be fundamentally different. The depth and intensity of a woman's motherly feeling is associated with the length and flow of her menstrual period. She has more different hormones than man, and the internal glandular secretions cause marked changes in her behavior often related to emotional instability—she laughs and cries more easily.

A summary of studies over time related by Dr. Katherine Dalton in *The Premenstrual Syndrome*, show a large portion of crimes committed by females are clustered in the premenstrual period—along with suicides, accidents, a decline in the quality of school work, decline in intelligence scores, visual acuity, and response speed.

Indeed, men and women are different in every cell of their bodies. The difference in the XY chromosome combination is the basic cause of development into maleness or femaleness. Perhaps because of this, a woman will outlive her male counterpart by three or four years in the U.S.

These, together with the list that follows, are only some of the differences between men and women. Taking these differences into consideration makes it easier to understand why men and women have difficulty communicating. These differences should not become excuses for failing to communicate, but should be used to wake us to the need to work at communication.

Pain shared is halved. Joy shared is doubled. —*D. Corkille-Briggs*

Man	Woman
Man normally has a higher basal metabolism. He is turning on the air conditioner when she is wrapped in a blanket.	Woman has a lower basal metabolism. She stands higher temperatures, is cold more easily.
Man has a smaller stomach, kidneys, liver and appendix, and larger lungs. In brute strength, men are 50% above women.	Women have a shorter head, broader face, chin less protruding, shorter legs, and longer trunk.
When the working day in British factories, under wartime conditions, was increased from 10 to 12 hours, accidents of men did not increase at all, women increased 150%.	Woman's blood contains more water (20% fewer red cells). Since these supply oxygen to the body cells, she tires more easily and is prone to faint.
Men's brains are specialized—the left side of the brain tends to handle verbal tasks and the right side handles spatial tasks.	The connecting tissue in a woman's brain is thicker, allowing for faster cross-over of information.
Men are attentive to things and more likely to be distracted by novel objects.	Women are better at perceiving subliminal messages and better at remembering details.
Men are more analytical—they think more abstractly. They have a knack for taking a situation out of context and analyzing it.	Women have a more complex thought process. They are more observant of the context around an experience. They can take in more information, on different levels.
Men seek closure in a group situation. They desire direct communication.	Women are comfortable with open ended conversations and complexity.
Men have difficulties communicating sadness.	Women have a hard time expressing anger.
Men tend to interrupt more often and speak longer.	Women tend to be better listeners.

The American Culture of Divorce: Just Whom Does It Hurt?

Adiscussion about relationships would not be complete without tackling the difficult issue of divorce. No one is surprised to hear the divorce rate in the United States has grown. The suddenness with which it has grown is the shocking part of the story. In the 1940s, only 14% of women who married eventually divorced. The passing of only one generation saw a surge to nearly 50% of marriages ending in divorce, and many women opting to have children out-of-wedlock. In the period from 1970 to 1992, the proportion of babies born outside of marriage went from 11% to 30%.[1] Some estimates today say 65% of marriages end in divorce.

American psychologist John B. Watson made a forbidding prediction in 1927: "In fifty years, unless there is some change, the tribal custom of marriage will no longer exist." Ten years later sociologist Pitirim Sorokin forecast that " . . . divorces and separations will increase until any profound difference between socially sanctioned marriages and illicit sex relationships will disappear."[2]

We like our freedom, and the rhetorical question often asked "Whom does it hurt?" has been answered by a large and growing body of research with several profound findings. In her book, *The Abolition of Marriage*, Maggie Gallagher writes;

The overthrow of the marriage culture and its replacement by a postmarital culture is the driving force behind almost all of the gravest problems facing America—crime, poverty, welfare dependence, homelessness, educational stagnation, even child abuse. Above all, the decline of marriage is behind the precarious sense of economic instability haunting so many Americans in this time of statistical economic abundance, low unemployment and inflation, rising GNP and personal income.[3]

THE FAMILY AND POVERTY

A popular radio talk show host received a call. The woman was asking for counseling about her economic situation. She was hoping to find a way to start a home business so she could quit work and stay home with her newborn child. As the host dug into this young woman's story, he found that although she had only one child and a young marriage, her husband had been married before and was paying a large portion of his income for child support, leaving just $500.00 a month for this new family. Sadly, this new mother must work; they could not afford the economic down time of starting a new home business.

---

1 Amara Bachu, *Fertility of American Women: June 1994* (Washington, D.C.: Bureau of the Census, September 1995), xix, Table K.
2 Martin King Whyte, *Dating, Mating, and Marriage* (New York: Aldine de Gruyter, 1990), 1.
3 Maggie Gallagher, *The Abolition of Marriage: How We Destroy Lasting Love*, (Washington, D.C.: Regenery Publishing, Inc. 1996), 4.

Lest you think that the ex-wife and children are living it up at this ex-dad's new family's expense, consider this: the stamp of our divorce culture is downward mobility. "Affluent kids slip into the middle class. Middle-class children experience the strains of blue-collar life. Working-class children slide into poverty, and the poor become trapped in a permanent underclass."[4] Marriage is the one institution that research has shown is a deterrent to poverty. A few years ago, economists David Neumark of the Federal Reserve Board and Sanders Korenman of Princeton University found that married men earn from 10 percent to 50 percent more than single men of comparable age, race, education and skill level. After carefully controlling for a number of factors, what they found is that there is "a productivity effect of marriage."

CHILDREN

One sad truth about divorce is the devastation to children. In addition to financial security, children need a stable and safe home environment in order to thrive. Studies show marriage is a significant protective factor against child abuse. For example:

- *The National Health Interview Survey (1988)* by the U.S. Department of Health and Human Services found that children from disrupted families are at a much higher risk for physical or sexual abuse than children from intact, married-couple families.[5]
- A 1994 study in the *Journal of Comparative Family Studies* found that, out of 52,000 child abuse cases, 72 percent involved children living in a household without one or both biological parents, even though such households comprise roughly a third of all households with children.[6]
- A 1995 published study of 1,000 students found that only 3.2 percent of the children who were raised with both biological parents had a history of maltreatment. However, a full 18.6% of those in other family situations had been maltreated.[7]

WOMEN

Poverty is, of course, major problem for women of divorce, but without a doubt the greatest issue is domestic violence. While the incidence of domestic abuse between married couples is extremely low, the incidence of domestic abuse between unmarried cohabiting couples is high.

- One survey found that more than two-thirds of domestic violence offenders were ex-spouses (35 percent) or boyfriends or ex-boyfriends (32 percent). Only 9 percent were current spouses.[8]

---

4 Ibid.
5 U.S Department of Health and Human Services. National Center for Health Statistics. *National Health Interview Survey*. Hyattsville, Md. 1988.
6 Cathrine M. Malkin and Michael E. Lamb. "Child Maltreatment: A Test of Sociobiological Theory." *Journal of Comparative Family Studies*. Vol. 25, 1994, pp. 121–130.
7 Carolyn Smith and Terence P. Thornberry. "The Relationship Between Childhood Maltreatment and Adolescent Involvement in Delinquency." *Criminology*. Vol. 33, 1995, pp. 451–479.
8 Ronet Bachman. "Violence Against Women." U.S. Department of Justice. Office of Justice Programs. Bureau of Justice Statistics, NCJ-145325. January 1994, p. 6

- The Justice Department also found that never-married women are far more likely to be assaulted than married women, and divorced or separated women are three times more likely to be assaulted than married women.[9]

Taking into consideration all possible variables, a relationship that is being worked on is generally the safest place to be.

MEN

Numerous studies show that marriage is a societal good. A typical study is found in the *American Journal of Sociology* stating married couples have longer lifespans than unmarried people. The author concludes that "for both sexes, the hazard of dying falls significantly with marital duration, suggesting a cumulation of the benefits of marriage over time." Researchers say their findings are hardly surprising: "The relationship between marriage and death rates has now reached the status of a truism, having been observed across numerous societies and various social and demographic groups."[10]

Scholars at the National Institute for Healthcare Research (NIHR) recently compiled a report showing that divorced men are especially likely to experience health problems. When compared to married men, divorced males are twice as likely to die prematurely from hypertension, four times as likely to die prematurely from throat cancer, and seven times as likely to die prematurely from pneumonia.

According to the NIHR, divorced men also have significantly higher rates of depression, substance abuse, auto accidents and suicide. "Being divorced and a nonsmoker is only slightly less dangerous than smoking a pack or more a day and staying married, observes NIHR president Dr. David Larson.

Divorce is not a politically correct topic. We do like our freedom. And there are times when divorce is necessary. But perhaps in light of all of the research, it is time to rewrite the old adage: Married, early to bed, early to rise, makes man, woman and child healthy, wealthy, safe and wise.

---

9 "Criminal Victimization in the United States, 1992." U.S. Department of Justice. Office of Justice Programs. Bureau of Justice Statistics, NCJ-145125. March 1994, p. 30.
10 Lee A. Lillard and Linda J. Waite. "'Till Death Do Us Part': Marital Disruption and Mortality." *American Journal of Sociology* 100 (1995), pp. 1131–1156. Cited in "Living Longer, New Research." *The Family in America*. Rockford Institute. July 1995.

Prescription for Ailing Lovers

Linda Zink[*]

Aday-long seminar, sponsored by UCLA Extension, was billed as an introduction to a five-week course to be offered by Dr. Irene Kassorla during the spring quarter.

Dr. Kassorla's message for the day (aside from telling mothers to "get out of the house, and away from your children" and giving at least one divorcing couple feelings of guilt and inadequacy because they were "throwing their marriage away like Kleenex") was the importance of giving "honest positives."

An "honest positive," Dr. Kassorla explained, is any truthful comment that makes the other person feel good about himself.

For a variety of reasons, Dr. Kassorla said, "even the healthy parent delivers practically no honest positives to his youngster. His folks may be praising him to the sky behind his back, but the kid doesn't know that. Instead, all he gets is the 'nos' and 'don'ts' and criticisms that make the 'no goods' ring up in his head."

Dr. Kassorla came upon the importance of honest positives while doing undergraduate field work in psychology at UCLA Medical Center. After a brief time of watching the autistic children on the ward receive comfort and attention for undesirable behavior, the then-unknown student decided the staff was going about the treatment backwards and as a result was making the parents crazier than they were.

"I'd see a child come in who was a two percent head banger. Because the child was rewarded—or got attention—when he banged his head, he'd be a 100 percent head banger by the end of a month. In the meantime, he was ignored when he did something good or normal."

At least one staff member had confidence in her application of positive reinforcement in the treatment of autistic children. She got a patient and a chance and the result was the first recorded therapeutic interaction with an autistic child.

Dr. Kassorla had similar successes with disturbed adults while pursuing her Ph.D. at the University of London. In one instance, she treated a 52-year-old man who had not spoken for 30 years. Within a month she had him talking again.

"In an hour of therapy, I would give the patient about 200 honest positives and about four negatives. And most of my negatives consisted of not saying anything at all."

---

* Reprinted by permission from Independent Press-Telegram.

Later, Dr. Kassorla began using the honest positive approach in her work with healthy adults. According to more than one audience member who had worked with her, the results of the treatment were "fantastic."

"I guess that I've learned to feel good about myself working with the doctor," one woman said.

"She's really a terrific person," remarked another. "And her method makes sense."

According to Dr. Kassorla, the healthy parent or spouse reverses her ratio of 200 honest positives to four negatives. Most people, she said, confuse giving love with giving directions. They nag or punish when they could be getting better results with honest positives.

Dr. Kassorla admitted, however, that learning to give honest positives isn't easy. She warned the audience, "You will make mistakes, you'll fail nine out of 10 times . . . but when you're successful or even when you catch yourself giving a negative instead of a positive, give yourself a kiss on the cheek."

Although a firm believer in being straight-forward in her dealings, Dr. Kassorla said she never volunteers negative information. When confronted with a situation where she must be honestly negative, she says she precedes any negative statement with three honest positives and follows it up with yet another honest positive. She suggests the same formula for expressing anger.

"I don't below the belt anyone. If the Hunchback of Notre Dame came up and asked me how I liked his back, I wouldn't tell him, 'Look hunchy, beat it.' I'd tell him I liked his smile and his sense of humor or something and then I'd tell him that I really wasn't too fond of his back."

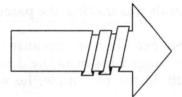

The most important phase of living with a person is respect for that person as an individual. —*M. C. McIntosh*

When Your Ex-Lover Won't Let Go

Sheila Anne Feeney[*]

After being dumped by her husband, a woman bought the $150,000 house next door to him. She devoted her days and nights to watching and annoying her ex. When women visited him she would gather the children and loudly admonish them to look. This was easy, because she had also installed mobile spotlights, which she trained on any woman who visited. The man's attorney was hopeful that he could get a court order to unplug the spotlights, but her scrutiny proved unbearable. Eventually, the man gave up and moved.

The two taut thrillers "Fatal Attraction" and "House of Games" have been drawing box-office crowds who want to see spurned female protagonists get even with men who do not reciprocate their affections.

But while hell hath no fury like a woman scorned, experts say that interpersonal terrorism following a breakup is not the exclusive domain of females. Although expressions of romantic obsession may vary between the sexes (men are more likely to become violent and be direct in their harassment; women are more likely to pen a "poison" letter and act anonymously), both men and women are capable of lashing back at an ex in ways that can range from the self-demeaning to the deadly. The spurned party can vent his rage and despair in acts that can make the former lover's life hell.

Statistics are not kept on the various and subtle forms of terrorism a spurned lover may exact, but there is a feeling that such behavior may be on the rise. "Maybe people are more neurotic," says attorney Raoul Lionel Felder. In nearly three decades of practice "I didn't come across it as much before as I have in the past couple of years."

Dr. Robert Jay Lifton, professor of psychology and psychiatry at City University and John Jay College of Criminal Justice in New York, suggests that such behavior may be attributable to an absence of consistent and clear principles to guide social relationships. A person unfairly victimized in a business deal can seek justice in court, but no tribunal exists to hear crimes of the heart.

"We lack a structural set of social arrangements to resolve severe human and sexual conflict," Lifton says. When there is no way for a person to seek the square shake to which he feels entitled, he is more likely to resort to vigilante-type actions.

Other psychiatrists concur that often it is the lover who feels betrayed and emotionally swindled who is most likely to obsessively seek reconciliation or revenge.

Theories differ over why some people are unable to bounce back from the normal "postdepartum" blues that descend after a loved one bails out, but the capacity for vengeful or bizarre behavior lurks in all of us.

"I've seen well-adjusted people act and do crazy things when they are emotionally distressed about another person with whom they are in a real or imagined relationship," says divorce lawyer Judith Bader-York. Even the most accomplished people, she says, "can engage in unstable behavior."

Lifton suggests that lovers who won't let go "are people who are particularly susceptible to the fear of falling apart. One may see the relationship as one's whole life—and the severance of the relationship can become associated with death."

Violence is most likely, Lifton continues, when the person "feels his or her own life threatened in some actual or symbolic way." When feeling worthless and under duress, he says, rage and anger are safer to experience than the "fear of falling apart."

Even hateful communication can be perversely satisfying to someone suffering from love withdrawal. Felder observes that harassment is often a misguided method for an embittered ex who finds hostile communication more rewarding than none at all.

The problem, [Dr. Edward M.] Shelley explains, is that "it gets you nowhere. It doesn't get your lover back and it doesn't solve anything."

While obsessive thinking may not get someone into the overt trouble that compulsive behavior causes, Shelley points out that it is self-defeating. The lovelorn woman whose mind reels with ruminations about her previous sweetheart is not able to fairly evaluate any other candidates for the vacancy.

Someone who feels emotionally short-circuited from an abrupt breakup may believe that the person who pulled the plug owes them an explanation. A polite phone call to the ex requesting a meeting at his or her convenience—and talking things over without recriminative remarks—can often help heal the wounds.

"It's surprising how many times a jilted lover is able to get a good response" with this method, says Shelley. "It's amazing how reasonable people can be when they are treated reasonably."

Diagnosing Your Relationship

PURPOSE:

To identify strengths and weaknesses of a specific relationship that you are in.

PROCEDURE:

1. Select a relationship that is important to you (family, friend or significant love relationship).
2. For each statement below place an initial on each line as to how it relates to the relationship you have selected.
3. After completing all statements, review each one and analyze how satisfied you feel using the rating scale.

Rating Scale		
S	=	Satisfactory
OK	=	Acceptable but not exceptional
D	=	Somewhat disappointing

You may have marked an item low on the continuum and like it that way. Or you may have marked an item high but feel uncomfortable about it. One person's intimacy is another's anxiety!

1. *Cooperation*
   A. We identify, define and solve our problems together. We respect each other's competence.
      Rarely . . . . Often
   B. We work together as a team without competing or putting each other down.
      Rarely . . . . Often
   C. We make decisions together. We make the most of what each of us has to contribute.
      Rarely . . . . Often
   D. We share our opinions, thoughts and ideas without becoming argumentative or defensive.
      Rarely . . . . Often
   E. Overall, I am satisfied with our mutual respect and cooperation in thinking, deciding and working together.
      Rarely . . . . Often
2. *Compatibility*
   A. We accept and work through our differences to find a common life style with regard to our social and public images.
      Rarely . . . . Often
   B. We accept and work through our differences to find common values with regard to religion, morality, social concerns and politics.
      Rarely . . . . Often

Gerald L. Wilson, Alan M. Hantz and Michael S. Hanna, adapted from *Interpersonal Growth Through Communication*, 1989; William C. Brown Publishers.

C. We accept and work through our differences with regard to our social life and choice of friends.
Rarely . . . . Often

D. We accept and work through our differences so that we are able to share a basic approach to roles and rules.
Rarely . . . . Often

E. Overall, I am satisfied with the way we deal with our differences, maintain a life style and share values.
Rarely . . . . Often

3   *Intimacy*
A. We often play together. We put fun into what we do together.
Rarely . . . . Often

B. We express our emotions and feelings openly and freely. We say that we are scared, sad, hurting, angry or happy.
Rarely . . . . Often

C. We tell each other what we like and dislike. We ask openly for what we want from each other.
Rarely . . . . Often

D. We "let go" with each other. We play, relax and have fun with each other.
Rarely . . . . Often

E. Overall, I am satisfied with the level of openness and intimacy in our relationship.
Rarely . . . . Often

4.   *Emotional Support*
A. We listen, understand and empathize with each other's disappointments, hurts or problems.
Rarely . . . . Often

B. We encourage and support each other when one of us is making basic life changes or trying new behavior.
Rarely . . . . Often

C. We take responsibility for nurturing when either of us is sick or hurting.
Rarely . . . . Often

D. We are emotionally supportive of each other when either of us feels anxious, dependent or in need of care.
Rarely . . . . Often

E. Overall, I am satisfied with the nurturing and support we give to and receive from each other.
Rarely . . . . Often

DISCUSSION:

1.   What relationship strengths were you able to identify from this analysis? What weaknesses?
2.   What communication areas would you like to work on in this relationship?
3.   Overall, how satisfied are you with the information you have discovered about this relationship and why?
4.   What have you learned from this analysis that can enhance other significant relationships in your life?

Ad Inexplorata

As I travel
Baggage becomes heavier
until you offer your hand
guide my belongings with ease
with a smile.
I project a future of smiles,
move toward a long flight
together—side by side yet,
we each have a window seat.
Suddenly, I want nothing
but the view—open space, brightness.
I soar away, ask for blanket,
to place my barriers.
Unknowingly you drift.
The turbulence grows.
Jet engines, the constant roar
of life, work together
toward a flight of success.
We both hear, if we listen
I close the window shade halfway
you float back in
our defenses are down
we engage in the landing.

By permission, *Tracy Schleder*

Self-Disclosure Questionnaire

PURPOSE:

To discover how much of ourselves we disclose to other people.

To realize that different people affect what and how much we disclose of ourselves.

PROCEDURE:

1. The answer sheet on the following pages has columns with the headings "Mother," "Father," "Sibling" (brother or sister), "Female Friend," "Male Friend," "Spouse," and "Significant Other."
2. You are to read each item on the questionnaire; then indicate on the answer sheet the extent that you have talked about each item to the person, that is, the extent to which you have made yourself known to that person. Use the rating scale provided.
3. Be sure to think of only one person in each category throughout the entire survey. Do not, for example, skip from one friend to another. Select one person for each category and then answer according to what you have talked about with the person.

ATTITUDES AND OPINIONS

1. What I think and feel about religion, my personal views.
2. My personal opinions and feelings about religious groups other than my own (e.g., Protestants, Catholics, Jews, atheists, etc.).
3. My views on the present government—the president, government, policies, etc.
4. My personal views on sexual morality—how I feel that I and others ought to behave in sexual matters.
5. My views on the question of racial integration in schools, transportation, etc.
6. My views on social movements (e.g., women's rights, gay liberation, ecology action, affirmative action, etc.).

TASTES AND INTERESTS

7. My favorite foods, the way I like food prepared and my food dislikes.
8. The kinds of movies that I like to see best, the TV shows that are my favorites.
9. The style of house, and the kinds of furnishings that I like best.
10. The kind of party or social gathering that I like best, and the kind that bore me or that I wouldn't enjoy.
11. My favorite ways of spending spare time (e.g., hunting, reading, cards, sports events, parties, dancing, etc.).
12. To what extent I use alcohol/drugs.

WORK (OR STUDIES)

13. What I find to be the worst pressures and strains in my work.
14. What I feel are **my** shortcomings and handicaps that prevent me from working as I'd like to, or that prevent me from getting further ahead in my work.
15. How I feel that my work is appreciated by others (e.g., boss, fellow workers, teacher, husband, etc.).

16. How I feel about the choice of career that I have made, whether or not I am satisfied with it.
17. How I really feel about the people that I work for, or work with.
18. My own strengths and weaknesses as an employee.

MONEY

19. Whether or not I owe money, if so, how much?
20. All of my present sources of income (e.g., wages, fees, allowances, etc.).
21. My total financial worth, including property, savings bonds, insurance, etc.
22. My most pressing need for money right now (e.g., outstanding bills, some major purchase that is desired or needed).
23. How I budget my money, the proportion that goes to necessities, etc.
24. To what extent money is important to me.

PERSONALITY

25. The aspects of my personality that I dislike, worry about, that I regard as a handicap to me.
26. Things in the past or present that I feel ashamed or guilty about.
27. What it takes to get me really worried, anxious and afraid.
28. What it takes to hurt my feelings deeply.
29. The kinds of things that make me especially proud of myself, elated, full of esteem and self-respect.
30. The things about my personality that I would really like to change.

BODY

31. How I wish I looked, my ideals for overall appearance.
32. Whether or not I have any long-range worries about health (e.g., cancer).
33. My present physical measurements (e.g., height, weight, waist, etc.).
34. My feelings about my adequacy in sexual behavior, whether or not I feel able to perform adequately in sex-relationships.
35. Whether or not I have any health problems (e.g., allergies, headaches, heart condition, etc.).
36. The physical characteristics I admire about myself.

BEHAVIOR

37. What the various roles that I "act out" are.
38. The extent to which I like or dislike these roles.
39. Which role is most like me and why.
40. The extent to which society's stereotyping influences my behavior and interaction with other people.
41. To what extent do I play "games" in order to be socially accepted.
42. To what extent tactile communication (touching) plays in my communication behavior.

Communication

43. To what extent do I say what I am really thinking at the time.
44. To what extent do I use profanity for shock value.
45. To what extent I use nonverbal communication for social gain (e.g., possessions, dress, appearance, cues, etc.).
46. My strengths relative to self-confidence in expressing my opinions.
47. The aspects of my communication I like (e.g., straightforward, clarity, organized, etc.).
48. Whether I am self-conscious about speaking in public or not and why.

Self-Disclosure Rating Scale

3	I have talked in full and complete detail about this item to the other person. This person knows me fully in this respect, and could describe me accurately.
2	I have talked specifically to this person, yet have felt hesitant to talk in complete detail. This person knows me well, but not fully in this respect.
1	I have talked in general terms about this item. The other person has only a general idea about this aspect of me.
0	I have told the other person nothing about this aspect of me.
–3	I have lied or misrepresented myself to the other person about this aspect of me.

Self-Disclosure: Answer Sheet

	Mother	Father	Sibling	Female Friend	Male Friend	Spouse	Significant Other
1							
2							
3							
4							
5							
6							
7							
8							
9							
10							

	Mother	Father	Sibling	Female Friend	Male Friend	Spouse	Significant Other
12							
13							
14							
15							
16							
17							
18							
19							
20							
21							
22							
23							
24							
26							
27							
28							
29							
30							
31							
32							
33							
34							
35							
36							
37							
38							
39							
40							
41							

	Mother	Father	Sibling	Female Friend	Male Friend	Spouse	Significant Other
42							
43							
44							
45							
46							
47							
48							
Totals							

DISCUSSION:

1. Who do you reveal yourself to the most?
2. What is it about these relationships that causes you to reveal yourself?
3. Who do you reveal yourself to the least?
4. Do the roles that you and the other people assume in your daily lives affect your self-disclosure in your relationships with them?
5. What kinds of things do you reveal the most? The least?
6. Does the amount of self-disclosure with each person satisfy you, or should there be more self-disclosure with certain people and less self-disclosure with others?
7. Did the results of the questionnaire surprise you? If so, how/why?

Too Close for Comfort—
A Rising Fear of Intimacy

Cathy Lawhon[*]

Newport Beach psychotherapist Dr. Pat Allen defines intimacy as "being willing to make and keep contracts and commitments." Unfortunately, she and colleague Dr. James Prescott say, fewer and fewer people are willing to make and keep agreements. And those who are trying are struggling.

"People are phobic about intimacy, either physical intimacy, mental intimacy or both," says Allen, a prominent speaker and therapist who describes herself as a blend of feminist Gloria Steinem and Marabelle Morgan of *Total Woman* fame. "Some people are phobic at the initiation level, where they are not willing to even make the contract. They're the casualties. Then there are people who tentatively make the contract, then pull out of it."

The intimacy outlook wasn't always this grim. But single-parent families, dual-career families bent on acquiring status and possessions, the sexual freedom encouraged by birth control and the repression of sexual pleasure imposed by monotheistic religions have helped to create a society that all too often finds intimacy painful, Allen and Prescott say.

The discomfort with intimacy begins at the physical level and extends to the emotional level.

"Because we don't know how to be physical," Allen says, "we don't know how to be emotional. We are animals first. We have to start with bodies and then work our way up to human."

"A useful model," the Irvine-based Prescott says, "is to go back to a baby and look at the intimacy and spontaneity, joy and happiness that come from that very close physical relationship with the mother and that very basic caring and nurturing and compassion. Those things influence very much the kind of commitments they'll be able to make.

"That's where Shere Hite (in her recently released book *Women and Love)* so misses the boat by dumping on men as being solely responsible for the lack of intimacy," Prescott continues. "She diminishes the very important role of women as mothers."

Children raised without touching and physical intimacy develop an aversion to or an avoidance of intimacy, says Prescott, who experimented with isolation-reared monkeys during his 1966–1980 stint with the National Institute of Child Health and Human Development in Bethesda, Md.

---

[*] By permission, *Orange County Register*

"For monkeys, pleasure becomes pain, affection becomes violence," Prescott says. "Humans experience that to a lesser degree, developing an impairment to experiencing pleasure through intimacy."

Like the monkeys who grew up without mothers, infants in dysfunctional families become adults with a limited capacity for intimacy. Few parents purposely deprive their children of physical intimacy. But pressures of modern society sometimes make it difficult, especially for single parents, to give them adequate attention.

"If you go to a grade school now, 64 percent of the kids are raised in one-parent homes," Allen says. "Every little girl under age 10 who doesn't have tactile closeness to her father is going to be a deprived, hostile female. These abandoned girls are turning into castrating females who are producing castrated males. We're going in circles.

"Little boys have an over-connection with mother. That little boy has an inability to give. If a boy is raised with Dad, he's got his role model, but is disconnected from mother."

Babies who spend eight to ten hours a day in infant care centers while both parents work grow to distrust intimate relationships too.

"There's no way these kids are getting their emotional needs and basic trust met," Prescott says. "They're lined up in those cribs and they become apathetic and depressed. Infants need to be held and stroked and moved. And they need that intimate connection of breast feeding with the mother."

In Jungian terms, the child growing up with two career people is stuck in a family of two fathers, Allen adds.

"I say that in a healthy family, one of the members has to be responsible for the status and security. In our culture that has been the man. The other member is responsible for the sensuous and sexual needs of the family. In many families, nobody is doing the sensuous and sexual except for the little Mexican lady who's coming in from Tijuana. And she may be an absolute love and may indeed be a lifesaver for these kids. But you've still got a real screwed-up deal here."

Is it possible for both mother and father to provide status and security and fill the sensual and sexual needs of the family? Absolutely, Allen responds. It's even OK if the dad fulfills the sensuous and sexual needs. But neither scenario is common. "In our money-grubbing society," she says, "we value money and power more than love."

Ironically, however, sexual freedom for women has also aided the demise of intimacy, Allen says.

"I believe we're still reverberating off the (birth control) pill movement," she says. "When women became capable of casual sex, it immediately lifted sanctions that used to require women to be very, very careful about the reason they had sex. Men and women could both practice casual sex, which negated intimacy. I'm teaching women to know their integrity and what their standards are, then stand by it. You don't go to bed (with a man) until you have longevity, exclusivity and continuity."

While the dearth of intimacy diminishes happiness within marriages and other romantic relationships, on the job and between friends, it also profoundly affects society. Prescott maintains that children who are deprived of intimate, physical contact become violent adults who abuse spouses, children and themselves.

"Studies suggest that during formative periods of brain growth," Prescott says, "certain kinds of sensory deprivation—such as lack of touching and rocking by the mother—result in incomplete or damaged development of the neuronal systems that control affection.

"Since the same systems influence brain centers associated with violence, in a mutually inhibiting mechanism, the deprived infant may have difficulty controlling violent impulses as an adult."

Self-abuse shows up in the addiction to alcohol and drugs, even suicide.

"Children in non-bonding families have what we call ontological insecurity," Allen says. "It's a disbelief in their right to exist. It's the precursor for schizophrenia or depersonalization. It leads to the ability to die without regard."

"And people are drowning their emotional pain in drugs and alcohol," Prescott adds. "They're stuck in the gratification phase, and that's the only way they can get it."

Unfortunately, Allen and Prescott can suggest no quick-fix solutions to becoming a more intimate and less troubled society, short of increasing general awareness. It's a huge task that they try to tackle by sponsoring day-long training sessions for intimacy and affectional bonding. Allen also hosts free group-therapy hours at 7:30 p.m. every Wednesday at a neighborhood community center, where she gets "about 500 people a night asking questions about how to find love."

But a meaningful move toward a more intimate society must begin with providing loving, stable environments for children, they say.

"The only appropriate reason for divorce is violence, or if you're becoming physically, mentally or emotionally ill in the relationship. And I mean certifiably ill as diagnosed by a doctor or therapist," Allen says. "Any other reason is based on some egocentric, prideful decision about what is expected and what is assumed."

Prescott's other suggestions for raising happy, intimate humans include making sure the child is wanted.

"I like to use the foreign-language analogy," Prescott says. "Any newborn can learn any language in the world and speak it like a native if it's exposed to the language in the period of brain development for encoding language. But once you pass a certain point, there is no longer a neural blueprint for that language and the child will always speak it like a foreigner with an accent."

Relationship Roles

PURPOSE:

To examine the different purposes that different significant relationships serve in our lives.

PROCEDURE:

1. For each situation below list three people whom you would select to meet the situation.
2. List these people in the order of whom you would call on first, second and third.
3. Explain why you picked each person.

Situation:

You are stranded 200 miles from home and need someone to drive your brand new sports car to you. Whom would you ask?

Person	Reason
1.	
2.	
3.	

Situation:

You are going out of town for two weeks and need someone to stay at your house and take care of your pets. Whom would you ask?

Person	Reason
1.	
2.	
3.	

Situation:

You have been offered another job and feel very uncertain about taking it. Whom would you discuss this with?

Person	Reason
1.	
2.	
3.	

Situation:

You just broke up with a person that none of your friends or family likes very well. Whom would you share the news with?

Person **Reason**

1.

2.

3.

Situation:

You have just been informed that you are the winner of the Readers' Digest Sweepstakes. Whom would you tell?

Person **Reason**

1.

2.

3.

DISCUSSION:

1. Was it difficult selecting people for any of the situations? Why or why not?
2. How does the situation change the way we communicate with others?
3. What did you learn about these relationships and the roles they play in your life?

Connections

1. Smile! It makes your face light up and your eyes sparkle.

2. Say hello to strangers. It feels good to be acknowledged.

3. Look people in the eye when you are with them. Show them they are your present priority.

4. Remember and use people's names when you speak to them. It makes them feel valued.

5. Focus on the positive. Everyone has something to contribute that is useful.

6. Praise freely—but require a request for criticism.

7. Be tolerant. There are as many opinions and preferences as there are people.

8. Give freely to others. The best reward is knowing you have made a difference.

9. Be enthusiastic. Passion is contagious and magnetic.

10. Have patience. Have you ever had a bad day?

R E A C T I O N S

1. List three examples of relationships in your life where your communication has been influenced by the stage each relationship is in. Describe how communication is used in these relationships.

2. What kinds of barriers do you encounter that make it difficult to maintain important relationships?

3. How does self-disclosure influence your relationships?

4. How does understanding the role of communication in relationships help you establish and maintain meaningful relationships in your life?

Job Search Skills

DEFINITIONS

A perfect time to apply your communication skills is during the job search process. For example, the networking process will afford you an opportunity to use both your verbal and nonverbal skills as you meet people who will give you information about their particular field and perhaps help you join them in that world. Clear and thoughtful writing in your cover letter and resume will attract attention of prospective employers who will invite you to an interview. Finally, the employment interview offers you the opportunity to manage both your verbal and nonverbal communication skills.

✴ Cover Letter

A letter adapted for a particular end which highlights one's background with specific items that most relate to the needs of a prospective employer. You tailor your experiences to the employer's anticipated needs.

✴ Resume

A selective, well-organized synopsis of your education, accomplishments and special skills. The resume is a brief sales device designed to communicate your value as an employee.

✴ Networking

The art of making and using contacts who can help you reach your objective. You identify people who can supply you with important information and resources.

✴ Employment Interviewing

A highly concentrated face-to-face meeting designed to determine the interviewee's qualifications and determine a job "fit."

———————— ✩ ✩ ✩ ————————

THE IMPORTANCE OF JOB SEARCH SKILLS

The Bureau of Labor Statistics estimates that the average worker will have six employers in the course of a lifetime. The average worker searches for a job once every three to four years.

Generally, the harder you work at job hunting the quicker you will find employment. Many people begin the job search process and fail to compete in today's workplace because they are ill equipped without a basic understanding of how to network, write a resume and conduct themselves in an interview.

BARRIERS TO GETTING A JOB

In this section, we will present the major mistakes that prevent job seekers from getting hired.

10- TO 12-HOUR WORK WEEK

For a person who is unemployed, job hunting should be a 40-hour work week. You must not burn out after a few hours to return home to wait for that "phone call." You must talk to people to get leads. Don't be surprised if you meet someone who will change your life.

FAILURE TO NETWORK

Networking is making and using contacts. Job hunters are not always willing to develop and pursue leads from contacts. Friends and acquaintances will give you referrals which are most effective job sources.

CANNED OR POOR RESUMES

You must get an interview to be hired. In order to get an interview you must write a well-prepared resume and a cover letter which is original and well-focused. These items are screening devices for the personnel department. You will be eliminated from consideration as an applicant if they don't indicate you are qualified and would be a good employee. This initial impression is an indication of what can be expected from you after you are hired.

POOR INTERVIEW TECHNIQUES AND/OR PREPARATION

Good physical appearance creates a positive self-image and self-respect. You must reflect a positive attitude. During the interview you must listen attentively and sell yourself by showing enthusiasm. You must communicate that you know and care about the job. Your responses must address the specific needs of the employer. It requires preparation to discover the problems of the person who has the responsibility to pick you for the position in the organization. It is most important to practice interviewing.

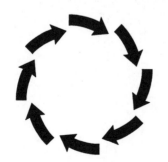

The impossible is often the untried. —*J. Goodwon*

NETWORKING

One key element which promotes professional success is networking. Networking refers to establishing contacts with individuals who can help you succeed in your endeavors. Many jobs are attained through word-of-mouth rather than through classified advertisements. Thus, the more people you know that are in related fields the better chances you have at being successful. How does one network? Four specific ways include colleges and professors, part-time jobs, organizations and volunteering.

Going to college and doing well is important for many career opportunities. When you go to a four-year college or university, you should ideally pick the best college you can for your major field of study. You should distinguish yourself in that program by achieving rank in the top 10 percent of your class. You should also get to know and work with and for your professors and prove your abilities to them so they will be willing to recommend you when you graduate. Remember, these are important people who are well networked. You should also have one or more of these people become your mentor. Mentors are guides who help you make the right moves to be successful. Thus, do not just attend school and go home!

Another suggestion while in college is to become active in campus activities, organizations, athletics, student governments, etc. Many organizations look for these kinds of involvement because they want well-rounded individuals working for them.

Getting a part-time job in the field you want to enter while you are going through college can be a great help in being successful. For example, if you are majoring in accounting, get a job with an accounting firm. The biggest and/or best would be ideal. While there you should become the best part-time employee the company has ever had. For example, arrive at work early; leave late and work hard. Even if your job is a low level one to start you will be distinguishing yourself as a unique person and will advance and quite possibly create a good position for

yourself within that company. Perhaps you will also find someone in a position above you who will become a mentor. You should also look for positions the company may not have and create that position which you feel they need and you can fill. Then go sell it to management—many people obtain very good jobs through this method.

Organizations are an excellent way to network, especially if you take leadership positions within them and become known as a "doer" who is committed and successful. Examples of organizations in which you could become active are clubs associated with your major in college. For example, if you are a finance major, join the finance club and become an officer such as the president. Become a very active leader and do things such as bringing onto the campus successful professional people in your field to speak to your group. Get to know these people and impress them. There are also state and national organizations which are affiliated with your major field. For example, future teachers may want to become student members of groups such as the National Education Association and California Teachers Association.

Becoming involved in civic organizations is also a good idea. Examples are Rotary, Lions, Kiwanis, Soroptimist, American Association of University Women and breakfast business networking clubs. In these organizations you are not only networking with successful people, you also have the opportunity to "give back" to your community through service projects.

Volunteering is another way to "give back" to your community as well as get to know other successful people. You may want to volunteer in political campaigns, hospitals, Special Olympics, Red Cross, United Way, for example.

In summary, networking is important to your professional success. Not only do you become acquainted with people, you contribute to your community and expand your social skills and build lasting friendships.

The 1-2-3s of Resume Update

Dianne Vozoff[*]

Let's face facts: it's the rare professional who likes to while away the hours pondering the subtleties of an old resume. Once you're comfortable in the right job, basic instinct seems always to point you toward the nearest closet and its highest shelf, where the pitiful thing can be stashed for future use. If you're curious about your own knack for translating career know-how and personal charm onto looseleaf paper, take a few minutes and quiz yourself.

True	False		
_____	_____	1.	The cardinal rule to effective resume writing is: More is Better.
_____	_____	2.	The best resume extensively outlines all your professional achievements.
_____	_____	3.	A career objective at the beginning of your resume is not necessary because the thrust of the entire document should suggest your professional ambitions.
_____	_____	4.	What's in your resume must always take precedence over how it's said.
_____	_____	5.	A good resume is flexible enough to cover various job options within your professional field of interest.
_____	_____	6.	A well-done resume paints a clear sketch of who you are as a person—your height, weight, race, age, sex, marital status and hobbies—so that an employer will know whether or not you're right for the company.
_____	_____	7.	Employers like to see that you're a person concerned with things other than just your job, so always include as much volunteer work, continued education and association involvements as possible.

True	False		
———	———	8.	All resumes should contain the complete names, addresses and telephone numbers of personal and professional references.
———	———	9.	Even the best resume tends to get boring, but you can relieve the drudgery by varying visual format and mixing grammatical style.
———	———	10.	To help your resume stand out from the hundreds an employer may receive, have it printed on an extra-heavy, tastefully colored paper stock. Consider a distinctive typeface and a unique layout.
———	———	11.	Asking friends and professional associates to read and critique your resume is not always a good idea because their input can easily confuse you and cloud essential issues.
———	———	12.	Your resume should be accompanied by a cover letter if you're sending it out "cold," but if it's sent in response to a specific ad, the employer will know why you're sending it.
———	———	13.	A cover letter is primarily intended to repeat the more pertinent points of your resume.
———	———	14.	It may take a lot of hard work, but it's possible to write a resume good enough to secure for you the job you want.
———	———	15.	It's necessary to spend the time and money to update your resume only when you're actively seeking a job.

(See answers in article below)

The truth of the matter is that a resume is a resume is a resume, and there's only so much that can be done with anyone's. It's equally true, however, that if you're ever to be a fully active and prepared executive, you need one—and a good one—on hand, all the time. An up-to-date resume not only guarantees you immediate application to any worthwhile career opening that should come your way, it forces you to begin the process that all successful professionals must eventually master: regular assessment of what you've accomplished, what you're doing right now and where you want to head from here.

The most important thing to remember when you're updating is that you're doing just that: updating, not extending. At every step along the way, be prepared to discard items which five years ago were relevant, even brilliant, but no longer help to reinforce your professional profile. Just because you've been involved in a particular field for 17 years, don't assume that you need a page of resume to reflect each 12-month period. Edit. And edit again. Then type the whole thing and edit some more. That's the key to successfully updating.

In case you're straining at the bit over the results to this little quiz, you should know that the answer to every question is "False." Each illustrates a popular myth in resume lore, and as such, each is a trick question designed to make you doubt what you thought you knew, might have known or just plain guessed to be the case. If you answered "True" to any of the questions, you're heading for a foolhardy move come resume season. And a wrong resume move can produce only a limited number of consequences—all of them unnerving, unsatisfying or simply uneventful.

With such murky terrain ahead, would you care for a pointer or two?

1. The resume rule of thumb is not "More is Better." 2–3 pages is a good length.

Don't ramble, don't try to overimpress. No resume should be a three-ring circus enticing, enthralling and entertaining employers beyond the boundaries of human imagination. Be sedate, be professional, be concise. That's what employers look to find. So, again, edit until you have one solid, representational page of professionalism.

2. Falling for the misconception that a good resume must extensively outline all professional achievements is how so many people end up with one the length of Fifth Avenue. A strong resume gets down to basics immediately, and it highlights only those professional achievements which strengthen candidacy for the available position. Although there are exceptions to the rule, those achievements (if you have them under your belt at all) are usually your most recent. You should mention a major career success from, say, 10 years ago only if it can dramatically reinforce an image of progress, dedication and expertise.

Again, remember to edit for professionalism, not ego gratification. Even if the project you managed was outrageously impressive, 14 years ago is a long time. Don't continue to commit it to paper if it doesn't help to pull your resume together today. Be content that you, a few close friends and a grateful former employer know the secret.

3. You should always—repeat, always—state a career objective at the beginning of your resume or in your cover letter. If you take nothing else from this simple exercise, remember at least this one fundamental rule. And if the best objective you can think of is "Finding an interesting position with a growing company," go back to your scratch pad and begin again.

A well-written career objective at the beginning of your resume or cover letter tells any employer that you know what you want from your next job. Employers like that sort of professional focus—provided you make your interests relevant to theirs. Be specific. Your professionalism will be reflected in how articulately you can state your own ambitions.

When you first sit down to update your resume, spend a lot of time on the career objective statement. Keep reworking it until you're satisfied that it does in fact say something and that it accurately reflects your current goals. In essence, if your career objective is clear and tight, all other updating work will fall automatically into place. Each word that follows will be included to support that initially stated career aim. Without this essential element, your resume can only meander through years of 9-to-5. And the people least fooled into thinking you'd be a good addition to a growing company will be those employers you'd like most to impress.

Remember, too, your career objective should change every so often—if for no other reason than that you've theoretically reached the goals you set for yourself five years ago. When you sit down to review your resume and find that, even after all this time, you're no closer to reaching your old goal, it's a good thing you've decided to work on your resume. Because you need a new job.

4. What's in your resume is more important than how it's said. Wrong. Ironically, how you explain what you've done is, in the end, far more important than the achievements themselves. This is not to say that professional achievements are irrelevant. They do, after all, explain why you're presenting a resume in the first place. But you must convey your ability in a way which is meaningful to employers and makes them notice you for what you've accomplished.

Think of it this way: if you've bothered to go through all the effort involved in updating the content of your resume, you might as well go the next step and upgrade the way in which you convey your accomplishments. Action words. That tired old resume phrase must take on a lively meaning now. The more experienced you are, the more powerful your words must be. In updating, make sure your resume uses words that reflect responsibility, management authority, commitment, growth, strength and intelligence.

5. No resume is flexible enough to cover all bases. After years of professional experience, you've no doubt accumulated varied enough knowledge and expertise to confuse even yourself—if you were to read it all in a list.

As you prune your old resume to make room for more pertinent information, categorize professional experience. Chances are, all past positions have afforded growth in several areas. Then you can draft several resumes, each highlighting different areas of experience. In this way, you're likely to discover the need for two, three, maybe even four different resumes, each one supporting different career objectives and relevant to different fields and companies.

A multi-purpose resume is a lazy resume. It says too little to an employer and doesn't help you much in understanding your own professional growth. Instead, keep several up-to-date and specific resumes on file. They will allow you the luxury of career mobility. When you see an ad or arrange for an informal interview, you can choose the best resume from your repertoire and then tailor it further, if necessary, to the specific company.

This approach also has a hidden advantage: if, as you categorize, you see that you've accumulated years of employment but no transferable skill, you're on your way to escaping the dreaded Professional Rut.

6. If you're bothering to tell a prospective employer your weight, height, race, age, marital status and hobbies, you might just as well include your favorite dessert and brand of laundry detergent. People tend to include this sort of information to illustrate how well they'd fit into the employer's corporate image. The problem is obvious: what if you miss the mark? Unless you're absolutely sure that Widget Manufacturing is looking specifically for people

into sky diving, don't mention it on your resume. List your credentials and let them call you in for an interview based on those impeccable qualifications.

7. It's not always wise to indicate a lot of volunteer experience, association memberships or even continued education on your resume. When you first start your career, it's crazy not to include it on resume. But as you become more seasoned, more specialized and more professionally sophisticated, employers like to see your resume reflect almost obsessive dedication to your work. Too much volunteer experience or association activity can reflect poorly on your image as a top-flight professional. As you update your work experience and find the need to include more and more career information, delete the "extras" from your resume. This doesn't mean going whole hog and listing nothing at all; it means listing with discretion.

For example, if you're interested strictly in socially oriented work and feel confident that employer interest would be piqued if they knew that you were black, then continue until retirement to list your NAACP membership. Likewise, mention of a prestigious professional association membership couldn't hurt.

8. List 3–5 references in alphabetical order. List them by name, title, business address and phone number. Use people with crdibility such as past employers, professors in your major, etc.

9. The only boring resume is one which says nothing. Even if it's laden with impressive experience and the most remarkable design since the wheel, your resume will turn off an employer if it's written with inconsistent verb tenses or poor sentence structure. It should be easy to read, say what must be said, and then end. Period. Mixing style and repeating information is not the solution to a boring resume. Instead, rewrite it and tighten it up until it speaks fluent Actionese. That's what makes a resume exciting. At its hard-nosed core, a resume is a document, not an original work of art.

10. Be unique. Use a pastel color paper or an original design. Do not hand in a resume that looks like everyone else's.

Again, updating your resume means increasing its ability to quickly communicate your professional value. If you try to bowl recipients over with scented, cobalt blue parchment that's been embossed with your family's coat of arms and then covered with fancy Gothic type, you'll succeed. They will be bowled over. And your resume will bowl right along with them directly into the nearest wastepaper basket.

11. If you don't feel that you can ask your friends and associates to read and criticize your resume without confusing or clouding issues, then perhaps you've aligned yourself with the wrong people. These are precisely the individuals who know you—perhaps no better than you know yourself, but certainly more objectively. They are the people who understand your field. You've worked with them and shared important achievements with them. If you must, chase them down and corner them in your den with hot coffee until two in the morning. But get them to read your resume and help you update your new composite. If you find their help confusing, then you were already confused. Use their input as a beacon light leading you out of a dark and dangerous fog.

12. You always need to send a cover letter with your resume! Whether you're mailing it "cold" or in response to a specific ad, a cover letter must accompany every resume you send out because most employers will look for it. And they'll be unfavorably impressed if it's missing. Besides, a clear, friendly, profes-

sional, sparingly informative letter will reinforce your image of experience, confidence and know-how.

13. Not only is it not the primary purpose of a cover letter to recapitulate your resume, but at no time should it rehash information that's available elsewhere. The cover letter gives you your moment to shine. That's the appropriate place for revealing just a little of your unique personality (you know, the one that's going to be an intelligent addition to the company). If your resume is a formal document—and it should be—think of your cover letter as a short conversation: here you can highlight something of special significance in your resume. If you're at a total loss for words, just say hello and-please-get-back-to-me. But to recapitulate what's already on your resume adds nothing to your chances of getting an interview. It's a waste of time—yours and the employer's.

14. Perhaps the most common career development myth is that a really good resume can secure a worthwhile job. No resume can do that, so don't design or expect yours to accomplish the impossible. Nobody is hired because of their resume, only interviewed. The best professional resume is a sophisticated, modern-day calling card. As such, its sole function is to take you another step toward the personal interview setting. And there, in that one-to-one interaction, you will no doubt enlighten the employer to the indisputable fact that, yes indeed, you are the best candidate for the job.

15. Even if you're happily employed at a company which seems to offer unlimited growth potential, you should still take your resume out once a year, dust it off and read it as if you had just been canned. Could you send it out with only a single date change? If so, you're not growing. The energy you expend updating is never wasted, only stored for wiser, future use.

In professional circles, there is a right and a wrong way of doing just about everything. But there is room for self-expression—provided you express who you are in language which employers understand. Following the suggestions outlined in this article is only a beginning to the long process of updating your resume. As you work and rework your composite, you'll find that rules which at first seemed rigid become magically flexible. That's as it should be. Bend them, twist them, stand them on their heads until they feel right to you. But never be so bold as to break them outright. Unless, of course, you want your career to gather dust just like a useful resume—the one forgotten on your closet shelf.

RATING SCALE

If you answered "False" to all 15 quiz questions, even if you got a couple wrong, consider yourself a whiz kid. If you're currently employed at anything other than book editing for a career development publishing house, you're hiding a needed light under a bushel basket.

10–12   False answers puts you in the Resume Titan category. You're obviously one of the big kids.

7–9   False answers suggest that you're in need of some brush-up reading. But don't feel bad; most of us are only human.

6   False answers or less and you're a sad statistic, a Resume Monkey. Have another banana and hire a professional to write your resume for you.

Cover Letters and Resumes

PURPOSE:

To examine sample cover letters and different types of resumes.

PROCEDURE:

1. Read the resume guidelines and sections listed below.
2. Read and consider the one sample cover letter.
3. Consider and compare the three sample resumes. Bear in mind that the format should match the nature of the job.
4. Correct the one problem cover letter.
5. Correct the one problem resume.

DISCUSSION:

1. What factors influence the choice of a resume format?
2. What is the purpose of a cover letter?
3. How does one decide what to include in the resume? The cover letter?

Note: Always keep a copy of any letter/resume you send. You may want to refer to such information later when you are called for the interview. You may also want to build on either item as a rough draft the next time out.

RESUME PREPARATION GUIDELINES

Do's

1. Keep to two pages (maximum).
2. Use quality paper and type it or print it.
3. Make it succinct, impactful and use "action" words. (It should sound "exciting.")
4. Remember, it is a "sales" tool.
5. Type it very neatly, preferably using a computer program such as Word. Lay it out carefully. Format and readability are important. (Some programs have templates for resumes.)
6. Keep it in the third person; make it "flow."
7. List career objective, education (if degreed), experience (with most recent chronological items first) and miscellaneous.
8. Show favorable information.
9. Write in short sentences and in plain English.
10. Proofread it!

DON'TS

1. List salary data/history. (Use separate sheet if requested.)
2. Be too wordy and too long.
3. Use "I," "me," etc.
4. Show information which could be unfavorable.
5. List sex, age, marriage status, or hobbies.
6. Falsify information. (Think about what is not said.)
7. Put anything in unless it puts you in a favorable light.
8. List race, number of children, religion-related information.
9. Try to use one resume for a "catch-all" which will suffice for any and all types of jobs.

SECTIONS TO BE INCLUDED IN YOUR RESUME

Personal Information
    Name
    Address
    Phone(s)
    Objective: As specifically as possible describe which position you want to fill (You can put this in your cover letter.)

Educational Background (list first only if you have no work experience)
    Schools Attended (most recent first)
    Dates of Attendance
    Degrees Awarded/Major
    Honors Received
    Grade Point Average (If to your advantage)

Work Experience Data (list before education if you have work experience)
    Places of Employment (most recent first)
    Your Job Title(s)
    Work accomplishments (use action verbs)
    Inclusive Dates of Each Employment (year only)

Professional/Honorary Associations in which you hold memberships

Interests and Hobbies (anything you can do well)

COVER LETTERS

A cover letter should accompany a resume. The cover letter is extremely important because it can generate an interest in you as a candidate for a job. You need to be as specific as possible and use appropriate examples of what you have done in order to catch the attention of the reader.

East Willow Ave.
Inglewood, CA 90027
April 15, 1998

Personnel Director
The Irvine Company
Newport Center Dr.
Newport Beach, CA 92663

Sir:

I wish to express my interest in the position of Personnel Representative which I saw advertised in the *L.A. Times.* I fulfill all of the basic qualifications listed in the position description. I have two years of experience working in the Personnel Department at Hughes Aircraft. As Assistant to the Director of Human Resources at a large school district, I also had the opportunity to become experienced in the area of training and development. In addition to these skills, I have screened, interviewed, and referred candidates for employment in a wide variety of job classifications.

I currently hold an A.A. Degree in Business Management and will receive my B.A. in June with Personnel Administration as my major. I minored in economics and have a fine mix of academic preparation and practical experience for success in a business-related environment.

My resume details the above mentioned experience as well as other skills I possess that may also be attractive to your company. I look forward to meeting with you to discuss in depth my abilities and your company's needs. I will call you in two weeks.

Thank you for your time and consideration.

_____

Gary B. Swelt

Home Phone: (310) 432-1167
Bus. Phone: (714) 911-7621

Enclosure

SAMPLE RESUME 1

Roberta Tracy
Walnut St.
Colleyville TX 76000
Home Phone: (817) 498-3775
Work Phone: (817) 597-9086

OBJECTIVE: A professional level position in personnel

EXPERIENCE   Over 17 years of general personnel experience in business and industry
SUMMARY: with specialization in college recruiting.

EXPERIENCE:

1983–Present   Miller-Berger Construction
                   Employment Representative

                   Responsible for recruitment, selection and placement of all
                   company employees as well as new employee orientation.
                   Accomplishments: Designed college recruitment brochure to attract
                   college graduates to company management positions. Designed and
                   implemented new employee orientation.

1979–1983   Colleyville Water and Power
                   Employment Clerk-Interviewer

                   Responsible for accepting and screening applications, writing
                   follow-up correspondence and interviewing clerical personnel.
                   Accomplishments: Designed interview follow-up letters as well as
                   interview appraisal sheet. Administered and scheduled typing tests.
                   Participated in new employee orientation.

1978–1979   St. Theresa's Hospital
                   Employment Clerk

                   Responsible for accepting and filing applications and Equal
                   Employment Opportunity cards as well as preparing and delivering
                   weekly jobline phone message.
                   Accomplishments: Developed efficient application filing system.
                   Designed internal job posting format and system.

EDUCATION: A.A. Speech Communication, Austin Community College 1994
                   B.A. Business, Baylor University (in progress)

MISCELLANEOUS:

Dean's Honor Roll 1993 and 1994
   • Officer: Student Speech Communication Association
   • Member: Personnel and Industrial Relations Association (PIRA)

SAMPLE RESUME 2

Gary B. Swelt
Portray Place
Orange, CA 92633
(714) 499-7621

CAREER OBJECTIVE

Personnel Management

Personnel Administration

- Monitored performance evaluations
- Assisted in wage and salary upgrades
- Supervised clerical staff of three job classifications
- Provided input into department budget
- Conducted panel interviews
- Recruited for various position classifications
- Interviewed and referred candidates for vacant positions
- Coordinated generalist employment functions

Training

- Performed training needs assessment
- Facilitated new employee orientation program
- Conducted in-house workshop for employees on motivation
- Planned in-service training

Employment

Employment Coordinator, Taco Bell, Inc., Irvine, CA 95–Present
Personnel/Training Asst., H.B.U.S.D. Huntington Beach, CA 94–95
Personnel Clerk/Receptionist, Hughes Aircraft, Torrance 90–94
Yeoman, Ship's Office, U.S. Navy, San Diego, CA 86–90

Education

B.A. Personnel Administration, California State Univ. Long Beach, 1993
A.A. Business Management, Orange Coast College 1988

Affiliations

Toastmasters International, Club #233 Newport Beach Chapter
American Society for Personnel Administration

SAMPLE RESUME 3

The following two formats illustrate creative alternatives to the traditional resume. They might work well for someone going into a field where creativity is admired.

COLLAGE FORMAT

PROCEDURE:

1. Form a collage of pictures on a poster board.
2. Take a black and white snapshot of your pasteup.
3. Have the picture printed on the paper of your choice.
4. Personal information can be printed on either the reverse side of the collage or on separate pages to be inserted inside.

Caution: Do some homework before using photographs. It may be considered illegal for a future employer to use it.

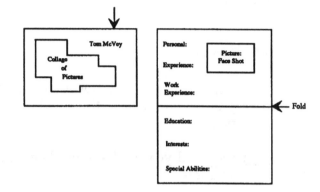

Nothing succeeds like the appearance of success.
—*C. Lasel*

PROBLEM COVER LETTER

The following letter has numerous mistakes. Find and correct them, because any of them could be quite damaging.

January 23, 1998

Mr. Harold E. Spring, President
Product Market, Inc.
Anywhere St.
Thistown, Iowa
52004

Dear Mr. Spring,

I am sending you with this letter my own Resume because I saw your add in the Times. I would very much like to have this job. I am working part-time in sells and would really like to move up.

In the past several years, I have worked over 175,000 hours in the sales and marketing of Stayway products.

I am contacting you because your company looks to be in need of a man with my incomparable experience to work on a full time basis. If so you may be interested in some of the things I have done.

For example, during the past year, I have singlehandedly sold over $5,000,000 worth of computer equipment and services throughout the United States. Due to these sales, I have been the number one salesman for Allied Computers for the last year.

During the last five years, I have been responsible for over $25,000,000 in retail sales for products raging from tools and hardware to sophisticated computers.

If this kind of experience would be invaluable to your company, I would love to talk with you.

Fondly,

Harrison L. Smith
Sycamore Street
Anytown, Arizona 92651

PROBLEM RESUME

Gene A. Allen

This resume contains numerous mistakes. Find and correct them.

RESUME

Wheat Lane
Anytown, New Jersey
80091

Date of Birth:	7/7/56
Height:	5' 11"
Weight:	189
Health:	Very good
Sex:	Male
Marital Status:	Single

EDUCATIONAL EXPERIENCE

High School Diploma (1974)
Seal High School
GPA: 2.0

Bachelor of Arts (1978)
Emory University, New York
Major: Business Administration
GPA: 3.0
Activities: President of AEO Fraternity
Varsity Football

Master of Science (1980)
Emory University, New York
Major: Economics
GPA: 3.0

WORK EXPERIENCE

1980 to 1988	Position:	Administrative Assistant
	Place:	Vanderbilt University, New York
	Duties:	Assisted college president with all his duties.
1988 to Present	Position:	Executive Director, UNICEF
	Place:	Baltimore, Maryland
	Duties:	Worked with 480 employees; in charge of in-service training and coordination of 53 field offices
	Supervisor:	Dr. M. L. Singe

REFERENCES—will be furnished on request

OUTSIDE INTERESTS—racquetball, astrology, bridge, sailing, skiing, and wood working

Brainstorming for Resumes

PURPOSE:

To brainstorm some ways to create effective resumes.

PROCEDURE:

1. In small groups think up as many possible suggestions for resumes as you can.
2. Brainstorm at least 20 action verbs that can be used for accomplishments. Examples include designed, presented, developed, created.
3. Get back into a large group and present your ideas to the class.

DISCUSSION:

1. What types of resumes were most and least effective? Why?
2. To what extent would it be important in tailoring a specific resume to a specific job?

INTERVIEW PREP KIT

Once you have been notified that you are to have an interview, it makes good sense to prepare. An interview is not a "spontaneous" event. It is a sales experience. You must use your interview time to convince the company that you are the one for the available position. Careful preparation will help you display yourself well.

Your interviewer may have a copy of your resume in advance. For some jobs, usually hourly rated, resumes are not requested. It is useful, however, to have some ready in any case. You will usually fill out an application blank in advance. Take care in filling out applications. Take all the time you need to guarantee precision and accuracy.

Once you enter the interview, pay attention to the amenities. Watch for directions about where to sit. Take the cue from the interviewer about whether you are to exchange names and shake hands. Wait for him to start the interview—do not blurt how eager you are to go to work.

Dress Carefully

Do not convey messages that you do not intend to convey. A great many decisions are made about us based on the way we dress. For example, if we are wearing excessively expensive clothing to an interview, the interviewer may conclude that we tend to live beyond our means. If our clothing is "scudsy," excessively "sexy" or "studlike," the interviewer may get some interesting ideas but they will usually not have anything to do with the job. The best advice is to dress discreetly, using quiet, semi-dark or dark colors, with little ornamentation. Keep cleavage to a minimum. Make sure slacks and pants are not too tight. The clothing need not be high fashion, or even new. But it must be neat and clean, appropriate to the occasion.

By permission, Dr. G. M. Phillips; Penn State University

Prepare Yourself with Information about the Company

Many companies provide a brochure for prospective employees. If your company does, you can get the following information from the brochure. If there is no brochure, check at your local library to find out about the company. If both of these alternatives are unavailable, feel free to ask for information at the interview.

Knowledge about company

✓ Name, location, size of the company and type of business
✓ Types of jobs currently available
✓ Conditions under which you might work
✓ Nature of the training program
✓ Opportunities for education and advancement
✓ Promotion policies
✓ Whether there is a union
✓ The fiscal history and employment stability record of the company
✓ Turnover rate and prognosis for permanence
✓ Whether travel or relocation is required
✓ Salary offered, job description, qualifications for the position
✓ Nature of the community in which the company is located
✓ Employee benefits

You should be suspicious of any company that is unwilling to provide this basic information. Be careful in asking about it, however. You do not want to give the impression that #12 is more important than #3 or #5. Consider the impact of the questions on your potential future employer.

Prepare Your Remarks for the Interview

Your interviewer will use the interview to size you up to see if you are qualified, will fit into the company and have the kind of personality they are seeking. Given that you are equally qualified with your competition, whether you are hired or not is at the discretion of the interviewer. Generally, people who are sloppy, inarticulate, excessively heavy, smokers, drug or alcohol users, unconcerned, and who cannot prove what they assert or "lip off' to the interviewer do not get hired. There is no affirmative action procedure for these people. However, heavy people can reduce, sloppy people can dress neatly and inarticulate people can learn speech skills.

There are certain types of questions which are currently illegal. If you are asked these kinds of questions you face a moral problem. You might blow the interview if you do not answer them. If you answer them, you may answer them wrong. You always have the right to protest to the local employment service. Any employer who asks these questions may actually be trying to discriminate, but most likely they are unaware of the specifics of the law. Be careful.

Discriminatory Questions

1. Employers cannot ask you what your name was before you changed it.
2. Employers cannot inquire about your birthplace, or the birthplace of any member of your family.
3. Employers cannot ask you to disclose your ancestry or national origin.
4. Employers cannot ask for your age unless, for some reason, it is a bona fide criterion.
5. Employers cannot ask you to name your religion, the church you attend or state the religious holidays you observe. S/he can declare the days of work required, so that you may choose not to accept the job if it violates your religious commitment.
6. Employers cannot ask about the citizenship status of anyone except you. They may ask if you are a citizen or whether you intend to become one.
7. Employers cannot ask any questions at all about your relatives. They may ask you for the name of someone to notify in case of emergency.
8. Employers cannot ask about your national origin or race.
9. Employers cannot ask questions about physical handicaps unless it is specifically relevant to the job. They can require physical examinations.
10. Employers cannot ask you to report times you were charged with felonies or misdemeanors, but they can ask you to report convictions.
11. Employers cannot ask about marital status, children, expectations for children, cohabitation, your spouse, etc. They can assert the conditions of employment and let you choose.
12. Employers cannot ask you to disclose memberships in organizations which would disclose your race, religion or national origin.
13. Questions about sexual preference are not always illegal.
14. Employers can question you intensively about your education, job qualifications, work experience and they may require you to take whatever examinations can be justified for the position.
15. Employers can inquire into your character, including use of drugs and alcohol, hobbies, outside activities.

Under the Buckley Amendment, you can get access to your personnel file. If you are having trouble gaining employment, you may find this useful. You can discover the kinds of invidious information that might be interfering with your ambitions.

To prepare yourself best, get a one-minute speech prepared on each of the following topics. When you do, you will have an answer to the questions most frequently asked in interviews.

1. My educational achievements in high school and college.
2. What I am interested in.
3. My skills are . . .
4. How I can be motivated to do my best work.

5. The kind of criticism that helps me most.
6. How I have demonstrated leadership.
7. My vocational goals now, five years from now, 10 years from now.
8. I am mature because. . . .
9. My past work experience has been. . . .
10. I am a creative person because . . .
11. How I can help your organization.
12. Why I am interested in your company.
13. My extracurricular activities qualify me because. . . .
14. My volunteer activities qualify me because. . . .
15. What I have learned in the past few years.
16. I have read the following books and they are about . . .
17. I read the following magazines regularly because . . .
18. How I have gotten along with my previous employers.
19. What I have learned on my previous jobs.
20. My school grades do/do not estimate my ability because. . . .
21. The kind of work I am most interested in . . .
22. I can get along well with people because . . .
23. I can demonstrate that I want to get ahead by. . . .
24. How I get along with people from various backgrounds.
25. Why I am your best choice.

Do not talk about how badly you need the job. Do not run down other candidates. Be responsive to the interviewer's questions. If you do not understand a question, ask him/her to restate it. Try to integrate your prepared remarks to meet interviewer questions. Be terse or ignore altogether illegal questions.

Employers will evaluate you on: communication skills, definitive handshake, neatness in appearance and on application and vita, promptness, responsiveness to social cues, good manners, directness in answering, economy of expression, whether you appear organized and have your future planned. They will look for willingness to work, qualifications for the job, courtesy to past employers, interest in and knowledge about the company, desire for permanence, maturity, social awareness, decisiveness, sense of humor. They will reject you for excessive garrulity, nonresponsiveness, flippancy, temper and arrogance, name dropping (never drop the name of a company officer on a personnel interviewer. If the job is a set-up he has already done his work). Any interviewer may reject you for any reason. It is sometimes wise to ask if you can call or write (in the event you don't get the job) and get some evaluation of your performance in the interview.

After the interview, find out how you will be notified. Do not call the company unless you are asked. If you are told to, call exactly when requested. Companies do not like to be pestered. If the company does not notify you on time, wait a discreet 24 hours and go on with your search. Companies are not always reliable, but it won't help you get a job if you tell them off about it.

JOB INTERVIEWING

DO	DON'T
Have a neat, conservative appearance	Look casual, sloppy
Look interviewer in the eye	Look at other things while talking or listening
Appear calm and relaxed	Fidget with anything or shift in chair
Show interest and enthusiasm	Indicate lack of interest in the company
Be assertive and tactful	Be overbearing or very meek
Use proper English	Use slang or swear words
Speak clearly and loud enough	Mumble to yourself
Have specific professional plans and goals	Appear to be just rambling around
Be willing to compromise	Overemphasize money
Know what salary the job generally pays	If your record is poor, be prepared to explain
Make the most of your scholastic record	Make excuses or evade issues
Be direct and honest	Fool around and show poor manners
Act mature and courteous	Give a limp or aggressive handshake
Give interviewer a firm handshake	Condemn past employers
Treat past employers with respect	Say you loaf during vacations, didn't like school work or indicate in any way that you are lazy
Indicate a strong desire to work	
Show a sense of humor when appropriate	Act like you're shopping around or only want the job for a short time
Know what you're talking about—knowledge of area and job responsibilities—give short clear answers	Be frivolous or cynical
	Give vague, indefinite, long-winded answers
Show high moral standards	Indicate low morals, radical views or prejudices
Do your homework—find out all you can about the company	Indicate that you know nothing about the company and what it does
Be on time for interview	Be late, without a *very* good reason
Ask questions and show vitality during the interview. Remember, this is a two-way street.	Be apathetic or afraid to ask questions
	Forget to thank the interviewer
Show appreciation to interviewer for his/her time	Get frustrated and irritated
Keep a cool head in answering all questions	Be unprepared—take it for granted that you've got it made
Be prepared to answer *all* kinds of questions—rehearse with someone. Use a video tape.	

REJECTED? HERE'S WHY![*]

1. Poor personal appearance
2. Overbearing—overaggressive—conceited "superiority complex" "know it all"
3. Inability to express himself clearly—poor voice, diction, grammar
4. Lack of planning for career, no purpose and goals
5. Lack of interest and enthusiasm—passive indifference
6. Lack of confidence and poise—nervousness—ill at ease
7. Failure to participate in activities
8. Overemphasis on money—interest only in best dollar offer
9. Poor scholastic record—just got by
10. Unwilling to start at the bottom—expects too much too soon
11. Makes excuses—evasiveness—hedges on unfavorable factors in record
12. Lack of tact
13. Lack of maturity
14. Lack of courtesy—ill mannered
15. Condemnation of past employers
16. Lack of social understanding
17. Marked dislike for school work
18. Lack of vitality
19. Fails to look interviewer in the eye
20. Limp, fishy handshake
21. Indecision
22. Loafs during vacations—lakeside pleasures
23. Unhappy married life
24. Friction with parents
25. Sloppy application blank
26. Merely shopping around
27. Wants job only for short time
28. Little sense of humor
29. Lack of knowledge of field of specialization
30. Parents make decisions for him
31. No interest in company or in industry
32. Emphasis on whom he knows
33. Unwillingness to go where we send him
34. Cynical
35. Low moral standards
36. Lazy
37. Intolerant—strong prejudices
38. Narrow interests
39. Spends much time in movies
40. Poor handling of personal finances
41. No interest in community activities
42. Inability to take criticism
43. Lack of appreciation of the value of experience
44. Radical ideas
45. Late to interview without good reason
46. Never heard of company
47. Failure to express appreciation for interviewer's time
48. Asks no questions about the job
49. High pressure type
50. Indefinite response to questions

---

[*] Negative factors evaluated during the employment interview and which frequently lead to rejection of the applicant
By permission, *The Northwestern Endicott-Lindquist Report* published by The Placement Center; Northwestern University, Evanston IL.

Sample Interview Questions

Dr. Frank S. Endicott*

The following list represents those questions most frequently asked by job interviewers.

What are your future vocational plans?

In what school activities have you participated? Why? Which did you enjoy the most?

In what type of position are you most interested?

Why do you think you might like to work for our company?

What jobs have you held? How were they obtained and why did you leave?

What courses did you like best? Least? Why?

Why did you choose your particular field of work?

What percentage of your college expenses did you earn? How?

How did you spend your vacations while in school?

What do you know about our company?

Do you feel that you received a good general training?

What qualifications do you have that make you feel that you will be successful in your field?

What extracurricular offices have you held?

What are your ideas on salary?

If you were starting college all over again, what courses would you take?

How much money do you hope to earn at age 30? 35?

Do you think that your extracurricular activities were worth the time you devoted to them? Why?

What do you think determines a person's progress in a good company?

What personal characteristics are necessary for success in your chosen field?

Why do you think you would like this particular type of job?

Do you prefer working with others or by yourself?

What kind of boss do you prefer?

Are you primarily interested in making money or do you feel that service to humanity is your prime concern?

Can you take instructions without feeling upset?

Tell me a story!

How did previous employers treat you?

What have you learned from some of the jobs you have held?

Can you get recommendations from previous employers?

What interests you about our product or service?

Have you ever changed your major field of interest while in college? Why?

---

* By permission, *The Northwestern Endicott-Lindquist Report* published by The Placement Center; Northwestern University, Evanston IL.

When did you choose your college major?
Do you feel you have done the best scholastic work of which you are capable?
How did you happen to go to college?
What do you know about opportunities in the field in which you are trained?
Which of your college years was the most difficult?
Did you enjoy your four years at this university?
Do you like routine work?
Do you like regular hours?
What size city do you prefer?
What is your major weakness?
Define cooperation. Do you demand attention?
Do you have an analytical mind?
Are you eager to please?
What job in our company would you choose if you were entirely free to do so?
What types of books have you read?
Have you plans for graduate work?
What types of people seem to rub you the wrong way?
Have you ever tutored an underclassman?
What jobs have you enjoyed the most? The least? Why?
What are your own special abilities?
What job in our company do you want to work toward?
Would you prefer a large or small company? Why?
Do you like to travel?
How about overtime work?
What kind of work interests you?
What are the disadvantages of your chosen field?
Are you interested in research?
What have you done which shows initiative and willingness to work?

Note: If you take the time necessary to write out brief answers to each of these questions in the list, it can help you clarify your own thinking and establish ready answers.

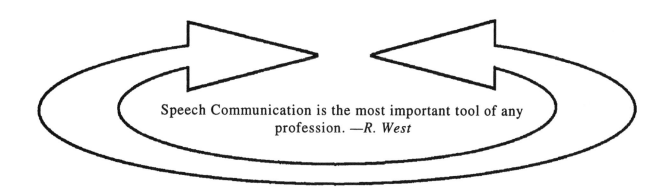

Speech Communication is the most important tool of any profession. —*R. West*

RESUME WORKSHEET

Before you write your resume, complete the following worksheet. If you keep this form and update it periodically, you will find creating a resume less of a chore.

Personal Information

Name:

Address:

Phone Numbers: Home:

                       Work:

Educational Background

Degree:

Major:

From:

Date:

Honors:

Affiliations:

Degree:

Major:

From:

Date:

Honors:

Affiliations

Degree:

Major:

From:

Date:

Honors:

Affiliations:

Outside Interests

Work Experience

    Position:

    Place:

    Dates

    Duties:

    Supervisor:

    Position:

    Place:

    Dates

    Duties:

    Supervisor

    Position:

    Place:

    Dates

    Duties:

    Supervisor:

Professional Organizations

References

    Name:

    Title:

    Place:

    Address:

    Phone Number

Name:

Title:

Place:

Address:

Phone Number

Name:

Title:

Place:

Address:

Phone Number

Ideas for the design of your resume:

REACTIONS

1. Using the questions found in the Interview Prep Kit, prepare yourself with information about a specific company or agency in your city. List that information here.

2. Make a list of friends, relatives and acquaintances to be part of your network.

3. You have met a person at a party. Prepare the answer to either one of these questions: "What type of work do you do?" or "What do you intend to do with your major when you graduate from college?"

4. Make a list of the most impressive things about you.

Selected Readings

Be Your Best by Linda Adams, Holbrook MA: Adams Media Corp.

The Adams Job Interview Almanac and CD Rom by Robert Adams, Holbrook MA: Adams Media Corp.

Stand Up, Speak Out, Talk Back: The Key to Self-Assertive Behavior by Alberti and Emmons: Simon & Schuster

The Confidence Course by Walter Anderson: Harper Collins

Creative Aggression by Bach and Goldberg: Garden City, NY: Doubleday, 1974

Jonathan Livingston Seagull by R. Bach: Avon

Listening Behavior by L.L. Barker, Englewood Cliffs, N.J.: Prentice Hall, 1971

What Do You Say After You Say Hello by Eric Berne, NY: Grove Press, 1972

What Color Is Your Parachute 97 (or the latest edition) by Richard Bolles, Berkeley, CA: Ten Speed Press, 199–

Asserting Yourself by Sharon Bower and Gordon Bower: Addison Wesley

The Feeling Good Handbook by Dr. David Burns: Penguin

Self Esteem by Dr. David Burns: Penguin

Bus 9 to Paradise by Dr. Leo Buscaglia, Thorofare, N.J.: Slack; New York, N.Y.

Love by Dr. Leo Buscaglia (and other books by this author): SAA, 1972

Chicken Soup for the Soul, Volumes 1, 2, 3 or 4 by Jack Canfield and Victor Hansen: Health

Chicken Soup for the Women's Soul by Jack Canfield and Victor Hansen: Health

Dare To Win by Jack Canfield and Victor Hansen: Health

Don't Sweat the Small Stuff ...it's all small stuff by Dr. Richard Carlson: Publishers Group West

You Can Be Happy...No Matter What by Dr. Richard Carlson: Publishers Group West

How to Win Friends and Influence People by Dale Carnegie, New York: Simon and Schuster, 1986

Journey to Ixtlan by C. Castaneda, New York: Simon & Schuster, 1972

Emotional Intelligence by Daniel Coleman, New York: Bantam Books, 1995

How to Survive the Loss of a Love by Dr. Melba Colgrove, Dr. Harold Bloomfield and Peter McWilliams, New York: Leo Press, Dist. by Simon & Schuster, 1977

The 30 Secrets of Happily Married Couples by Dr. Paul Coleman: Adams Media Corp

The Seven Habits of Highly Effective People by Stephen Covey: Simon & Schuster

Smart Women, Foolish Choices by Dr. Connell Cowan and Dr. Melvyn Kinder, New York, N.Y.: CN Potter (1985) Dist. by CRO

Ask Barbara by Dr. Barbara DeAngelis: Doubleday Delacort

Secrets About Men Every Woman Should Know by Dr. Barbara Deganelis: Doubleday Delacort

Love for a Lifetime by Dr. James Dobson: Spring Arbor

What Wives Wish Their Husbands Knew About Women by Dr. James Dobson (and other books by this author): Spring Arbor

Pulling Your Own Strings by Dr. Wayne Dyer, New York : T.Y. Crowell Co., 1978

Real Magic by Dr. Wayne Dyer, Samuel Weiser

The Sky Is the Limit by Dr. Wayne Dyer, Samuel Weiser

Word Play: What Happens when People Talk by P. Farb, New York: Knopf, Dist. by Random House, 1973

Body Language by J. Fast, New York: H. Evans, 1970

Man's Search for Meaning by Victor Frankl: Simon & Schuster

My Mother, My Self by Nancy Friday, New York: Delacorte Press, 1977

Men are from Mars, Women are from Venus by Dr. John Gray: Harper Collins

Mars and Venus on a Date by Dr. John Gray: Harper Collins

Black Like Me by J.H. Griffin, Boston: Houghton Mifflin, 1977

Beyond Culture by E.T. Hall, Garden City, NY: Anchor Press, 1976

The Power Is Within You by Louise L. Hay, Santa Monica Ca: Hay-House, 1988

You Can Heal Your Life by Louise L. Hay, Santa Monica Ca: Hay-House, 1988

Napoleon Hill's Key to Success by Napoleon Hill: Fawcette

Think And Grow Rich by Napoleon Hill: Fawcette

The True Believer by E. Hoffer: Harper Collins

Celebrate the Sun by J. Kavanaugh, Los Angeles: Nash Pub, 1973

What Makes the Great Great? by Dr. Dennis Kimbro: Doubleday/Delacort

14,000 Things to be Happy About by Barbara Ann Kipfer: Workman Publishing

The Essential Book of Interviewing, Armold B. Kantor: Random House

Clam Plate Orgy by Dr. Wilson Bryan Key, Englewood Cliffs, NJ: Prentice Hall, 1980

Media Sexploitation by Dr. Wilson Bryan Key: Englewood Cliffs, NJ: Prentice Hall, 1976

Subliminal Seduction by Dr. Wilson Bryan Key, New York: New American Library, 1974

I Ain't Much Baby—But I'm All I've Got by J. Lair, Garden City, N.Y.: Doubleday, 1972

Language of Wisdom and Folly by I. Lee, San Francisco: Int. Society for General Semantics, 1967

The Birth Order Book by Dr. Kevin Leman: Dell Trade Books

Were You Born for Each Other? by Dr. Kevin Leman: Dell Trade Books

100 Best Companies to Work For by Robert Levering and Milton Moskowitz: Penguin

Dress for Success by John T. Molloy: Warner Books

Dress for Success for Women by John T. Molloy: Warner Books

How to Be Your Own Best Friend by Newman and Berkowitz: Ballantine Books

1984 by G. Orwell: Signet Books

A Guide To Confident Living by Dr. Norman Vincent Peale (and other books by this author), New York: Ballantine Books

Enthusiam Makes the Difference by Dr. Norman Vincent Peale: New York: Ballantine Books

Power of the Plus Factor by Dr. Norman Vincent Peale, New York: Ballantine Books

The Power of Positive Thinking by Dr. Norman Vincent Peale, New York: Ballantine Books

The Positive Principle Today by Dr. Norman Vincent Peale, New York: Ballantine Books

Treasury and Joy of Enthusiam by Dr. Norman Vincent Peale, New York: Ballantine Books

The Different Drum by Dr. M. Scott Peck (and other books by this author): Simon & Schuster

The Road Less Traveled by Dr. M. Scott Peck: Simon & Schuster

The Road Less Traveled and Beyond by Dr. M. Scott Peck: Simon & Schuster

In Search of Excellence by Dr. Thomas Peters: Warner Books

Passion for Excellence by Dr. Thomas Peters: Warner Books

How Could You Do That? by Dr. Laura Schlessinger, New York, NY: Harper Collins

Ten Stupid Things Women Do to Mess Up Their Lives by Dr. Laura Schlessinger, New York, NY: Harper Collins

New Passages by Gail Sheehy: Bantam Books

Passages by Gail Sheehy: Bantam Books

Pathfinders by Gail Sheehy: Bantam Books

The Language of Love by Gary Smalley and John Trent. Ph.D. (and other books by these authors), New York: Pocket Books, div. Simon & Schuster

The Two Sides of Love by Gary Smalley and John Trent, Ph.D., New York: Pocket Books, div. Simon & Schuster

When I Say No, I Feel Guilty by M.J. Smith: Bantam Books

Millionaire Next Door by Dr. Thomas Stanley and Dr. William Danko: Longstreet

Interviewing: Principles and Practices by J. Stewart and Cash: Brown and Benchmark

You Just Don't Understand—Men and Women In Conversation by Dr. Deborah Tannen: Ballentine

Why Should I Hire You? Seven Proven Steps for Getting the Job You Want by M.R. Thimpson, JIST Works

Johnny Got His Gun by D. Trumbo: Bantam

Cover Letters That Knock Em Dead by Martin Yate, Holbrook, MA: Adams Media Corporation

Interviewing by Martin Yate, Holbrook, MA: Adams Media Corporation

Knock Em Dead 1997 (Job Seeker Handbook) by Martin Yate, Holbrook, MA: Adams Media Corporation

Resumes That Knock Em Dead by Martin Yate, Holbrook, MA: Adams Media Corporation

8 Weeks to Optimum Health by Dr. Andrew Well: Random House

Spontaneous Healing by Dr. Andrew Weil: Random House